HELENE GROVER

Sometimes the Music

© Helene Grover 2021

Helene Grover asserts the moral right to be identified as the author of
'*Sometimes the Music*'.

Cover design and typeset by Green Avenue Design.

Published by Cilento Publishing, Sydney Australia.

All rights reserved. No part of this publication may be reproduced, stored in a retrieval system, or transmitted, in any form or by any means, electronic, mechanical, photocopying, recording or otherwise, without the prior permission of the publishers.

Disclaimer: This is a work of creative non-fiction. All of the events in this memoir are true to the best of the author's memory. Some names and identifying features may have been changed to protect the identity of certain parties. The author in no way represents any company, corporation, or brand, mentioned herein. The views expressed in this memoir are solely those of the author.

ISBN: 978-0-6450004-8-1

To Allan Goldring, my beloved godson

CONTENTS

CHAPTER 1: Playing with Memory 1

CHAPTER 2: War and Peace 7

CHAPTER 3: Oceans Away 14

CHAPTER 4: Barefoot Boy 23

CHAPTER 5: Career Explorations 31

CHAPTER 6: The Pied Piper Piano Player 52

CHAPTER 7: Some Days Have a Massacre 59

CHAPTER 8: Journey Into Madness 68

CHAPTER 9: Moving In 73

CHAPTER 10: From Shanghai To Sydney 83

CHAPTER 11: Jazz Time 99

CHAPTER 12: Paddington Jazz Festival 110

CHAPTER 13: Love And What Came With It 119

CHAPTER 14: George Cables Tour 131

CHAPTER 15: Woman of Mystery 141

CHAPTER 16: A Few Drops of Sherry 149

CHAPTER 17: Dizzy Gillespie Concerts 153

CHAPTER 18: Joe (Bebop) Lane 162

CHAPTER 19: Jungle Juice 174

CHAPTER 20: My Mother and My Russian 192

CHAPTER 21: Moving to Woop-Woop 198

CHAPTER 22: Trying to Adapt in Suburbia............................ 206
CHAPTER 23: Jamming With Branford Marsalis.................. 213
CHAPTER 24: Pentridge Prison.. 218
CHAPTER 25: Lost Laughter 226
CHAPTER 26: Move to Coogee.. 233
CHAPTER 27: Laughter Found 238
CHAPTER 28: PARIS... 247
CHAPTER 29: Santa Barbara 251
CHAPTER 30: Much Ado About Laughter 256
CHAPTER 31: A Gun – A Festival.. 269
CHAPTER 32: Drying Out 279
CHAPTER 33: Keeping Abreast.. 288
CHAPTER 34: Bob Dylan Concert 293
CHAPTER 35: Oye, Oye, Oye 298
CHAPTER 36: Heroes and Villains 304
CHAPTER 37: Liquorice Allsorts.. 314
CHAPTER 38: End Play... 323
CHAPTER 39: The Last Lily 328
CHAPTER 40: To Hell and Back... 336
CHAPTER 41: The Music Stopped
– Monday 11th October 2010... 342
CHAPTER 42: Funeral 347
CHAPTER 43: Sea Change 355
THE WARRIOR... 360
ACKNOWLEDGEMENTS 361

CHAPTER 1

Playing with Memory

"Life is a lot like jazz – it's best when you improvise"
– George Gershwin

Silence brought me the memories, music made them dance.

A slate-coloured metal roof was my childhood playground – it jutted out from the open French windows I had climbed out of to play with my favourite toys. Close by inside, my father quietly read his daily paper.

The silence of this peaceful Paris day was broken by the man upstairs sticking his head out of his apartment window and dangled down a piece of string towards me, shouting, "I'm taking your dolly." I was four years old and too young to consider this an empty threat, I frantically clutched Pierrot, my porcelain doll to my young chest and dived through the partially open window, breaking it into jagged fragments.

Glass shattered into the room, a piece of it dug into my father's leg, another tore a gash on my arm, and we both ended up in a bloody mess.

This is one of my earliest memories and plunges me into alleys of time to retrieve for you the kaleidoscope of my existence.

I have to tell you, writing about your life is like riding a ghost train. You pay at birth, get on the rickety open train and go through dark tunnels where ghosts of the past pop out to scare the daylights out of you. Now and again, wispy skeletal fingers of memory brush your face, and you keep going along in the darkness, until a break happens, and you roll out into the daylight again to see people standing mindlessly staring at you while waiting for their own ride. Then back you go into the tunnel of half-forgotten memories where yesterday's demons pull another scream out of you.

Remembering my childhood, I often felt as if I were two different little girls: a defiant one, poking out her tongue, thumbs on the side of her forehead wiggling her fingers in a gesture of "I don't care, you can all go away," and the defeated child standing head bowed in the corner, hands behind her back, alienated from carefree kids busy with everyday nothingness.

I didn't choose to emerge at a time when war exploded across Europe, and myriads of people, including my parents, ran for their lives.

Oh for goodness sake! It's too early in our relationship to subject you to such melancholy. But how else would you know where I came from, apart from the womb, of course.

France, the twenty-first of August, Nineteen forty-two, was not the most welcoming place and time to be born.

I have no memory of bombs pouring from the sky, or sirens wailing as Paris was bombarded, warning the inhabitants to run for shelter. What I have, is an unspoken sense of something broken in me.

Who would want to be born at a time like that? I didn't want to leave my embryonic safety, and battled my mother's womb for a long time before I emerged into a world where hell's demons trampled all over my birthplace, leaving death in their footprints.

My father couldn't be present for my birth; he was involved with the French resistance fighters. Fate also kept us apart when he died.

When I think of all the turmoil and fears, I can finally understand and accept that at my age, I still have to sleep with either some kind of sound or light in my bedroom. These fears have never left me.

I can't envisage this time of history to include music. The notes would have choked with the sounds of Paris being ripped apart and if I knew for sure there was a God, I would say, "Hey mister or madam, couldn't you have made life less complicated? Couldn't you have left pain and killing out of it all? Did you really have to see how humans react to your experiments?"

It's taken me a long time to figure out why the people who came into my life appeared, disappeared, stayed, taught me, gave to me, took from me and left me with more questions than answers. I'm writing this book to make sense of it all, share with you my most challenging parts, and mostly, to tell you about the one person who took up a quarter of my existence, and barrelled me through some of my greatest lessons. This was the man who brought me music, pain, tears and excitement.

My memory is pregnant with his music born every moment his fingers touched the keyboard.

By the time I met him, I was old enough to know better than to go chasing pretty butterflies over unknown walls and places. Constrained by my mother's fears and her illiteracy, all I wanted to do was find ways to avoid the boredom of an ordinary life.

I spent a total of twenty-six intermittent years with Serge Ermoll, musician, composer, martial arts man, enfant terrible of jazz and incorrigible alcoholic. I cried a deep, wide lake of tears and spent a fortune on therapy trying to figure out how and why I repeatedly returned to the cycle of a relationship seeped in verbal abuse, anger and the erosion of my self-esteem. I wonder now, how strong was love's glue that contained such a sticky mess.

We had adventures, experiences and exciting events. Yet, there was a destructive force as well. My curiosity of chasing pretty butterflies over unknown walls became the struggle with this man's emotional hawks.

I wonder now, if I could have made better choices.

♪♪

I can't imagine living in a world without notes filling the air, drifting into my ears like fingers reaching into my emotional layers.

Some people just listen to music, others create it. I did both, and inside that world, I found many creative individuals.

My half-brother Phillip was responsible for the first song I heard. He came home with a relic gramophone that had a large funnel, and out of it tumbled the deep voice of Paul Robeson, singing *"Old Man River,"* in a language I didn't understand. Phillip told me it was English and the man whose voice magically floated in the air was black, same colour as Phillip's friend who often came for dinner and played hide-and-seek with me. There were few spaces to hide in our small all-purpose living room.

My family's favourite instrument was the violin, and my father promised to send me for lessons one day. He did his best to keep his word but sadly, fate didn't allow it. However, I can imagine the agonies my parents would have had to endure listening to screeching strings during my hours of practice. Maybe a few interested refugee mice might have stuck around.

We knew it was housework time when my mother, who loved opera, warbled in her high-pitched voice, *"Die Fledermaus"*, an operetta about a bat, and drove us bats hearing her.

Notes tumbled through my life, preparing me for an eclectic taste in music with a diverse collection of genres: Singers, bands, melodic, classical, invasive, rock, country, haunting tunes, or discordant noises scratching at ear drums. I was into whatever took my fancy at the time; popular songs from the charts or recordings of birds, waterfalls and other noises of roaming wildlife.

Long before music seduced me, I had to move beyond childhood nightmares and grow up quicker than most children. I had to learn much more than school could ever teach me, beyond writing, reading and arithmetic. First French, and later English. But, these were the basics, not really the coping tools necessary to take me through who I was and where I was heading.

CHAPTER 2

War and Peace

"Observe constantly that all things take place by change and accustom thyself to consider that the nature of the Universe loves nothing so much as to change the things which are, and to make new things like them."

– Marcus Aurelius

Sirens screamed behind me. The more I tried to get away from them, the more they chased me up the street into the next street. Dodging cars, the howling noise followed me around another sharp corner. The pursuit continued until I was cornered in an open car park. My noisy pursuer was an unmarked sedan with several men inside. One of them ambled out, came towards me and tried to open my locked car door. Irritated, I shouted out, "Who are you, what do you want?"

"Police, open your door."

"Show me your badge."

Standoff. I was trapped, I had a moment of panic when he fished inside his jacket, pulled out his badge, and held it up.

I felt safe enough to roll the window down and ask, "What do you want, Officer? I wasn't doing anything; until you started chasing me."

"Open your boot."

"What for?"

"You seem to be in a mighty hurry, young lady. You beeped the car in front of you and forced the driver to go through a red light."

"Was there a red light, Officer? So why do you want to look in my boot?"

"We've just had a complaint a thief rushed out of the shopping centre, and seeing you are in such a hurry…"

"Is that all?" I laughed and popped open the boot. "You can have a look. I don't steal things."

He looked in the boot, then at my license and smiled. "Do you make a habit of being chased by police sirens?"

I felt more relaxed. "No, Officer, not recently," and the whole incident was over.

But it wasn't, not for me, not in the compartments of my lost childhood where the howling of sirens was accompanied by a desperate need to escape.

This time I was a grown-up woman living in Australia, a long time and distance away from the origins of my fears. Perhaps these remnants were left in me to create defiance towards authority.

♪♪

On the eighth of May, nineteen forty-five, Charles de Gaulle, leader of the Free French Forces, announced the end of World War Two in France.

My parents and our family often talked about those harsh years of terror: running, hiding and leaving the city for safer places. They were locked in their memories with reminders that we were all fortunate to have survived. Conversations were about how my parents had escaped Paris taking with them a few pieces of clothing thrown hastily into a battered suitcase, their dangerous journey through France, and the Gestapo boarding the train to check personal papers. Anyone they considered suspicious was hauled away for interrogation.

Fear, the common companion on the train tearing across the countryside, took its fodder of displaced people with their meagre possessions to places far away from the bombs and invaders of Paris.

Cramped together with other passengers in our carriage: my father, mother, an elderly grandmother and few weeks old me, were dispersed throughout the train, just in case any of us would be taken and never seen again, They felt it important for some of our family to survive and create future generations.

I wonder if coincidence led my family to settle in Souillac in the Dordogne Valley until war's end, and if serendipity led me to discover recently that Souillac has an annual jazz festival, founded in 1976 by an American GI who had helped liberate France.

If I were writing a fiction novel, I would have invented this connection between the first few years of a little girl's life in a town in South Western France, and her ultimate connection to a jazz musician, a pioneer of Free Jazz in Australia, similar to the French double bass player,

Henri Texier, who appeared in the 2019 "Souillac en Jazz" Festival. Strange. N'est ce pas? But I am writing about real life, about me, and the people who have been part of this factual adventure.

A rat-infested barn was our new home until the end of the war. The rats often ran with impunity across the overhead beams, their long tails hanging over the edges, terrifying me with their twitching, whiskered noses and round little eyes looking down at me. My father told me they were kittens and were frightened of us because we were so big and made a lot of noise, and because Papa said so, I lost my fear.

Funny how what we learn as kids stays with us. Nowadays, when a rat runs across the beams of my backyard veranda, I shout 'Hi mate, wait till my pest control people leave you some juicy titbits."

Just over two years old, I was too young to carry memory, and oblivious of the turmoil around me, I played like any other normal child, yet, buried in the hidden places of my psyche began the foundation of an indefinable something scratching at me for the rest of my life. Who knows if it may have influenced the choices I ultimately made.

My father, clever with his hands, with a limited number of tools, made all kinds of things for the local farmers: soup-ladles, fry pans, rolling pins, plant holders, and bowls. He exchanged these items for fresh produce such as milk, eggs, cheese, vegetables and fruit, providing my mother with enough ingredients for her to create delicious meals.

We didn't return to Paris until the end of the war when people picked up the broken pieces of themselves to reconstruct their tomorrows.

We can never go back to what was, no matter how much we long for the before time; returning home, to a place or person, is inevitably different. Fresh memories impose themselves on the old ones, and we either adapt or slowly disintegrate.

My parents; veterans of many changes, found a new place to live, a compact two-bedroom first-floor flat at the end of a cobblestone courtyard in the suburb of Mairie des Lilas.

The apartment had a living room, a separate kitchen with a fuel stove. The extended roof, where the drama with my doll had played out, was our outdoor outlet. We had no bathroom or hot water, so we had to go to the local bathhouse for a proper shower. Without the luxury of a toilet, we had a makeshift potty under the bed, and in the morning, my mother carried it down the corridor, past other apartments, down a long flight of stairs, to empty the contents into communal outdoor hole-in-the-floor toilets.

The one time I went with my mother on her potty emptying mission, it coincided with our neighbour from upstairs, also carrying a full potty, accompanied by her young son, Pierrot, my first puppy love. I wonder if that little boy also almost died with embarrassment, like me? Mind you, the two of us were in a heap of trouble when discovered in the coal cellar with our pants down, trying to figure out why our whatsists were different from each other.

There was no privacy living in a cramped space with my mother, father and brother. My five-year-old cousin Louisa sometimes stayed with us and peed in the bed.

A short walk to the next suburb of Porte des Lilas, my father established his small sheet metal atelier where he made coal bins, baths, and other tin items. Although a craftsman, he didn't earn much so couldn't afford to buy me toys. Instead, he made me a doll's table, chairs and a crockery set all out of metal. I loved my personalised playthings, made just for me by my dad. He also bought me gifts from the local flea market: old half-used paint tins, raggedy dolls, an egg timer which I thought was great until my mother took it away to use for its original purpose.

He made practical things for my mother, a rolling pin, baking trays, and creative pieces out of copper and pewter: vases, flowerpots and other household ornaments. Dad made them all in his workshop filled with rich smells of old iron, rivets, hammers and tools. He cut pieces of metal, pounded them into shape, put on his protective glasses and gloves, and lit a blue flame that spurted out of the acetylene torch as it melted the bonding metal into useful and beautiful objects.

The smell of rusty metal brings back my childhood in my father's magical workshop. I spent a lot of time there, watching him, or tinkering with odd pieces of metal, sometimes scribbling in a huge ledger in his minuscule office.

The memories of the war lingered, followed by food scarcity and the rebuilding of lives that would never be the same again. Everyone was trying to recover from the horror years. People had lost families, friends, homes and the life they had before. The scars remained for too many years, invisible inside the emotional playgrounds of grownups and children.

At night, my nightmares were filled with German soldiers and packs of wolves rushing out from behind the bedroom door, until the screams and tears of my fears woke me up and my father hugged me back to sleep.

CHAPTER 3

Oceans Away

"One of the gladdest moments of human life methinks, is departure upon a distant journey into unknown lands"

– Richard Burton

My parents had lived through enough troubled experiences to give them the strength to adapt.

"Eat your soup, Helene, you are not leaving the table until you're finished." My big brother Phillip ordered. He insisted that I finish every last bit of my meal, including a potato with a black eye. "We starved during the war so we must be grateful, and eat everything in front of us." I resisted and both of us obstinately stayed at the table long after my mother had cleared it and washed up.

I wonder if that obstinate child in me, the one who hung on for hours over a dodgy potato, became someone that obsessively hung onto lost causes.

A rhythm settled in our home. Dad toiled in his workshop, mum baked and kept a super clean home, Phillip went to his draftsman's job, and I struggled with school.

We weren't prepared for letters from my other half-brother Charles encouraging us to migrate to Australia where he had settled with his new wife. He wrote letters full of glowing descriptions of a new world, safe from wars, with enormous potential, and two new grandsons. He added that although a long way from Europe, this fledgling country would welcome my father's sheet metal trade and offer a profitable income.

Surrounded by my mother's delicious food at the dinner table, our family was in endless discussion about this migration lunacy. My parents had been through enough of being proverbial wandering Jews crossing the continent from their distant homelands: Dad's long trek from Russia to England, mum from Poland, Germany and finally France, where they met and married. Hadn't they moved enough?

I was too young to be included in the decision of whether to move again, but my parents were faced with an agonising dilemma of whether to stay in the comfort of our close family and the life we knew, or sail into a completely different environment. I have no idea what prompted the final decision, possibly the prospect of my father seeing his new grandchildren from the offspring of his first marriage. Whatever! We were moving to Australia.

Pierrot, my baby-like porcelain doll, had to come with me, along with my parents meagre belongings: pots, pans, a feather doona, a few household items, all packed into old suitcases and a large wicker basket. Impossible to see were the invisible pains of leaving home and family and everything they knew of their surroundings: Shops, streets, neighbours, sights and smells of home.

How does one say goodbye, probably forever? Goodbye to all the nooks and crannies of an entire life? Other migrants will understand the feelings, the deepest places of themselves, what it means to uproot your existence and reconstruct it in another country. As a nine-year old, I had fewer problems dealing with this.

We boarded the train from Paris to Naples, embarked on a migrant ship, "The Sydney" and sailed towards the bottom end of the globe to a land, at the time, vastly unknown in Europe.

As far as I was concerned, none of this mattered; I was having fun on the big ocean liner, dashing around the decks with other kids. I was too young to notice how sad my mother was as she kept repeating, "I am going to faraway seas, and never coming back."

Around the same time, a seven-year-old boy, Serge, was sailing with his mummy and daddy, from Shanghai to this same Promised Land.

My father was sixty-six, my mother in her fifties when we landed in Sydney in 1952 on a scorching January day and were bewildered that at this time of year, there was no snow.

Emerging from the long sea journey, the first thing we saw, were big green vehicles with rods attached to overhead wires and moving slowly along a track. We had never seen a tram before, the forerunner of many new things to grapple with, especially the language. Peculiar foods unpleasantly bombarded our taste buds. Gone was the rich, runny Camembert now replaced with soap-like cheese, and I took a long time to develop a taste for the brown goo called Vegemite. Square pieces of cardboard disguised as bread, were replacements from our crusty baguettes.

No matter what, we had to adapt. I tackled school; my mother found a kitchen job in a deaf and dumb school. She did very well there and learnt more sign language than English. She took a long time to learn the language, but she tried. "Ferry sorry, I no speaking zo good," she smilingly told people. She refused a job washing dead bodies in the Jewish morgue. Her reasoning was, "If I worked in a place like that, I'd be so frightened they would probably find two dead bodies in the morning."

Dad found work in a sheet metal factory and was made foreman that first year.

Australians didn't know how migrants viewed the new country. John O'Grady, under the pen name of Nino Culotta, described a part of it in his book, "They're a Weird Mob", and over the years, it sold close to a million copies. I still have one on my cluttered bookshelves.

A sort of pecking order emerged. People arriving from France were considered glamorous, whilst Italians and Greeks were perceived as house builders and green grocers – important for the development of the nation. Australians hadn't experienced the ravages and anti-Semitism of Europe and were kinder to us. I received some good-natured fun from Aussie kids, *Oolala mademoyselle*. But never anything like the venom directed at me when

I was six years old in Paris, and called a *'sale Yupain'* (dirty Jew) by a nasty woman in our building.

Just the same, we felt like aliens from a different planet. We couldn't get on a train and in a few hours return home to everything familiar. It seemed like we had travelled on a rocket to Mars, planet Earth was far, far away. We had landed at 6 Toyer Street, Tempe where we shared a bedroom in a two-bedroom house with Charles, his wife, and their two little boys. Funny how things don't turn out to be as we expect! The reality was quite unlike the letters to my parents, All they wanted was to work, save, and find a place of their own, Yet, here we were in the Promised Land with a hopeful future ahead of us, but our plans were waylaid and our hopes crashed when my father was diagnosed with stomach cancer and became terminally ill. Our difficulties were now like being attacked from all sides by swarms of bees.

Dad was put in palliative care and my mother went by tram to visit him daily after work. Whenever I tried to go in the ward to see him, the nurses shooed me away. In the fifties children under fourteen were not allowed to go in and see a dying relative. The watchful nurses were oblivious to the joy on his face when he saw me, or the rip in my little heart when I was pulled away from him.

My father died within one year of our arrival in this brave new world.

He would have said: "Dust in the earth and then nothing."

The photograph on my sideboard keeps my father's face vivid in my memory; I can almost feel the soft, loose skin of his face I used to love to pinch as a child, or pull the tendrils of grey hair across his head.

After that, everything changed. The isolation from family was poignant in the way my mother and I had to cope with it all.

I was ten years old and had to grow up instantly, becoming my mother's manager, financial consultant, interpreter, writer of letters, and negotiator for anything that came up.

Children of migrants often have to deal with interpreting for their parents grappling with the new language. I believe it's a two-edged sword. On the one hand, we learnt to be self-sufficient at an early age, and on the other hand, we lose a little part of our innocent childhood.

I couldn't wrap myself up in a kind of grownup swaddling, so I suffered layers of invisible vulnerability, at times raw and exposed. Experiences such as the death of my father, adapting as a child to a new country, and my mother engulfing my growing-up years with fearful overprotection were probably elements that prepared me for Serge and the sea-saw years of pain and love.

♪♪

In the early sixties, the suburb of Erskineville was considered an inner city slum area where rent was cheap.

Our tiny terrace was set in a narrow, unwelcoming street, squashed in a row of similar houses, facing a dilapidated, disused factory. A few years after my father's death, my mother bought the house for four thousand pounds. This was a huge sum for my mother who only earned six pounds a week. I was still at school with no way to contribute financially. I can't imagine how she managed to save although I remember her endless requests to turn off the light when I left a room, and that we heated water in the concrete tub in the kitchen and carried it with buckets to the paint-peeling metal bathtub. But for the first time in her life, my mother owned a house. We painted it, decorated it, and fitted into our new way of living.

Every Friday afternoon I picked mum up from work and we went to Paddy's Markets where she bought a live chook to take home, slaughter it a few days later, pluck its feathers, and make a delicious meal from the murdered fowl. We often laughed about how one peak hour Friday, riding home in the tram, my mother desperately tried to restrain her newly acquired chicken from poking its head through the holes of her string bag while it was attempting to peck a woman sitting next to us, until, to our horror, the captive flew out and all over the tram, chased by a frustrated conductor who eventually caught it by the feet. It entertained the other passengers, while the children howled with delight.

Scorching summer Sundays, we had picnics at Bondi Beach. I swam and rode the waves while mum prepared the food and gossiped with her newfound friends. We then crushed into crowded buses and went home.

Relaxed from a glorious summer day at the beach, we opened the back door and were confronted with a winter wonderland. Don't be silly! There is no snow in Sydney around Christmas time. Aboriginal kids from next door had climbed the fence and tipped out all over the garden, my mother's entire collection of plucked chook feathers. That was the end of her doona-making plan and she didn't have the heart to start all over again, so we had to make do with Aussie doonas.

I left school at fifteen with only an intermediate certificate. I had done well learning the language, Australian history, and composition but maths was my Waterloo. Mum wanted me to go on with studies but I argued it would be better for both of us if I got a job and contributed to the household. Crazy really, as a teenager I had more pressing needs like clothes, girlfriends, boys and writing songs.

My mother insisted I do Jewish and had no concept of the discomfort it brought me living where we did. Existing on Four pounds and eight shillings a week, our house in Erskineville was the best she could do. Most of my social peers lived in the better areas of the Eastern Suburbs and it seemed boys judged you by your address. I learnt that lesson painfully from a handsome young man who had driven me home one night after a dance at the Synagogue. He looked at my home in disdain, and asked. "When are you moving?"

Surprised, I answered, "We're not moving, I live here."

"You mean permanently?"

Whether the romance might have blossomed if I had lived in a more expensive area, I never found out since he disappeared after that night. This was the first time in my life I was confronted with social or financial status.

One of the factors that endeared me to Serge was that he didn't give a damn about finances, status or anything reeking of snobbism, although he was particular about the playing capacity of his fellow musicians.

Amongst the relationship experiments I moved in and out of, I was never wise enough to make reasonable choices. My university of life came from living it, as well as reading streams of books. I had an insatiable need to know stuff, and still do.

CHAPTER 4

Barefoot Boy

"There can't be any large-scale revolution until there's a personal revolution, on an individual level. It's got to happen inside first."

– Jim Morrison – The Doors

I grew up painfully. My body objected, my mother objected, I objected, to anything and everything. There was one person who didn't: my girlfriend Carole, another rebel and my mother sure objected to her. Carole wanted to be a singer, and I poked around writing songs. The music was our bonding glue. Carole plunged in the deep end with boys, and I barely wet my toes.

Teen years with my mother were a disastrous battleground. I was too young and self-absorbed to understand what she had to cope with as a single mother with no family support and little income.

My challenges were the changes in my body, and what was I going to do now I was almost grown up.

♪♪

In the mid to late fifties, British EMI Records dominated the Australian music market, until Festival Records was established and Johnny O'Keefe became the first Australian singer to attempt breaking into the USA market, although that didn't happen. He became 'The Wild One' of Australian rock establishing the very first pop TV show on Channel Two, *Rock Around the Clock*, where I appeared a few years later.

The era was a time of music evolution in this country. Up until then, most of the pop music in the charts came from England or the States. Australia was in exploration mode; record companies started up and looked towards local talent.

Offspring of early migrants from the United Kingdom and Europe provided a powerful influence on the local recording industry. Years later I learnt that I was an integral part of the first wave of Australian music, and the first female to write a hit song.

During those challenging years with my mother, and my body, all I wanted to be was a singer. I had a pretty, out of tune voice, so I became a songwriter instead, and still maintain this was a fluke. Carole chased a professional singing career.

Most songs people write live in forgotten obscurity, it was a miracle mine found its way beyond my teenage dreams.

Wedged between the upper rung of a tall ladder and the ceiling in the hallway of our house, I sang. The acoustics bounced my voice around, making it sound better than it actually was. I spent a lot of time up there, belting out the latest hit parade songs and scribbling new ones. Pad and pencil propped on my knees, I gave birth to 'Barefoot Boy.' I didn't have a plan; the song just ran away from inside my imagination.

I couldn't figure out why my ceiling vocals irritated my mother. "You coming down from up there, or you'll break your neck," she shouted at me in Yiddish, interrupting my creative moments.

My mother's best possible future for me was simple; first, become a competent secretary, then find a nice Jewish boy, get married, have children and be a super housewife. I viewed this as unbearable boredom.

I was rebellious enough to sidestep my mother's restrictive plans, and had fun flings with boys my mother disapproved of.

Hanging out with Carole, I kept writing songs, and engaged in loud screaming matches with my mother.

Despite my dubious singing voice, Carole and I became 'The Diabolos.' Two teenagers wearing on-stage tight, low-cut blue dresses, fake ponytails, and knotted scarves tied sideway on our necks. We vaguely matched. At least we were about the same height: short with big boobs.

"C'mon Helene, we're going to Suzie Wong's in the city to sing in a talent quest." Carole insisted, she was enterprising enough for the two of us.

"Wish we'd have rehearsed more. What are we going to sing anyway?"

'Barefoot Boy of course! You wrote it. It's a good song and you never know who might see us there." We had rehearsed long enough not to make utter idiots of ourselves.

We won the talent quest at Suzie Wong's. Goes to show; all it took to change my life was, an instinct to write, a need to be different, a promising song, a determined friend, and a couple of judges to see the potential. This culminated in Festival Records signing me up.

What does a wet behind-the-ears star-struck teenager know? Certainly it wasn't how to navigate the difficult arena of the recording industry or the whims of its managements. I lost the battle to record my own song, which turned out to be better with the lovely voice of upcoming young singer, Noeleen Batley.

Meetings I had with the Artists and Repertoire man at Festival Records were marred by having to dodge his advances. Staying in his good books and his hands out of my cleavage or my pants was a perpetual juggling act.

My next A. & R. man, Johnny O'Keefe helped many of us fresh, keen, new talent make our way in the rock and roll industry, and with him, I didn't have to deal with uncomfortable come-ons.

It took months for 'Barefoot Boy' to reach its final vinyl stage and played on radio. The single was released in 1960. At sixteen, I was overwhelmed by the sudden fame of having a number one hit song, conceived at the top of a ladder and later reach an audience across the country. Instead of becoming a singer, I became a songwriter, and played with words for the rest of my life. After that, I restricted my out-of-tune singing to watery vocals in the shower, where I sounded fabulous and the neighbours probably cringed.

Noeleen also recorded my next song; "Ice Cream Man" released the following year.

Carole married four times (or was it five?). She had a few kids. Her second husband was the drummer in her band. For a few years, they made their base in Vietnam and performed for the troops. She eventually divorced this husband, married number three, and went to the Middle East where she learnt belly dancing. She came back to Australia and became a solicitor, and opened a belly dancing school. A whole fascinating life could be written into another book, but in mine, condensed into one paragraph. Sorry mate.

I'd love to give that precocious young Helene a kick in the butt right now, for feeding her monster of self-importance at the time. Yet, I understand that appearing on National television, having interviews on radio and mainstream newspapers, could inflate the ego of a sixteen year old.

My sense of self-importance puffed up even more when the record company management set up a meeting for me with Lyle Richardson, the manager of singer, Bruce Gillespie whose hit song "Velvet Waters" had run its course. They hoped I would write another hit for him.

We were meeting at Teen Canteen, a crowded teenage hangout in Pitt Street. Wrapped in my new pale grey mohair coat with a fake fur collar, together with my newfound ego, I was under the delusion I was a big time celebrity. I walked in, my head somewhere in the "I-think-

I'm-the-greatest" place, didn't see the step in front of me, tripped and went sprawling all over the floor, ending my slide ride right in front of Lyle and Bruce. What an entrance! The sharp needle of deflation pierced my puffed up ego.

I sure was having an exciting life.

Nothing came of the meeting, but I learned an important lesson, mohair coats and an overblown sense of self-importance don't make you famous. By the way, Bruce disappeared into obscurity.

♪♪

My mother was singing her own hit tune from her complaint hit parade, 'I no like dis moosik business, is like a prostitute ting. No good for nice girl.' This led to gigantic screaming matches, slammed doors and not speaking with each other for days.

A never-ending catch phrase I threw my mother for most of my life, "Leave me alone, mum," fell on deaf ears.

"I no leaving you alone if you not good girl." Oi vey! My mother, the perpetual pain and guardian of the life she wished for me.

Time to leave home. Years later, I regretted I had been such a shit, leaving without a word, and sneaking off while mum was at work. My reason not to leave a note was because she couldn't read and phones weren't in every home yet. I was gone for six months, leaving her to worry whether I was still alive. I now think of that selfish me, chasing my own needs with little regard for the one person who cared about me the most. Yet, one way or another,

I paid the price. My mother extracted the payment by constantly repeating how much she had worried about me. Her lament went on for years, pouring gallons of guilt on my already fragile psyche.

Carole and I were seduced by the night bustle of Kings Cross. We had office jobs and could afford a one-bedroom flat in Tusculum Street.

At last, I opened my teenage wings and flew into freedom with my new carefree lifestyle. No more creeping home around two am after a night out to hear my mother's voice in the dark, "You tink I no can hear you?" And in the morning face a day of little sleep and a banal office job.

Unhindered by pesky, demanding parents, and a walking distance from the daily nightlife, we often hung out in a little jazz club in Brougham Street, the El Rocco.

Tucked behind the main stretch of neon signs, where the crime centre of Sydney existed with its vice, prostitution, strip and gambling joints and the first gay cabaret, Les Girls, the El Rocco nestled in a pocket between the city and Kings Cross. A narrow flight of downward steps led down to a smoky, dimly lit underground firetrap room where black and white photos of musicians hung on the walls. The stage had a piano with enough space for a small band. The place probably wouldn't have fitted more than sixty people, most, sitting around tables. Yet, the El Rocco survived as an iconic venue of early Australian jazz featuring fledgling musicians.

Maybe, some nights, when Carole and I sat sipping our coffees and listening to jazz, a handsome blonde piano player was exploring his chops on that small stage, but we were not yet connected to each other's radar. Besides, Serge was busy with band fans and, as I learnt later, local prostitutes, while I was busy dragging home or dodging amorous advances from a string of unwanted boyfriends.

Finances became tight and I moved back home where everything was the same as before, only now, my mother had extra fuel about how much I had made her suffer. She tagged in, that it was time for me to settle down, have a 'normal' life and forget all about this crazy song-writing business.

If only my father had been alive, I felt he would have been the one to nurture my creativity and my passion for music. Would he have approved of my random choices of people in my learning process? I wonder what he would have made of Serge Ermoll, the music man that took me through the emotional pits of my most difficult odyssey. And, if I were to learn anything in life, it was to be the hard way, with one of the most challenging human beings I could find.

My destiny drew me to enter through the gate of this relationship, that challenged everything I was and believed.

CHAPTER 5

Career Explorations

"Our finest moments are most likely to occur when we are feeling deeply uncomfortable, unhappy or unfulfilled. For it is only in such moments, propelled by our discomfort, that we are likely to step out of our ruts and start searching for different ways or truer answers."

– M. Scott Peck – The Road Less Travelled.

You would think a hit song on the charts and much publicity would project some change in one's life. It didn't work that way. All I could do was continue with typing jobs and scribbling more songs.

The biggest change I made was to get married on the twenty-seventh of October 1967.

I had a couple of silly reasons to get that gold ring on my finger. One was that my girlfriends were getting married, including Carole, and the other, more important one, was to give my mother the satisfaction of me hooking up with a Jewish man. I think many young women get seduced by the wedding. You know, the dress, the big do. I went for the whole catastrophe; long white satin dress, fluffy veil, bridesmaids, ritual at the Great Synagogue and the glass breaking. Followed by the mediocre dinner at some overly expensive wedding venue in the city, which my mother could ill afford and became a contention with the in-laws. So, I had the wedding, followed by two boring years of domestic blah in the suburbs. If you were to ask me why it ended, I would say I had told my husband with the thinning hair, if he ever went bald I would divorce him. I didn't wait that long, he still had considerable hair on his head by the time I left.

After my divorce, I sailed to Europe for a year to visit my family in Paris first and on to work and explore London. Both cities excited me in different ways, but as a divorced young woman in my mid-twenties, I embraced the exciting British hippy era by buying the widest bell-bottom trousers and round John Lennon glasses in a trendy Carnaby Street shop, and became an instant pseudo-hippie. A friend invited me to stay with her in Golders Green, which was convenient for a little while, particularly when we shared watching Neil Armstrong's landing on the moon on her small black and white television.

I found an easy temp job with The Burma Oil Company. My new typing pool boss was amused that this Aussie girl took her work seriously. "That's not urgent, you can stop typing and tell us all about you and Australia, Helene." The next day, she taught me how to play tiddlywinks. I flopped on the floor with the other typists and flipped little coloured disks around. I can't remember if we ever got our work done, but my stay in London was great. Five days of doing little to earn my wages, and weekends exploring the city with my Japanese neighbour, Fumiko.

I was reluctant to return home to Australia a few months later.

♪♪

By my early thirties, I was drifting, and considering career options.

You either get on your destiny's train and let it take you to your unknown horizon or you stay at the same uneventful station until you die. Opportunity gave me the choice to ride into a theatrical career and I landed in the play, "Whose Afraid of Virginia Woolf". I had no training, but with a formidable director, who bullied the pants off me, I gave a reasonable performance. No! No sex involved, my director was gay.

My new director cum theatrical agent went on to cast me in his next production "The Killing of Sister George", where I played a larger than life character with a heavy European accent, Madame Zelda who predicted people's futures by reading their jewellery. Don't get me wrong, I didn't choose to be a complicated character. I took on what was available at the time and even managed to get paid for it. The cheek of it!

Finding a taste for being in front of an audience, I fast tracked my acting career beyond casting sessions and futile conversations with my new theatrical agent and reshaped Madame Zelda into Madame Zelia.

I gave Madame Zelia a gestation period of experimenting and looked for the right vehicle for her to deliver whacky predictions. I considered different body parts until I arrived at knees – What better place than the close proximity to the naughty bits?

"I looking between your knees und see big potential." Or "You have such beautiful knees, I tink they can go very far in your life."

You've got to have *chutzpa* to go down a loony path and take others with you.

I pinched the accent from my mother's mouth, and a bad dress sense of: large fluffy blonde wig, long orange and purple kaftan, loads of jingling jewellery, massive rings on every finger, and a homemade carpetbag full of knee photos. I fabricated a background of a medieval ancestor who had supposedly invented the can opener to cut Joan of Arc's chainmail leggings to get a knee reading.

Madame Zelia also claimed to have read famous knees. "I vas in Hollywood, Schweetheart, und I tell you vat I see inside some actress knees, many have such lonely looking knees like dey schpending too much apart from each udder."

You can imagine the confusion all this caused with the media people. I must have been convincing because one Telegraph journalist believed my prediction she would quit her job and travel overseas; lucky guess because she already had her ticket booked. Did I see the future between her knees, or did I get a flash from somewhere higher? Maybe!

My agent asked me to come to her office to meet a potential client. Entirely in character, dressed as Madame Zelia, I drove myself over the Harbour Bridge, down a one-way street and almost crashed into a truck coming out of the car park. A policeman on a motorbike was hot on my tail. "Can I see your license," he asked when we had stopped; he leaned in my car window. Bugger, I thought, now what? Ah well, I look the part so might as well be it, and handed him my license, "Dis me, sometime." He was confused.

"You came down a one-way street, lady, that's illegal you know."

I put on a horrified look, "I do somezing naughty, ferry, ferry bad," and I smacked my hand.

He became more confused. "Look, lady, I won't book you this time but be careful."

"Oh, you such good boy, I do somezing for you, I reading your knees." I know, it was an odd thing to do, but I just had to. "You putting your knee in vindow und I telling you your fortune, maybe you meet beautiful young lady."

Honestly, he did it! That cop put his knee in my car window. I couldn't help myself, I had to take it further, "Schweetheart, I no can see your knee viz boot on, you taking boot off, und taking trouser up und then I doing reading."

He laughed, "Thanks for the offer … er…"

"Madame Zelia, I am knee reader, dis vy I coming to Australia to find sunshine knees."

He drove off with a puzzled look on his face, and I made my way upstairs to my agent's office, I told her about my little episode with the cop. After she stopped laughing, she rang her mate on the *Daily Telegraph*. The next day, a headline caption read, 'Police stir over Knee Reader.'

The next public appearance for Madame Zelia was set up for the media in Sydney's Hyde Park. A strangely dressed woman feeding the pigeons in front of the fountain made the seven o'clock television news.

Dressed in character for all interviews, my necklaces of fake coins banged on radio microphones. Mike Carlton suggested I take my jewellery off so not to jingle all over the airwaves. Listeners couldn't see what I was doing yet interviewers announced that I was in the throes of looking into their knees for a deep insight into their future.

Not all of it was fun, especially when my agent insisted I take a bottle of champagne to give to the musical director while on National television. I had no way of knowing he would shake the bottle, fizz up the contents and send a stream of frothy champagne at Stuart Wagstaff and me. We were soaked in bubbly. Doing my best to save face, I wiggled my finger and in a strident Madame Zelia voice, shouted, "You very, very naughty boy." Seen right across the country on daytime TV.

Not finished with frustrating me, my agent had another mess for me to deal with.

I hate dancing girls! My agent included a bunch of them to surround the singer hired as support act for my Madame Zelia show. This was the last straw, I pulled an ultimate Prima Donna during rehearsals, "That's it, I've had it. I'm not having any fucking dancing girls prancing around my knee routine, or I'm not doing the show." The dancing girls disappeared, and I made my agent disappear after I learnt that all of it was part of her contra deals with other agencies.

To think, years later, I hooked up with the 'enfant terrible' of jazz, yet, here I was, an enfant horrible of questionable fortune telling.

The clash of personalities between Madame Zelia and me became a burden, so I killed her off by banishing her wig and gaudy outfit to the bottom of my wardrobe, and was done getting between people's knees.

Not done with acting, I landed a one-day television gig with Robert Morley, the late, great British actor featured in dozens of movies. We were on a shoot together for a Heinz Soup commercial about vegetables and zucchinis and you could say, I was in the soup with him.

My short-lived acting career included a two-week children's pantomime tour of the Central Coast during the Christmas holidays. I was booked to perform and write two short scripts. I wrote, *'Professor Braintwaddle and Gollywog go to the Centre of the Earth'*, and *'Professor Braintwaddle and Gollywog go to Mars.'*

Our third show, *'Captain Caravan'* was written by our director. It featured a caped crusader. The guy who played Captain Caravan was frequently confused. Actually, the whole project was a bewildering experience.

I was cast for three roles: a devilish imp, a Martian queen, and a villain called Slippery Sam dressed all in black with a cape draped across my face. As Slippery Sam I made villainous cackling noises, I knew I was convincing because, during performances, kids rushed to the stage area and kicked me hard on the shin.

Every day during the tour, we set up four shows in different locations. A cardboard cauldron attached to the roof of my car, later became the cooking pot for me, as an imp, to be boiled in.

As a matter of fact, we all cooked in thirty-five degrees heat wearing heavy costumes and makeup all day. The other 'actress', dressed in her gollywog gear of black makeup and fuzzy hair, would not be politically correct these days.

Black skivvy, tights, blacked out face and red plastic horns stuck to my forehead for my devilish outfit, attached to my backside a long stuffed tail trailed behind me. My clothes stuck to my body, and my horns nearly fell off.

Buying lunch at a café and sweltering in our getups, we suffered while locals and holidaymakers dressed in skimpy swimsuits came in to buy food. I can't tell you if it was deliberate or not, but one of them trod on my tail.

The whole thing was a glorious debacle and came to a disastrous ending. Nobody got paid. I hope you understand that the challenges of being an imp cooking in a cauldron, knee misreads, and on-stage disasters are what prompted me to leave the performance side of being the 'talent' to become a talent promoter.

There is a continent of difference between being an agent and having one. Being an agent, you are in charge; you hold the reins of someone's fame and fortune. Having an agent, expectations are even higher, disappointments more soul destroying.

My girlfriends had husbands and babies, and I was entering the business of nursing talent.

Madame Zelia, Martian Queens and devilish imps eventually found their resting place in the archives of my career changes, and I moved on.

Change has a way of snowballing into something bigger and different than expected. We don't know where it can and will take us. Every new step moved me towards what was intended for me. As for 'him', his footsteps brought him closer to me.

I wasn't looking for a man. I wanted a life, and for tomorrow to be an exciting day.

For several months, I was employed by my ex-theatre director, as part time dogsbody in his theatrical agency for $20 a week. It wasn't for the money; I was more interested in the opportunity to be in the front line of casting sessions. I got two lines in a commercial, followed by a no dialogue, big boobies Italian lady role in a soapie. I missed out on being the chalk-breaking teacher in a Colgate long running TV ad.

The reality of it was, I put in more time than the $20 paid me, but I did gain experience in how to run a theatrical agency. Meantime, I found another folly to occupy me.

You would think a reasonably savvy person would have enough insight not to become embroiled in one act of trial and error after another. But no! Not this chick! Maybe I channelled a chook's brain.

Friends of a close friend of mine were conducting weekend song and dance classes for young performers, and asked me to write a script for their next production. They wanted a musical, biblical saga about Moses leading his people out of Egypt. I had never written an entire script before: dialogue, music, staging, and directing kids aged from about eleven to eighteen. You can see right here my capacity to bite off more than I could digest.

My mother, the creator of spontaneous words of wisdom, often claimed you couldn't dance with one backside at two weddings. I nearly could. This time, it came in the form of a planned trip for us to go to Israel. It coincided with my preparations for the show. If Jesus could walk on water, I could float in the Dead Sea, lurch across the country in a tourist bus, write dialogue and create songs.

In the midst of soaking in that amazing country and people, discovering a deep sense of belonging, and coping with irritating fellow bus travellers, I was not looking for romance. It jumped at me from nowhere, well, actually, at the edge of the Dead Sea. I was standing on the black mud and looking into the face of an ex-paratrooper Israeli soldier. Amos and I had a delicious whatchamacallit, my mother looming like a dark eagle to swoop me away from my newfound hero. Filled with passion and discovery, the romance was never meant to last longer than the brief time we had.

I came back to Australia with a completed script and ready to direct the saga of Moses in ancient Egypt. It encompassed; the princess who found him in the bulrushes, Moses asking the Pharaoh to let his people go, an arduous journey across the desert, the parting of the Red Sea, and finally reaching the Promised Land.

Writing the play, the songs and directing this biblical catastrophe, took up all of my creativity and sanity, but we got through it all, and it became a great success, with parents and the club staff, at least. Afterwards, for a while, I basked in the success of 'In the Footsteps of Moses.' The thought of it all now sends shivers of horror down my spine.

The teenagers from the show talked me into starting a new drama group. We formed the Sydney Youth Workshop where our productions were filled with their creative development and the delivery of social issue themes.

It can be such a lovely thing developing creativity with young people. It brought me a period of not just challenges, but also some of my greatest joys. The sense of knowing I was instrumental in making a difference in young people's lives, still brings me enormous satisfaction.

Inevitably, with the diversity of personalities, and other frustrations, I was often heard shouting orders, such as, "Okay guys, no dope, no booze, keep your pants on boys, and, Bobby, please don't give yourself an erection to go out on stage with."

Entertainment industry people I invited were impressed with the level of talent and the calibre of productions we presented. Consequently, some of the kids were cast in TV roles.

Life can be like playing hopscotch, jumping onto the next square towards a career. You count the moves and hope to reach the top curve in one almighty jump. I admire people who know at an early age what they want to be when they grow up. I never had a plan, but having to manage the latest development with my young talents and concerned parents, I took an unexpected turn, and opened a theatrical agency.

Hiring an office was too expensive. Instead, I turned my spare room into my new business space. Olive-patterned, mustard-coloured wallpaper and bright yellow furniture were neither a decorator's delight nor a setting for a professional-looking office. I rescued it with paint, a cheap plywood desk, and above it, nailed to the wall, a corkboard to showcase the headshots of potential artists. For a two-bedroom unit on the third floor, my new office had a degree of authenticity.

Acquiring a theatrical agent's licence, together with letterhead designs for business cards and stationery were my next move.

By the late seventies, I was established in the entertainment business, and at last I believed my life had become interesting and exciting.

If I had known a larger-than-life entrepreneur musician would overtake my space, I may have set up office on Mars, but guessing the future is a career for fortune-tellers and Madame Zelia was retired.

It took a load of energy to kick my business into a financially viable one. I often dashed down the three flights of stairs of my 'office' to chase after casting people and new talent to get work and an income.

During the day I made phone calls, hustled TV and film work. At night I went to clubs, pubs and other venues, where I listened to musicians, bands and entertainers. My agency needed diversity to survive, and I became a kind of human ferret foraging for suitable venues and managements.

I discovered the Longueville Pub in Lane Cove was hiring rock bands, and importantly, it paid decent rates for musicians. Armed with demo tapes, photos and negotiating skills blah-blah, I convinced the manager to hire one of my hotshot bands for a few weeks. I sure earned my ten percent management fee, although not enough for a life of luxury.

The Longueville Pub, at the time, was fundamentally a bikie hangout. "Would you like a drink, lady?" The voice behind me belonged to a longhaired, bearded bikie.

"Thanks but I'd rather not, I'm here on business."

He looked me up and down. I was dressed in my tight blue jeans, brown stiletto boots up to my knees, a cowl-necked blouse hugging my boobs, and red shoulder length hair. I felt quite presentable, dressed for business in a pub and looking after 'my guys'.

"Are you a working girl?"

"In a way. I manage the band and came to pick up the money to pay my boys." I somehow felt that I had to dispel any other idea the bikers may have had of me.

"Great band; you must be a good manager, so, let me buy you a thank-you drink."

I've never been much of a drinker, for no other reason than I'm not that keen on the taste of alcohol. "Lemon, lime and bitters will be great, thanks."

That was all there was to it; a biker, a drink, a band, fees and going home alone to get some sleep. Outside of this,

I squeezed in a social life, ephemeral romances, and time spent with friends.

I chose not to get involved with any of my 'clients'. Some were gay, others married, or had girlfriends. As for the available ones, you know the old saying; you don't do doo-doos in your own backyard. So there you have it, no boyfriend!

The more I plunged into the world of music, the closer I came to meeting that dusky piano-player I had overlooked years earlier at the El Rocco.

♪♪

Having set up Helene Grover Enterprises, I discovered a new free to air radio concept, and in true hustle fashion, I fronted the station manager for some airtime, considering I hadn't even formulated any kind of programme, what a *Chutzpah*.

Located at the side of the Paddington Town Hall where traffic rushed along Oxford Street, Radio Eastern Sydney was the first Community FM Radio station in the Eastern Suburbs. Staffed by eager volunteers, announcers, technicians, and an assortment of occasional office staff, all held together by a station manager, the only person to be paid. Most of us didn't know how to operate the equipment, and learnt as we went along.

It's marvellous when you don't know much, but think you do. My only radio experience had been of interviews as a songwriter with someone else pushing all the buttons.

The new station manager at 2RES was finding his way, just like the rest of us. We had no idea if we had any listeners or if there was interest in the subjects we offered. Some of our announcers had beautiful speaking voices but prattled on about obscure topics. While others, with interesting subjects, sounded like they needed drastic voice makeovers.

During dial twiddling, an odd person 'out there' called us.

I had found my niche, but without a crystal ball, I couldn't know I had opened the door to a chain of events leading to a massive disruption of my life.

Innocent of its role in my future, the station's management was keen to present a variety of community programs, so I suggested, "How about I put together a one-hour weekly French program? I'm French, and speak the language." And before I really knew what I was doing, I had plunged into an unknown territory.

Many people yearn for fame and recognition, whether it's performing, creating something or objecting to the state of the world. All chasing on air moments to be heard, and I guess I was no different.

How on earth did I think I could do anything with only one Edith Piaf record? And suggest running a program about a whole lot of knowing very little? This was way before computers, Google and modern technology.

In desperation I contacted Maurice, then president of the Sydney French Club and owner of a large French music collection.

A short, heavily accented Frenchman; Maurice, had once been my boss until I had enough of doing too much for too little pay, echoes of my theatrical agent. However, we remained friends and kept in touch.

Forgetting his English was overwhelmingly catastrophic, and with no radio experience whatsoever, I hired him for the unpaid radio job.

He was delighted, "Of course, ma Cherie, I am zo 'appy you ask me."

Maurice relished his role as the quintessential charming, hand-kissing Parisian gentleman. I tried to ignore his bow tie. I hate bow ties; they are like dead butterflies having futile relationships with collars. I asked Maurice to co-host my new French program and he was so excited about it, his moustache twitched with pleasure. What was I thinking?

"Ello et Bonsoir, dis is Monsieur Maurice and vee now play for yuu a beautifuuul chanson by Edit Piaf, I larf her ferry much, now you listen to enjoy dis music."

Mon dieux! I thought, would anyone understand his fractured accent? Then again, maybe no one was listening out there.

"G'day and bonjours, welcome to the French hour," I added, entering into a cross-continent battle, which included playing French music and community events.

During the station breaks, Maurice thought he was entertaining me with his saga of extra-marital affairs. More like showing off. "Helene, I am 'aving affair with a young pretty English girl."

"I need to know this because? And does your wife know?"

"Maybe, but I think she 'aving affair too."

Keeping me up-to-date with all these sexual exploits, Maurice's wife rang to tell me about her affair with a younger man.

Not fair really, I wasn't having even one tiny bit of anything with anyone.

Enough! Assez! A few months of hearing about extra-marital sexploits, listening to fractured English, and no feedback from anyone, not even one *oo-la-la et merci*, I had enough of *vive* anything French. Maurice and I had run our program as far as it could go, and I pulled the plug on the whole thing. I never did find out the outcome of his bedroom antics.

Of course I wasn't going to leave radio alone, now that I had tasted the feel of it. I launched into the next offspring of my vivid imagination, an all-Australian music program I named 'Music Makers', featuring upcoming local recording artists.

Familiar with the radio station's equipment by now, I felt confident enough to invite some of my musicians for interviews, and to play their latest singles we offered as giveaways that no one wanted.

An unlikely hare entered from somewhere in the music paddocks.

"Helene Grover Enterprises." I answered the phone in my best businesslike manner.

A bright cheeky voice drifted into my eardrum. "Tony Savage here. I've been listening to your Music Makers program. Great idea." Wow, one listener.

"I can help you make it better."

I almost hung up. Who the hell was this presumptuous, irritating person? But… my curiosity kicked in.

"Who are you? And what makes you think you can improve MY program?"

Mister super-confident came back with, "I'm in the music industry and have a lot of contacts." Ha! The magic word, contacts. In showbiz, contacts are everything.

Stepping out of nowhere, Tony Savage was another odd bod on my roller-coaster theatrical agency ride.

"Let me be your co-host, and I'll upgrade the program and help make it the best Aussie talent showcase around."

I hadn't even met the man, didn't know who he was, probably one of those self-made music promoters with a questionable background in an industry already full of hustlers with hot-air promises.

Eventually I met Tony: tall, tousled, in his twenties and just as vocal in person. "I know Michael Chugg and can get some of his contacts. I'll get us an interview with Michael Hutchence when INXS comes back from tour, and I'm sure I'll be able to bag Peter Garrett's new album and probably one of the 'Oils' for a talk."

Sometimes I could be incredibly savvy and at other times, incomprehensibly naïve. I come under a banner of, "Act now – repent later." But, I have to admit all this name-dropping seduced me. The man didn't, but we became program producers together.

"How about we crawl before we run, Tony? It's early days in the program, it has to settle first." I was excited his ideas could happen. Although Tony's hip hype didn't match the snail movement of the station, he ingratiated himself by bringing in stacks of singles, albums and gossip about what was happening in the Australian rock industry.

I liked our program's new name, *Musos on the Move*. We created a balance between interesting interviews interspersed with recordings of Aussie talent.

The source of Tony's income was a mystery. I hoped he wasn't a drug dealer. However, he had a lively personality and was a fun co-host to work with, chatty and knowledgeable about Aussie music. A few weeks into the program, he suggested we pre-record. "I have a mate who owns a recording studio where we can put together really tight professional sessions."

"Recording studios cost money, Tony."

"K.O., my mate, said we could do it at night, when he's not busy, it's his own studio so he can do what he likes."

"Where is it?"

"Out at Riverwood, it's called Riversound Studio."

"What? Who wants to go to Woop-Woop at night for an interview?"

"You know musos; they go anywhere for a gig."

"But this isn't a gig."

"It's promotion for them."

Soft, gentle, in his mid-thirties with initials for a name, I never found out what K.O. stood for, maybe knockout? Nevertheless, he was the innocent catalyst who opened the door of the grand opera that shaped the next few decades of my life.

The three of us spent entire nights pre-recording the one-hour radio sessions. Musos came in for interviews. We had fun, coffees and sandwiches, while K.O. twiddled with the dials, Tony talked at bullet speed, and me, wedged between them, enjoyed myself by conducting this programming orchestra.

All this crashed when I discovered the guys were up to something not *kosher*. They were cooking up a moneymaking scheme of syndicating the program to sell advertising.

"I'm calling K.O." I was beyond angry.

The fire-breathing dragon in me burst out, "You bloody idiots, how dare you, both of you, what the bloody hell did you think you were doing, K.O.? You didn't check with me. I don't do shit like that. I suppose you both thought you'd make a heap of bread out of it." I screamed into the phone, projecting blasts of anger into the innocent white mouthpiece.

"We were just checking things out and were going to tell you if something eventuated." K.O.'s soft voice was defensive and louder than usual.

"Bullshit. Is that why Tony paid you for recording time all those hours?"

"Er…well… He hasn't actually paid me…"

"Oh, I get it, you got conned too. I suppose he promised you a big cut from the sponsors." I finally understood.

"Er…mmm…"

"Go on, don't be gutless, K.O., at least tell me." I brought my voice down to a lesser roar.

"Yes, he did."

"First of all, the two of you had the gall to go down this track without telling me. The station management would be horrified if any person running a program tried to make money out of it, and would most likely kick us out once they heard of it. Besides, I like to keep my nose clean."

During the whole of my phone blast, K.O. was holding the phone out for another person who was quietly listening to me behaving like a screaming banshee.

Not that I believe in fortune telling, but a few years before, some of my girlfriends dragged me off to a tarot cum-palm reader, who predicted an exciting man was coming into my life. He claimed to see my hero riding a white horse on his way to me. It was taking an interminable time for my knight in shinning armour to arrive and I figured the horse must be lame by now.

How was I to know a rusty knight was listening to my angry expletives at the other end of the phone? Not a great first impression of me. However, my anger worked and talk of syndication was shelved.

I was totally unprepared for the gigantic changes about to happen in my already mixed-up existence.

CHAPTER 6

The Pied Piper Piano Player

In 1888 Robert Browning wrote his story of the Pied Piper:
"Hamelin Town's in runswick by famous Hanover city, the river Weser, deep and wide washes its walls on the southern side… and in did walk this strangest figure…with sharp blue eyes…"

The German legend tells of a time, around 1349, when the Black Plague besieged the Town of Hamelin with a plague of rats, and to rid the town of the vermin, the Mayor hired a charismatic stranger who played his magical flute and mesmerised the rats to follow. This Pied Piper led them to the river to drown.

When it came time to pay, the townsfolk reneged and in revenge, the piper played his flute once more, luring the children out of town, never to be seen again.

In 1984, when I reached forty, I met a modern-day Pied Piper. This one played the piano, charmed people and frightened the shit out of many.

Until then, my existence was relatively tame, not counting the war or the displacement of country or the loss of my father when I was nine. I can't count the nothingness of my marriage and divorce, and my lightweight footsteps tiptoeing through showbiz and theatrical types of people, as well as my strange habit of jumping in and out of Jewish life, mostly to please my mother who still had some kind of influence over me.

I loved working on the radio program, but as I already wrote, there were glitches.

"What's with the new black grand piano in the recording room, K.O.?" I noticed the magnificent, highly varnished instrument when I arrived at his studio.

"My new client organised it for a recording session."

"I didn't think it was to tap dance on." I couldn't help sarcasm.

"You're in the music business, have you heard of Serge Ermoll?"

"Who?"

"The great piano player, Serge Ermoll."

'Should I have?'

"He's a jazz pianist."

"I don't do jazz."

"Serge is organising an Australian tour and recording session for a German pianist, Joachim Kuhn."

"Good for him. Can we get on with it now K.O.?" I sensed his disappointment. I cut short his excited rave about someone I had no interest in. Yet, K.O. continued to bubble with hero worship. "Serge is an amazing musician himself. He's recorded a string of albums. What a guy! He's incredible."

"That's good, can we please get on with it now, and can you cut down fiddling with the equipment? It's taking so long to get through a one-hour program!" Studio engineers tend to mess about endlessly with sound equipment. I never figured out if it was necessary or another way to make extra cash.

The day yawned awake with the sun sliding its way above the horizon. I was tired, fed-up, bleary-eyed and washed out from another all-night radio recording session. The last thing on my mind was to meet another musician.

K.O. accompanied Tony and I down the stairs out of the studio. There wasn't anything unusual about this mid-week morning, yet a huge leap of destiny was poised to engulf me, and the moment I reached the street, my life changed forever.

"Want to go somewhere for breakfast Helene, and have a coffee to wake you up for the drive?" Tony asked me.

"No, I just want to go home, fall in bed and get some sleep. Hopefully, nobody will call me for a few hours."

The traffic had not yet pulsed awake on the main Riverwood road, and I couldn't wait to get into my compact red Laser parked in front of the building, and go home. But no, I couldn't stop the next moment.

"Here comes Serge, great timing for you to meet him." K.O. sounded excited and I wilted. I wasn't in the mood to meet jazz royalty out at Woop-Woop.

He looked self-assured as he walked towards us, hands in the pockets of his cropped fine black leather jacket. Jeans neither too tight nor too sloppy, covering a reasonably tall thickset man with an impressive head of tightly curled fair hair. I later learnt it had been permed. His face was almost hidden behind a very large moustache growing down the sides of his mouth and blending into a trimmed bushy beard.

He reminded me of those self-confident actors who dominate the stage with their overwhelming presence.

Normally phlegmatic, K.O. now flushed with excitement, introduced us, "Serge, this is Helene Grover." I held out my hand.

"So you're the chick, pleasure to meet you." He looked me in the face and took my hand in his large one. That's when I noticed he had the palest blue eyes.

I was not in a mental state to be clever, "Me too, K.O. told me a lot about you."

Taking it for granted, he responded, "He exaggerates."

The footpath had done its job for Serge and me to meet.

Tony and I got into my car for the forty-five-minute drive. Drop him off, and concentrate on not falling asleep on the way home.

"What do you think of Serge? I've heard all kinds of things about him," Tony asked.

"Right now, I don't care. He has a great sounding voice."

There was nothing more to say or think about. Serge was another entrepreneur musician I met during my busy schedule.

You meet someone interesting, and at the time you can't predict how it will evolve.

Had I known the impact this man would have on my life, I'd have covered myself in protective talismans.

♪♪

The next contact Serge made with me was when he phoned to ask if I could get his German protégée a few gigs around town.

"I don't do jazz," I responded.

"K.O. said you have a lot of contacts with venues."

"He exaggerates. I really don't think I can help you; jazz is not my kind of entertainment. It takes all my time to promote my own artists. I'm a one-woman agency, that's all."

"K.O. said you were a feisty lady and I heard some of it during one of your phone calls."

This was becoming annoying, "What phone calls?"

"When you were chewing him out about your radio program."

"He let you listen in? I'm going to have a few words with him about that."

Serge laughed; it was a kind of cough noise underneath his rich speaking voice, "But hey, I didn't phone to upset you, I just wanted to know if we can do some business."

"Mm… I don't know if I can do anything… I don't know what your guy plays like; I usually listen to the music before I book them."

"I can drop some cassettes over to you if you like."

"You can, but I don't promise anything." I responded.

"I've been off the scene for a while, that's why I'm into management at the moment, it's slow moving for me, I'm very much out of touch." His flow of words faltered, and I sensed a moment of vulnerability from him, but this was not a conversation to have on the phone. Besides, we were on two sides of the music environment – he was jazz and I was rock and roll.

The jazz world was in another stratosphere I knew very little about. I worked with actors, rock and roll bands, variety shows, the odd country-western singer and the latest craze, a breakdance team.

Initially our phone conversations held nothing more than business. However, there is a Jewish word, *beshert* which roughly means, if it's your destiny for something to happen, it will, otherwise, even if you trip over the person, nothing!

In previous years, Serge and my paths nearly crossed a few times, but we hadn't connected.

Not when my friend Carole got married and hired Serge's band for the reception. I was totally oblivious to the man at the piano. Nor when Serge was touring with Dig Richards who had recorded my song, 'Alice in Wonderland'.

We didn't know then that our lives would one day be intricately woven together, and that we'd flounder around in a complex cauldron of living.

I hadn't planned for romance to come crashing in on me.

As the relationship evolved, we had a lot to learn about each other. The events of my life impacted on our later interactions. Loss of family: my father, the endless battles with my mother, chasing career changes and surviving as a young woman in the entertainment industry scrambling for a living.

After my divorce, I worked and travelled like a mad-thing, to compensate for the time I had lost being married, and there wasn't a peep of any kind of romantic attachment.

Then, along comes this extraordinary charismatic being who did *not* sweep me off my feet.

CHAPTER 7

Some Days Have a Massacre

"Look, I really don't want to wax philosophic, but I will say that if you're alive, you got to flap your arms and legs, you got to jump around a lot, you got to make a lot of noise, because life is the very opposite of death."

– Mel Brooks

"Have you listened to the tapes I left in your letterbox? I came by the other day, but you weren't there." The rich voice came over my phone. For some reason, I found it exciting.

"I did, but why didn't you call first, I might have been around at the time."

"I was going into town and was in a hurry, so did you get a chance to hear Joachim play? He's top class. I hope you can get him a gig. His talent will make you look good too."

"I did listen, and I agree, he sounds great, but I really don't know much about jazz or where I could …"

Before I had a chance to say anything else, "How about I take you to lunch in Chinatown? We can talk about it when I come back from Melbourne. I've got some gigs lined up down there for Joachim, so I'll call you when I return. We can go for Yum-cha."

"Yum-cha, what's that?"

He laughed, "I'll definitely have to take you. I'll call when I get back."

I felt like a hurricane had just blown through my phone: a lunch arrangement with strange food in Chinatown, a jazz musician promoter hustling work from me. Here was food for thought, and before I had time to digest that, another phone call from a casting agency interrupted me and I had to go chasing a bunch of actors for a soapie.

Somewhere in the girly depth of me was a tiny whisper that Serge was an interesting man, but for now, an event making headlines distracted me. Nobody knows how something they plan to do will turn out, like a simple Sunday afternoon in a pub!

In September 1984, one of my muso clients rang me, "Can you come and listen to my band on Sunday, Helene? Maybe you could book us, as well as the regular solo gigs you get me."

"Where will you guys be playing, Richard?"

"We're doing an afternoon gig at the Viking Tavern in Milperra, this Sunday for Father's Day. Could you come and hear my band?"

"I'll do my best to be there," and seeing it was Father's Day, I thought I'd pay a visit to my dad's grave at Rookwood cemetery on the way to the pub.

Showered and ready, it wasn't premonition that stopped me from going to either the cemetery or the pub. I felt the onset of a cold, which prompted my last-minute decision to stay home and look after myself.

Richard phoned me that evening sounding very shaken. "Just as well you didn't come this afternoon, Helene."

I felt guilty. "I'm sorry, I wasn't feeling very well, and it's a long drive to Milperra."

"It was an absolute massacre at the pub."

"Why, what happened? Your band killed them, hey?"

"Not the band, we were just beginning to play when two bikie gangs started a massive shootout. At first, we heard shots outside and hightailed it into the toilets. We were there to play, not to get killed in a gang war."

"Are you and your guys okay, Richard?"

"Yes, we're all pretty shook up, but it'll be something to talk about later. I hope it doesn't put you off coming to see the band another time."

"Of course not. Shootouts don't stop me." Little did I know how much a gun would ultimately impact on me.

The headlines that night confirmed there had been a massacre between two gangs in the pub at Milperra, the Bandidos and Comancheros, all carrying heavy-duty weapons, rifles and shotguns. Eight people were killed and many were injured.

A different kind of massacre was about to enter my life.

You meet someone and have an interaction, something happens between you. Neither of you have any way of knowing what will evolve. You are simply two individuals attracted to each other. Maybe there is a puppet master playing with you just to see how human beings behave with the peculiar phenomenon of relationships and love. Cupid is just a baby shooting his toy arrows.

I wasn't ready for any of it. Even now I wonder what that elusive 'thing' was that pulled me down the path of what could have been. A need for an elixir of emotion, a promise of something yet unfulfilled?

♪♪

"I'm back from Melbourne; it was a great tour." Serge sounded sexy and excited on the phone. "I'm inviting you to meet Andrew Oh, my new protégé, he's a great saxophone player, comes from Singapore. I've also invited our finance guy. I want you to join us at the Emperor's Garden for a Chinese slap-up dinner."

Was that an order? "When? I don't know if I'll be busy."

"Tomorrow night, I'll pick you up. I very much hope you can make it."

That's better, I thought, I'm not big on being ordered around. "I don't have any other arrangements. I can meet you at the restaurant."

"No, I'll pick you up."

Going to strange places and connecting with all kinds of odd people was not unusual for me, yet, once we arrived and settled in the Chinese restaurant, I felt awkward. Although this meal was meant to be business, it felt more like a scene from Alice in Wonderland with an odd bunch of characters surrounding me: Musicians, producers, a financier, wives, ex-wives, new partners and an assortment of offspring.

The Mad Hatter's tea party could not have been more peculiar than my first Chinese meal with Serge Ermoll, musician, composer, and recent jazz entrepreneur. He presided over us, weaving an exciting story about his recent trip to Melbourne. Platters of Chinese food kept coming. "Audiences loved Joachim down there. But man, did he mess up my budget, leaving me with massive hotel and phone bills. He drove me nuts wanting a black piano instead of the white one provided by the venue." Excited, Serge was taking mouthfuls of food with his chopsticks and keeping us entertained. "We stayed at expensive hotels, and had nightly banquets in Chinatown or Lygon Street. What a great place! I hired a car, and organised cocaine for Joachim and the boys."

With the mention of cocaine, my thoughts drifted off to another time, when, as an agent, I was familiar with the frequent use of coke in the business and knew that some agencies budgeted for the drug in their client's fees. I had no need for heavy substances; I felt I was extroverted enough not to need babble powder.

Armed with a folder of my actors' photos and résumés for an upcoming commercial, I walked into my client's office to find him bent over a few streaks of white powder. "Hello Helene, I'm having a few lines." He offered me a rolled ten-dollar note as he straightened up from a great sniff up his face. "Want a line?"

I was caught between being a good agent looking after my people, and diplomacy. I declined the offer and nonchalantly sat down. "No thanks, you go ahead, I'm cool." It would have worked had I not dumped my folders on the table, sending the expensive white powder in all directions.

Serge's ongoing saga interrupted my cocaine memory. "Tony, our bodyguard, cum drug provider was close by. The girls crowded in on Joachim because he's an incredibly good-looking man, I think he swings both ways, he even made a play for me, but I told him to get fucked."

I couldn't help thinking that Serge was like King Arthur presiding at the round table, and in true chivalry, he paid for all of us.

We found a lot to talk about when he drove me back to my car outside the radio station. I made a quick decision. "I have to go to Wollongong University Friday; one of my boys is performing there, would you like to come with me? On the way, I'll be stopping for a meeting with the Bankstown Theatre Restaurant people, to negotiate performances for a breakdance team I'm managing. It might be useful for you to meet the management."

"You manage breakdancers too? You're full of surprises, Helene Grover. Yes, I'll come with you and I'll drive. My car is bigger than yours."

On our way, we stopped for my meeting. After I introduced Serge to the manager, he sat quietly while I negotiated dates and fees for my Dynamic Floormasters, a bunch of street boys who could spin on their backs and tops of their heads.

"Man, you can hustle," was Serge's first comment back in the car.

"I have to; it's my livelihood." I was pleased he had noticed I had skills other than yelling down phone lines.

Night was setting in on the long winding drive to the University of Wollongong. I had made that trip many times before, but it was a lot more relaxing and pleasant to have an interesting man at the wheel.

Later that night, Serge drove back to Sydney through the leafy South Coast, and we got to know each other better by sliding into companionable conversation. Something beyond words pushed itself to the surface of our interaction and although undefinable, it was there, ready to tap-dance on a platform of emotion.

Both used to nocturnal activities, it seemed normal that at three o'clock in the morning, he came in my place for a very late supper.

Our first up close and personal flowed on from spending many hours together, and for that imperceptible attraction between us to emerge. We had verbally covered a lot of interpersonal territory, until the hours dissolved making talk irrelevant, and for two extroverted individuals like Serge and me, when it came to up close and physical, we floundered. We had finally arrived beyond inhibitions and allowed our bodies to take over. Then we got some sleep. That was the beginning of our relationship.

For a long time, I had a longing for an exotic entrepreneur to share my dream. So here he was, and carried away by this golden plumed phoenix raised from the ashes of his past, I was transported on the flight with him.

My mother had to be told. "Mum, mum, I think this is it. I've met the right man, he's amazing." I blurted all this in Yiddish, our shared language since my childhood. By this stage, she had grudgingly shelved the idea that her only daughter would ever live a normal life.

"He's Russian, Mum, just like Dad was."

"Jewish?"

"No!" As if that really mattered to me.

I would have loved for her to understand that Serge being Russian was important for me, his presence in my life could fill the hole in my heart left by my father who had been my best friend, now lost to me forever.

"Your fader come from Russia, dis man is from vere?"

"Shanghai, mum, he speaks Russian."

"Ah probably from Cossacks, not good for Jewish people."

Nobody, not even my mother could burst my new bubble. I didn't care if he was Tartar or Cossack, red or white, Serge was bombarding my senses and this was all that mattered.

Our backgrounds had echoes of similarities. He was a jazz musician and promoter; I was a songwriter, and by the time we met, a theatrical agent.

I could only marvel that this exotic creature decided to tell me all about the pains of his past, of his parents, and why he had been out of action for the last couple of years. The risk of being swept up by this larger-than-life exotic being made me ignore a little voice inside calling for caution. I sent that unwanted voice off to shut up, leave me alone, and let this something unexpected and shiny, grab me.

During this early stage of getting to know him, I hadn't heard his music, had not made any connection with the sounds that came from his soul to his fingers. I was getting to know the man, his background, history, views about the world, even a hint of his mercurial nature, but not a note of this had yet reached my emotions.

CHAPTER 8

Journey Into Madness

"By and large, jazz has always been like the kind of a man you wouldn't want your daughter to associate with"

– Duke Ellington

My connection with Serge was like looking into a kaleidoscope, floating fragments of coloured pieces showing me parts of his discordant existence.

You couldn't call the beginning of our relationship romantic. Apart from our 'business' dealings, we didn't have a conventional courtship with dates and amorous flirting. All we had were some shared commonalities and the 'something else' not yet defined.

Serge fascinated me and I found it incredibly endearing that a man could talk so openly about his emotions, and the dark holes of his life. He jumped backwards and forwards about himself, his intensity overwhelming as he recounted, "I was living a daily hell of paranoia, going to hell and back with a two-year breakdown from the overload of alcohol and pills. My associate and I opened a swish detective agency on the North Shore and because we were smart and knew how to handle ourselves, we did very well."

"It must have been dangerous?" Great question, which helped to boost his ego and boast about his heroics of chasing after questionable characters.

"I'm a 4th Dan black belt karate champion, which is just about the highest grading, besides I have a gun license to carry a piece."

I knew 'a piece' was a gun, which made it easy for me to imagine him as a detective, and when he also mentioned his martial arts skills, it made me envisage him in the role of detective. Serge had chosen to emulate the crime-fighting fiction hero, Philip Marlowe, played by Humphrey Bogart in the 1946 movie, "The Big Sleep".

Too early to know the little boy in him was never far away, nor for me to understand he was a deeply troubled man. In comparison, the violence of my childhood was the Holocaust and the constant verbal battles with my mother were nowhere near as colourful as Serge's background.

I watched him absentmindedly pulling at his moustache when he told me about his two years of madness and paranoia, the result of an anonymous phone call to his office.

"I heard a sinister voice on the phone, and my whole life spun out of control, 'We will get you Mister Ermoll.' Maybe the words of the unknown voice may not have had such a devastating effect if I hadn't been doing a lot of booze, drugs, marihuana, acid, and Valium. Somehow the whole mix made me plunge into a mental breakdown, and my world fell completely apart; I was holed up at my parents' house in Punchbowl for nearly two years and virtually lived in their attic with my loaded gun pointing down into the room below in case 'they' were coming to kill me."

"Didn't your parents do anything to get you out of there?"

"They tried, but my mother was pretty well off the planet by then, and my father was busy with his own music world. They didn't know how to deal with my paranoia. All the psychiatrists I was taken to were useless. I even got talked into going to a disreputable ashram on the Central Coast, and literally ended up a tree to get away from the head guru who, it was later found, was a paedophile."

His pain attached itself to my feelings and disturbed me in a way I couldn't understand. I had never met someone with so much emotional baggage, and felt overwhelmed by the outpouring of his flight into that dark, incoherent world.

"Nothing could break through the curtain of my mental state until I was finally taken to see my mother's psychiatrist. I didn't want to go and it was a battle to get me to leave the house."

Hard to imagine how someone could drag this unwilling, and mentally disturbed hulk of a man to a therapist.

Shaking and paranoid, Serge was brought into the consultation room. Far from his own dark world, he couldn't tell his new therapist was blind. "I was a mess when I walked into Doctor Paul Merory's house, but you know what he did? First thing, he held out his arms and enveloped me in a long hug until the tears galloped down my face, my body heaved with emotional pain and release. I felt like he was taking me back on the road to sanity."

In that pivotal moment, the tall, lean and frail Doctor Merory brought Serge back towards recovery.

"I was sober for the first time in years. Paul helped me talk about my pains and how I had arrived at this point. I talked and cried about my childhood, complications with my parents, the mixed up world of jazz, but worst of all, the abuse I had put my body through with all the drugs and alcohol. Even though I came back from that fuzzy, crazy place I had been in for two years, I'm still not quite ready to play music. That's why I feel more comfortable being a promoter touring other musicians, like Joachim Kuhn, at least it brings me back on the scene."

Fascinated with Serge's history of descent into his mental hell, I saw him as a torn genius with a fractured soul.

As for me, I was living in my two-bedroom, third-floor apartment with beige walls, peach-coloured velour modular lounge, a dividing wall of mirror tiles, and a small veranda overlooking the distant ocean. Some people make plans, have goals, even have an idea of where they're heading. Me? I fell into what turned up next.

We live in the cocoon of our bodies where we can lock in our thoughts, feelings and memories, and hide from our own truths. We construct for ourselves versions of our stories, and if we were to stop our internal dialogues, we might hear the silent ones speaking from the caverns of our wounded psyches.

The more I became immersed in Serge's world, the dissentions with my mother and survival of my new business receded in the background, and I began to lose myself in a world where I believed was the exciting existence I had been yearning for.

CHAPTER 9

Moving In

"You can never cross the ocean unless you have the courage to lose sight of the shore"

– Christopher Columbus

We got to know each other as we talked about our childhoods, and discovered the commonalities that pulled us together.

1984 might have been George Orwell's view of a grim future, but for me, I faced the second half of 1984 with the belief I was heading for my brave new world, and what it did, was to flood my existence with a different kind of music.

During a dinner in Chinatown, Serge told me more about his return to sanity. "After that two-year madness, I needed to get back into action; I didn't have a plan, except I felt the need to move quickly. I've had these business cards printed." He pulled out one from the inside pocket of his black leather jacket and handed it to me. The card had a black silhouette skyline and the name, East Coast Jazz Productions, director: Serge Ermoll. "I couldn't afford colour printing, so I got some red stationary dots and stuck them on individually to give the card a Japanese look." I had to admit, it was very creative.

"Touring Joachim Kuhn was fun, although it threw me into massive debt with bills for hotels, car hire, dope and security. Being the new manager for Andrew Oh is much better. You met him the other night. He's easy going and a good commercial music player. Right now, I'm in the background, playing the keyboard and being the band's manager."

Serge was very particular about the calibre of musicians he worked with, piling high praise on "world class" ones or descending into remarks like, "He can't play for shit' or "He hasn't got the chops" or alternately, about one of his colleagues, "He flits over the keys like a fairy." When it came to his music heroes, he proclaimed effusive outbursts, "You're the greatest, man, and play the shit out of it."

Some musicians go for the booze, others the drugs. Although married to a pretty blonde Australian wife and the father of a young boy, Andrew loved the women. "I can't get the chick out of my head, man," he confided about his singer. "She's singing next to me at our gigs, and I'm sure she's sending me signals." The signals culminated into a torrid affair that broke up the marriage and was the catalyst for Serge and me to live together.

Funny how someone else's romance, marriage breakup, their moving from a house in Balmoral to an apartment in Manly, could be the impetus for a major life-change for me. However, this was the opportunity for Serge to move from his parents' cluttered fibro house in Punchbowl to the northern suburb, a short walk from the beach.

The sun was heading off into the distant ocean at Coogee Beach. We sat close together in my lounge room, he moved his arm around my shoulder, looked at me and just like that, asked, "You and I, we have something going together so, when I move to Balmoral, why don't you come with me. We could set up a joint office and pool our resources. It's a great place, Helene." Serge was great at presenting a sales pitch. "There's a separate entrance to an attached room, ideal for an agency. I'll have to wait only for a few weeks until Andrew and his wife move out."

Inside the safety of my personal cocoon, I wasn't prepared to make this kind of decision. I wasn't even sure about my feelings for this man sitting next to me, so how could I consider us living together? It seemed premature to be talking about it, considering there hadn't been any mention of love or any other emotion, but then again, musicians move to the sound of a different beat, particularly this one who seemed to live from moment to moment, and this moment was only a few weeks since we had met.

Living alone has its pros and cons, you can do what you want when you want, and if there's a mess, it's all yours. You play music you like, the awful nicotine smell permeating curtains and wardrobe is all yours until the day you decide to give up smoking forever. Then again, living alone is being alone, welcome solitude can become loneliness.

I fought an internal battle of whether to be cautious, or just go with the flow.

A sense of destiny compelled me, and in a reckless moment, "What about, in the meantime, you move in with me?" It was a gigantic leap for me. What I didn't say was, if it didn't work out at my place, I wouldn't have to move at all. He'd have to be the one to *schlepp* stuff in and out.

The reasons to change living arrangements were not as valid for me as they were for him.

My attraction to him fogged up any sensible reasoning. After all, I rationalised, people do it all the time; he'll bring over his stuff, we'll find a place for it and work out who puts what where, and accept or fight over who has supremacy over the new joined environment.

Whatever happened with Serge was never easy.

Initially, he moved in with a green plastic bag filled with his clothes, and a small brown one with personal stuff, and I thought, 'that was easy,' until a few days later, the whole office of his Eastcoast Jazz Productions arrived; desk, chair, files, posters and photos he immediately stuck on my ugly mustard-coloured wallpaper.

We had not discussed the details of Serge's move, and when I saw all that stuff invading my apartment's small office, something uncomfortable stirred in me. He had taken it for granted it would be okay to bombard me with all of his business and life. More of his invasive personality pulled me out of my girlish expectations.

The glorified entrepreneur musician was not as he first seemed. The sleek car he had driven me to Wollongong in had turned into a battered old bomb. His finance angel had flown off and it seemed as if the enchanted kingdom had vanished, replaced by stark reality.

Andrew's affair broke up his marriage. His wife stayed in the Balmoral place leaving Serge and me to stay put in my flat.

Who knows, if not for Andrew's one little affair, the story of Serge and Helene might have ended there.

How many of us can look back on our lives and consider that, if not for one event, life may have taken another direction? I wonder, what illusive elements shape our destiny, and we, the hostages live with the outcomes. I was not only naïve to have an almost stranger move in with me, but instead of waiting until this worked out, I was crazy enough to get seduced into a series of activities with him, and one could question whether I had lost my sense of reason altogether.

Not long after he moved in, he announced, "I'm meeting a venue owner at Bondi Beach. Why don't you come with me, I want to organise a few performances for Andrew and the band. It's in your field, will you help me with it?"

At last, one of my long-held fantasies, to jointly work on a promotion was coming true. I believed it couldn't get better than this. But the dream quickly crumbled.

A full moon danced and refracted into pieces on the calm, summer ocean. Across the road, along the stretch of Campbell Parade, was the Biltmore Hotel, a dilapidated residence that had been rejuvenated as a street level live music venue. Tourists and locals milled in a steady stream towards restaurants and cafes. Serge and I arrived for our meeting with the owner.

The three of us stood at the bar discussing booking dates and promotion strategies, familiar territory for me. I suggested, "I think some posters will be great to promote Andrew and the band." Serge dismissed my suggestion as if one would shoo away an unpleasant flying insect.

In an idyllic state of creative togetherness, I at first didn't notice that during the drive home, Serge was silent until the night exploded with his anger, "You made me look like an idiot. You really are a controlling bitch. Women are bitches."

Stunned and devastated, I blabbered, "I didn't mean to upset you, I was trying to help."

"Who asked you?"

"You asked me to come."

"Yes, but not to interfere." He aimed screaming bolts of anger at me confusing me about what to do, or say next. This was something new, I felt like a caged animal cringing behind bars. By the time we reached home, my silence had calmed him down, and he explained, "Look, I'm still emotionally very fragile after my two-year mental breakdown," and went on to describe the hell he had gone through.

Late nights for me, yes, but not usually so heavily charged with this kind of intensity and emotional outpouring. I was at the point of just wanting to sleep, and was unprepared for how demanding Serge could be, siphoning my energy to replenish his wounded psyche.

"I want to hear more about all that, but not right now. I'm so tired, I need to sleep."

"You don't give a shit." He became angry again, and I sensed I had to placate him, "Yes I do, I want to know more about what you went through and how you felt, but because I am so tired, I can't digest it all properly right now."

"Okay, I'm sorry, it's just part of my recovery." He petulantly let it be for that night and I couldn't go to sleep for a long time, ruminating whether I had made a mistake, nursing a new wound in my emotions, and should I call it quits in the morning. Then again, he did apologise, he did explain. Nobody is perfect and he is an exciting man.

How could this promising relationship, in its embryonic state develop into such an emotional force? In the following weeks, he found the triggers to pull my anger from me with his demeaning words knocking at the door of my indignation, until I retaliated with my own fiery responses engaging in futile verbal battles. It took me a long time to figure out the dynamics of our corrosive relationship, and my inability to run as far as possible from him.

Now, I wonder, how I could keep going, how I could allow the invasion of my sane mental state to be hijacked so badly?

Inside this temperamental, undisciplined man, lurked a lost boy; a small child whose tantrums were desperately in need of comfort, and when they were over, he became a loveable teddy bear again, wrapping me in his warm cocoon with hugs, huge bunches of flowers, full of apology and promising me better times ahead.

Just as sudden thunderstorms leave the sky with a colourful rainbow, mine transformed into the wild ride of Serge's promotional activities, and left me with little time or emotional strength to work with my stable of performers, as I became increasingly involved in his world of jazz.

The 'Mad Max' film crew had just completed the third movie, *Beyond Thunderdome*. Andrew Oh was cast as Ton Ton Tattoo, a blind saxophone player, in a scene with Tina Turner. As part of Andrew's new management team, I felt this provided us with an excellent media opportunity, and hopefully a film clip for his new album.

In the course of developing working relationships for my agency and making valuable contacts, I had worked very hard for close to ten years to gain a decent reputation, and was proud that Actor's Equity had recommended me to a production company who worked on commercials, films, and general entertainment. They became my most lucrative client. Doug, the boss, gave me a lot of work for my actors and especially my breakdancing team. I didn't share the same taste for booze and cocaine as Doug; nevertheless, we had a friendly working relationship.

To finance Andrew's album film clip, Doug offered to pitch a deal to one of his large company clients, and we arranged to meet at the City Hilton where Andrew and his band played.

The music was hot and so was the night, crowds mingled around the bar and dance floor.

Either drunk or nosed up with coke, Doug welcomed Serge and me with an overly friendly greeting by enthusiastically burying his face in my cleavage. 'Helene Darling, good to see you.'

I pulled his head away by the hair and gave him a hard smack on the hand. "Naughty boy, Dougie baby, get your head out of my tits." He looked sheepish, grinned a little and muttered an apology.

Amidst the music, the heat, the milling crowd, dancers, and laughter, Serge sprang into action. He grabbed Doug by the front of his shirt, ready to land a punch. "Listen here, you motherfucker; keep your face off my woman." Holy shit, I really didn't need this sudden act of chivalry. I had been handling bum pinchers and boob grabbers for a long time, and was quite adept at dealing with them with a martial arts type technique I had developed.

The three of us were locked in the middle of the dance floor in this crazy situation. I pulled Serge's arm back to stop any bloodshed. Not easy, I tell you. He was angry and chivalrous all at the same time. "Cut it out, Serge. You're my hero, thanks, but I'm cool." After he dropped his arm, I almost added, 'That's a good boy,' but felt this could have added more fuel and bloody noses.

Doug was too drunk or doped up to remember the incident, and our business arrangement was still intact.

My years in the entertainment industry brought me plenty of oglers, gropers, and indecent proposals. Dealing with all of it gave me enough resilience to find a sense of proportion and humour. No matter what field you are in, you have to take chances with people you do business with. It was even more precarious in the music industry.

Not every day a person fronts criminals and murderers. I never went out looking for them, nor did they seek me out. Let's just say I noticed them. Serge, on the other hand, encouraged them. It's not just in the music industry. Years ago, when I worked for a 'mate' in the *schmatta* (clothing) business, one of our clients offered to break arms or legs of delinquent account payers, for a price of course. No! I never engaged his services.

Close to the waterfront, the Manly Pacific Hotel was an ideal venue for entertainment and dining. I hoped to get Andrew a regular gig there. At the time I didn't know the well-dressed businessman on the other side of the desk from me was the notorious Andrew Kalajzich. He ultimately went to jail for organising his wife's murder.

You never know what murderous individual you may face across a desk. Ignorant of anything like that, I had bigger fish to catch, and did. Mister Kalajzich booked Andrew Oh to play at the hotel, and killing anyone had nothing to do with it. The kind of life I was leading by then, murder was the least of my problems.

Our Andrew eventually got himself a long-term gig at the Basement and I went on with other clients, projects and battles with Serge. I found myself juggling all the complicated elements of my life, his projects and moods, tight finances and what to have for dinner.

Serge had been living with me for only a few months, yet I was already flying high and low on the rollercoaster. As it rose and tossed me down again I was still attached to a kind of stable spot. In time, the hinges came undone and we flew off in all kinds of directions.

CHAPTER 10

From Shanghai To Sydney

There was a period which I refer to as the 'Golden Age of Jazz' which sort of encompasses the middle thirties through the sixties, we had a lot of great innovators, all creating things which will last the world for a long, long time

– Sonny Rollins

As diverse as my own existence was, I found Serge's much more fascinating, and began to write his life story. At first, the title was going to be, "Knight in Rusty Armour." This knight certainly had rusty hinges. He was thrilled with the idea, the title, and of course, the focus on him.

I couldn't possibly write about Serge in one go. Forty years of life takes time. I also had to deal with everyday work and workouts.

"Jesus Helene, turn that blasted music down, it's unbearable!" He came out of our bedroom wearing a white t-shirt he slept in. "What the fuck are you doing?"

"My morning aerobics," I answered him without stopping. "One-two-three," and did another body bend to the steady beat of George Benson's 'Broadway.'

"Turn it down, Helene, no wonder the people from the building behind, shot blanks up to your balcony the other day."

"They're a nasty bunch. Besides it's only for fifteen minutes, two, three, four. I'll turn the music down if you put the kettle on for breakfast."

"Good idea." He went to the kitchen, and I turned the sound down. He boiled eggs, made tea and toast, set the table. Nobody could boil eggs as perfectly as he did, exactly how I like them, not too runny, not too hard.

My workout finished, I sat down with him to eat breakfast. "Don't you like George Benson?"

"I do, but not so that people can hear him two streets away."

Eventually, I abandoned my lounge-room workouts; I've never been a dedicated exercise person anyway.

Writing about this man's life was another kind of workout.

Serge was born in Shanghai, and I learnt that Shanghai in the thirties and forties had flourishing communities of Chinese, Russian, French, and Jewish people. Artistically, it became known as *'The Paris of the East'* and was the hub of three art forms: Chinese cinema, animation and popular music. Combined with prostitution and gambling, it also was the centre for opium smuggling in the thirties. Many Czarist Russians fled there for safety.

During the turmoil of the Bolshevik revolution in Russia, Cossack pogroms descended on Jewish villages where young men were forcibly conscripted into the Russian army. My father was one of them, until he deserted. If he had been caught, he would immediately have been shot. He then made his way across Europe, reached England, established a new life and involved himself with politics and human rights movements.

Although both Serge and my father had Russian roots, each had made their life in other parts of the globe and they chose entirely different paths.

Serge senior pursued a music career and joined a vaudeville entertainments agency. He often boasted that he had been a regular performer at the prestigious Astor House, Shanghai's oldest running hotel. This venue had once hosted Charlie Chaplin, who, he proudly told us, became a close friend.

The many elements of Serge junior's life and history were so compelling that I felt it would be fascinating to share his life story through writing a book. The best times to write were after dinner. I sat at the table and wrote, interrupting him now and again to ask a question. Some nights, when the words poured out of his memory, I wrote so fast my fingers ached.

"You're asking me when did I start playing music! I was four years old, and for the next three years, my father taught me to play the piano, Chopin and other classics.

"I also have memories of snooker rooms my father dragged me to because he loved hustling. I was born in 1943, when after the Great Depression food remained scarce in China. To feed the family, Dad sometimes hustled pool for three days straight. My father was president of the musician's union in Shanghai, and took me with him to all their meetings. My mother never

looked after me because she was a high falutin' socialite who went around with all the upper crust people.

"She went to ladies' dos and all that kind of shit. That's all she did, and when I wasn't with my amah, our Chinese manservant, I'd be with my father. My parents led a decadent existence, they wore fine clothes, ate good food and attended endless social events; they also entertained many musicians and well-to-do figures.

"At that time, my father produced seventy-eight-inch vinyl records that circulated all over the United States under the name of Serge Ermoll and the Music Masters. He was recording for Columbia and Pathe Records, and was constantly sought after by the media, which made him a popular figure amongst the elite.

"We lived in the Avenue Joffre, the French sector, in a place called Hamilton House owned by Sir Victor Sassoon, a big international figure. I was enrolled at a French school, but my French studies were so appalling that the teachers had cut out rabbit's ears, stuck them on me and made me stand in the corner, in front of all the other kids.

"I can still remember the filth alongside the affluence, and places like Bubbling Well Road and the yellow, dirty Wampu River.

"Even when I was six years old I was a rogue. Man I was awful. I kicked one Chinese guy in the arse when he was playing marbles and made him fall flat on his face."

Finally, I am writing this book, and include the many pages of recording Serge's life he dictated to me, interrupted by our daily activities while trying to make sense of our relationship and the gigantic jigsaw puzzle of our individual natures. This was the beginning of the many times I put aside my own life and aspirations to focus on his, and only now do I question whether the pieces diminished me. All I knew was, being in the presence of an incredibly interesting man with a history, took my breath away.

Eventually my own life took on many pathways. Some were journeys of emotional recovery, whilst others, led to the discovery of new ideas, experiences and people who helped shape the more grounded person I eventually became.

We both had years of 'before us' times with other people and experiences and by the time we met, we were both on the forty-year old mark. This is the story of my experience with Serge Ermoll, Jnr., man, musician and undoubtedly "Enfant Terrible". My mother told me that I too had been an enfant terrible when I was little and prone to tantrums.

Whenever possible, I continued writing the saga of his life.

"I had everything I needed or wanted. Man, I had servants, toys, everything, except the one fucking thing I wanted the most, my mother and father home at night with me, but they never were. Then came the revolution. It brought in the communists who enforced a totally different concept of society than that of the right-wing Chiang Kai-shek. Many of our people returned to Russia.

"Others, like my parents, scattered to America, England, France, and Australia. I had already learnt a lot of English from the American tourists and army in Shanghai and was

told that in Australia, they pronounce the word "lady" as "lay-a-dee".

"Life had become very risky in China; if you hustled for food, it was perceived that you were dealing, and was considered treason. It could get you killed on the spot. My father was always a breath away from the firing squad.

"There was so much violence. I witnessed executions in the street where people were getting shot in front of me. I was so young, but I'll never forget seeing a policeman slice a woman up with his bayonet. I felt nauseated when I saw the blood spurting out of her. That image must have gone into some kind of internal storage tank that has affected me for life.

"My father decided that it was time to leave Shanghai, and we migrated to Australia in 1950 on the Chien Chai. Man, being on the ship with both my parents in one place was a lot better for me than in pre-war Shanghai. I had both my parents to myself with more togetherness than ever before.

Between mouthfuls of my cooking, Serge continued with his memories while I sat with pen and pad taking notes, and asked questions. He became irate when I interrupted him.

"I told you, weren't you listening? Too busy watching the fucking cat, man." Spencer had entered our lives by then. Puss had made himself comfortable on my peach-coloured lounge; curled up with his grey chin on his soft white paws, oblivious of his two humans at the dining room table. I pushed my biro onto the white paper, while Serge sprawled on his chair sharing his memories with me. Beyond the veranda, a sliver of ocean could be seen on the distant horizon and I continued to write.

During the forties and fifties Australia provided a safe haven for immigrants. My parents left the aftermath of war-shattered Europe whilst the Ermoll family escaped Shanghai before the Japanese invasion.

Fleeing from a life of plenty to face a new kind of hardship in Sydney's fibro suburbia, the Ermolls found it incredibly difficult to adjust. No more grand afternoons with elegant ladies for Serge's attractive mother. She was unable to adapt to menial work or the reality of her husband working in a factory. I had to hand it to the old man; he was a great hustler as he gradually made his way into Sydney's club land as a musician

We finished dinner and Serge continued, *"After we arrived in Australia I was enrolled at Ramsgate School. I'll tell you about fucking Australia, bunch of jhlubs (one of his favourite expressions for Australian slobs). And the food! Man! Kraft cheese that tasted like soap and if you managed to get olives, they were like bloody sheep turds."*

When I added that we too couldn't handle Kraft cheese, not after all the fabulous Camembert in Paris, he said, *"Yes, cool, but are we doing my life or what?"*

I felt miffed that my story was so easily pushed into the background whilst his ego pushed itself into the front seat again.

"The kids at Ramsgate School all ganged up against me, the new kid and all they could say was, 'Lets bash him up.' That to me was a reflection of what their fucking arsehole parents did to them. They instilled in their minds that new Australians were wogs, horrible people encroaching on their territory. I decided that after that first day at school, I'd get even with those

kids and, I got them one at a time, which got me incredible respect in that school. It seems that in our society you have to use violence and force. Look at Vietnam, Libya, and South Africa; anywhere you choose to look, it's all war and violence. Nobody settles a dispute with words. Not ultimately."

My experience was completely different. In my school, I had been the new French girl they were fascinated with. The other kids wanted to know what I brought for lunch and what Paris was like.

Dinner long over, we drifted into midnight. Serge's rich voice reached into the ethers of my apartment. We sat on the modular lounge, cat and notepad on my lap while he continued talking about his childhood.

Our unexpected battles pulled me further into his life. His dominant personality drew me into his turmoil. I was learning how he became a jazz musician, and the conflicts that surrounded him.

"When did the music start for you, Serge?"

"At first, my father couldn't afford a piano, so he bought me a trumpet with the money he had saved working at the Australian Paper Mills as a fucking labourer, can you believe it? It was an incredible shock for him to lose the glamour, prestige and recognition he'd had in China.

"I played the piano from when I was four, but later I took up the trumpet."

During the telling of his early childhood, Serge was excited, animated, and relished the attention. Then, like a calm ocean disturbed by the tides, his face crumpled into painful creases. His crystal blue eyes seemed to descend into a dark place where I saw glimpses of his pain.

"My father didn't start beating me until we came to Australia. I was about seven or eight. At first, it was because I was such a hooligan at school and got into so much trouble and it pissed him off, but at least, with that reason, I understood the punishment.

"It got worse. At first, he hit me with his hands and later on, he'd pull out his belt and too often beat me black and blue with it."

"What about your mother, didn't she try to stop him?"

"She tried at first. It was hard for her too. He didn't beat her, he just pushed her away, by that stage she was mentally retreating into a distant world."

"Did your father tell you why he beat you?"

"When he had a reason; like when I wagged school. Other times, I could see a look in his eyes, and when I got older, I felt that he actually got off on beating me."

"Your father seems like such a pussycat."

"Yes, he's good with women and besides he likes you. He beat me about the music too."

"You mean when you played? You were such a little boy."

His face twisted into a look of angry irony. *"That didn't matter. One time I couldn't play Chopin's 3rd Etude on the trumpet when he'd accompanied me, I must have played some wrong notes or something, so he beat me. Another time, I was asked to play at a party with relatives and friends, but I was too shy to play, so he dragged me outside and beat the living shit out of me with his belt, then he made me go back in the house and play for them.*

"The physical pain was not as tough on me as the pain of shame and embarrassment.

"That was when I began to have terrible aggressive feelings towards my father and sometimes even wanted to kill him. He beat me while my mother stood by helplessly, too frightened to do anything in case my father might decide to beat her too.

"I was a teenager by then, between thirteen and fifteen and still at school."

♪♪

"My grandmother also migrated here from Harbin, China. She lived with us in our government-funded house in Yagoona. She was the only person who intervened when my father started laying into me. Placing herself between him and me, she screamed in Russian for him to stop. I was so grateful for it that I thanked her in Russian, 'Spaciba Daragaia Babooshka' (thank you darling grandma) I was very close to her. She became the fundraiser for the Russian Community.

"See Helene, I had to bottle up all these emotions, even hate. It's like filling up a cylinder of gas, one day it explodes. I know that my father drank a lot, but underneath, whether it was booze or not, it was still him. I believe that he got pleasure from the beatings that made me become angrier and angrier.

"I took up boxing and used it to intimidate other kids, and that way I gained the power to form my own gang with a bunch of young kids. We wore masks and made up swords, got pipes and filled them up with gunpowder and a ball bearing, cotton wool on top so the ball bearing wouldn't fall out until it was fired. I don't know how we didn't blow ourselves up in the process of all that. We'd go out late at night, creep around and fantasise that we were some sort of hoods."

"You sound like you were a bunch of hooligans terrorising the neighbourhood, I can see why you were always in trouble. How long did that go on for?"

"Well Helene, I had to be the leader, and I had to be tough. It's the law of the jungle, you know. You're a female. You don't understand boy stuff."

"I don't understand violence, although there was enough in my background because of the war and generally girls didn't gang up to terrorize people in the streets."

"I was serious about my music though; it wasn't till later that I started practising the piano and listened to records a lot. My father made me practice and practice. He wanted me to listen to Louis Armstrong, and more of the traddie stuff, Jonah Jones and swing, Duke Ellington. Pretty good, but I got interested in contemporary music. I bought the Dizzy Gillespie album that my father said 'this guy plays outside the chords.' He wasn't really; he was just playing flat fives, raised nines, and augmented elevens. My father said it was a whole lot of rubbish, but I thought it was absolutely great. I played it over and over.

"My instrument was the piano, that's where I found that I could express myself musically the most. I was about sixteen and switched instruments from trumpet to piano.

"It was the music that gave me the emotional release."

I couldn't find emotional release from the ongoing epic of the raging battles between us, and writing about Serge's life seemed like a welcome distraction from the challenging parts of our relationship which was playing havoc with my emotions. There were times when I barely dried up my tears and pulled myself together to continue writing the story of his life. Okay, my dear reader, go figure!

"I found my life in my music just the same, even if it was by default and kept playing and doing what my father wanted me to. He eventually had me practice with Sonny Pratt, a young drummer.

I was about eight years old when Dad got Sonny and me loads of club work in every RSL, Leagues and Football Club in NSW."

"Did you get paid?"

"I guess we did, but the old bastard kept most of it and just gave us pocket money. He signed us up on Channel 7's Desmond Tester Show.

"Sonny and I were pretty excited to be playing on television with the American Mouseketeers when they came to Australia.

"Tommy Tycho had the Channel 7 Youth Show, so Sonny and I performed there too, with Lana Cantrell. Boy was she a stuck up demanding bitch. I was on TV all the time in those days. There was Lana, Brian Davies, Dig Richards and his brother Doug, Lucky Starr, The Delltones. Later, I ended up touring with Dig Richards who used to say to me, 'Why do you play this crazy way out music? it doesn't bring in any money. Stick with us, you'll get some recognition and make money."

This period of meeting Serge was not yet part of the game of serendipity, even though he was touring with his band, and backing Dig Richards who had recorded my song, 'Alice in Wonderland' which they most likely played as part of their repertoire. We never met then.

Still oblivious of the other's existence, we could also have met during Peter Allen's mini inclusion in our lives when Serge and I could have crossed music paths. Before he hit the big time and left his pseudo-brother Chris behind, Peter and I had attempted to write some songs together. Around that period, Serge was performing on the same bill as The Allen Brothers at the Sydney Yacht Club.

For the present, I was focusing on getting down Serge's story. *"I felt like I had come home when I discovered Miles Davis' playing trumpet on his album, 'Kind of Blue' and the incredible improvisations of John Coltrane on sax. They had a gigantic impact on my music, and influenced by the free improvisations of Coltrane I formed my Free Kata band, that I named from my Karate training.*

"I got a few live gigs and recorded some albums, which got into the archives of early Australian improvised jazz. Eddie Bronson on sax, and Louis Burdett, crazy, super talented drummer, were the exciting other members of Free Kata.

My philosophy was to express myself wholly and solely without restrictions or censorship, and it was through this music that I was able to finally let out all my pent-up emotions of frustration and anger. Boy, it used to upset a lot of people to hear it."

It took me some time into the relationship to understand Serge's bubbling cauldron of aggression, and where it came from.

"My Free Kata albums and concerts were all about that, I also needed to explode it all into a free form of improvisation. Would you like to hear the first album? I recorded a few."

Of course, I wanted to hear it, not just because he was now my partner, I also wanted to hear what his music was all about, and how he expressed his internal turmoil.

He put on the record, and throughout the flow of notes into the atmosphere I was mesmerised, not just with his amazing talent, but the way he expressed it.

In my third floor flat in Randwick, with a distant view of the ocean, I sat on a chair in front of the sound system, and for an uninterrupted time, I listened to Free Kata. This music reflected the inner layers of Serge's painful journey, and as I kept listening to his emotional roller coaster, it evoked in me my own visceral feelings.

Finally, it tore through anything I had heard before with its angry, aggressive pounding of notes that rose and fell through a catharsis of emotion, until it unexpectedly changed into something gentle, and I heard the redemptive quality of beauty.

At the end of the recording, I was drained. The construction of the notes and the jagged sound of the music had torn into an undiscovered place in me that had not experienced this kind of response in me before, and yet, I found meaning in it and respect for its creation.

Did it make me understand this human better? I think it did, but it changed nothing. We can understand someone, love, hate, empathise and all the other stuff, but it doesn't alter who they are, where they come from, and the delicate balance of the relationship you have with them.

"You know, Serge, I have a very eclectic taste in music, but had never heard of your Free Kata improvisation albums. How about we stop here and I'll make you a sandwich?"

"Yes, I'd like one, but you got nothing to make a sandwich with that appeals to me."

"I've got salami, there is…."

I was messing with a man who was mostly a carnivore, but also obsessive about food and only the kinds he liked, Chinese, Russian, European and most of my cooking, *"No man, fuck salami…I don't know why you buy that shit Danish stuff, get Sopresso next time, that's the real stuff."*

As I travelled through Serge's life with my pen and paper, the journey took us through hurricanes, storms, tempests and at least several earthquakes sweeping through our relationship.

My lion roared, paced, furiously tossed his thinning mane. His roars were huge, vocal sounds of agony and pain where the storms of his unresolved childhood lay buried, much too close to the surface.

Wanting to get a much better understanding of what Free Kata was all about, I contacted Paul (Pax) Andrew, a sax player friend of Serge's.

This is what Paul sent me:

"Serge was a great inspiration to us all. Back in '73 somehow I found myself listening to Serge Ermoll and Louis Burdett, down at the Rocks; creating something else, ripping the music apart and hammering the piano into crescendo after crescendo, followed by dramatic twenty-minute drum solos and honking squealing saxophone.

The very scary and ultra-dynamic Free Kata. A trio fronted by the sensational Eddie Bronson on tenor. I dug it though. Made me feel alive and on edge. Serge was a wall of energy yet always played the melody so beautifully, especially on a ballad or a song.

It was a real honour when I finally played with Serge in '85. He was playing tunes again by then. I mean form; blues, originals and standards all with his incredible touch.

Serge explained; "My deep lifeblood & love is free music, which is simply composing on the spot spontaneously, taking a walk outside the bounds of the metaphoric house of music & the boundaries of form, a walk on the wild side, a walk on the wonderful unpredictable path of beauty of spontaneity returning home after the excursion...home again. For all free music has form in itself & all music has time & rhythm, it's like my sensei used to say, "Experience is empty, innocence is full. There is surely nothing other than the single purpose of the single moment. A man's whole life is a succession of moment after moment, but if one fully understands the present moment, there will be nothing to do & nothing else to pursue."

Paul died of cancer, January 2019.

Throughout all my experiences and dialogues with Serge's colleagues and friends, I found people loved him, were in awe, were exasperated, were fed up, and as I will show you in the next part of his telling his story, there were even those who wanted to do him harm. I could have matched any of those sentiments as our relationship went through the whole gamut of emotions.

CHAPTER 11

Jazz Time

Well, jazz is to me, a complete lifestyle. It's bigger than a word. It's a much bigger force than just something that you can say. It's something that you have to feel. It's something that you have to live

– Ray Brown

When my darling godson Allan was a little boy, I read him stories and to make them sound fun and more interesting, I copied Victor Borg's phonetic punctuations, pulling my lips, tongue and mouth in a variety of shapes making odd ffts, and clicking noises to highlight commas, dashes and exclamations marks, until Allan giggled and shouted in delight, screaming for more. I loved it, not only because I could elicit so much delight in this sweet kid, but it also appealed to my sense of creating drama.

Allan is a grown man now and flies the world on important business. Now and again, we reminisce about those story times. He is a constant love in my life.

In my storytelling about Serge, there are no clicks or ffts; the childhood he brought in his narrative, was painful.

Especially when he talked about the beatings from his father that continued into his mid-teens.

When he was sixteen, Serge decided to *'get outa there'* and move to a damp-smelling converted laundry room. He took with him an old gramophone and continued to listen to what he felt was all the cool stuff, Chet Baker, Russ Freeman, Shelly Mann and Red Mitchell.

"I used to play the albums over and over. Stop, practice and try to get the chords until I got all the tunes down. I did everything; Brubeck, Mile Davis. Then I heard McCoy Tyner which blew me right out because he was so innovative on the piano. I wanted to be part of the great jazz innovators; the greatest were Charlie Parker, John Coltrane and McCoy Tyner who had learnt from Coltrane. They changed the whole concept of piano playing, and it prompted me to do that as well.

"When I discovered Bill Evans, I could understand that instead of playing tink-a-tinka-tink all the time, they broke and loped around creating rich harmony structures. I sat there practising and listening endlessly to all these people so I could emulate them. They were my greatest teachers.

I was losing myself in this new playground of jazz, but still had to do ordinary gigs, so I put together a trio that included myself on piano and Mike Lawler on bass, Mike played mainly with Dig Richards and the Delltones. Strictly Rock and Roll."

I interrupted him to ask, "What about alcohol? Were you drinking heavily at that time and were there any drugs around?"

"In those days I drank every day, but not a lot. It wasn't a crutch or anything. It was around, and everyone was doing it. My parents drank, my father a lot more than mum.

"I needed to stretch myself, experiment more with life and not just the music, so when I was sixteen, I headed up to Surfers Paradise. I went around town meeting as many musicians as I could and told them I was a jazz pianist from Sydney looking for a gig. Stan Bourne turned up at my motel and invited me to me play at the Southport Hotel. My boastful bravado landed me the gig, 'Stan, I gotta tell you the truth, I only know a couple of songs.'

"Without blinking he looked at me, 'When you're through with this job of mine, you'll know a lot of songs.'

"I couldn't read charts very well and had only a small repertoire, so I kept playing 'A Foggy Day in London Town' three or four times a night until finally, Stan asked me to play another song that I didn't know, and before I could say anything, he announced, 'Ladies and gentlemen, big drum roll, lights on Serge here, he is from Sydney, and he's going to play for us Rachmaninoff's Concerto in D Sharp Minor' and then Stan just walked off the stage.

"The applause started. Stan had gone to the bar and left me to play SOMETHING, so I started ad-libbing, improvising making it as dramatic as possible, the drummer came in at the end, playing pam, pam, pam, pam poom, padum, I did a lot of bullshit improvisations, and no motherfucker in the audience knew the difference. After that, I played every gig that I possibly could.

"I met Jim Anderson, the notorious underworld figure; he had a circuit of joints, and booked me to play in them. One day, as I was coming out of rehearsals, Jim pulled me by the front of my shirt, tickled my beard (all of three strands in those days)

and said in his heavy accent, 'None of yourrr…scooby-doo jazz in my cloob, son.' I told him that I wouldn't, but I did anyway."

"Seeing you were working for such a notorious character, were you aware of any criminal activities?" I asked.

My only boast about crime was that at a Jewish New Year lunch at a friend's place, I sat at the same table with the infamous crime boss Abe Saffron who also owned a string of nightclubs in Kings Cross, prostitutes and other nefarious businesses.

My lunch with a notorious criminal had no impact on Serge who wanted to go on with his story, *"All I gave a shit about was playing my music. I stayed in Surfers a while, bought some snazzy clothes including a sharkskin jacket, hung out with a voluptuous blonde stripper, and eventually moved back to Sydney."*

♪♪

Always enticed by music places, trendy activities, I occasionally went to the Mocambo, a well-established small jazz nightclub in King Street, Newtown. Less exotic than Kings Cross, but with a more artistic pulse than other suburbs, the main thoroughfare had single-lane traffic flowing past shops, a cinema, hair salon and a few pubs. The Mocambo provided a venue for some of the better-established jazz musicians and bands.

Again, the stars were not in alignment for Serge and I to meet. Even though we were around the same place and time, it wasn't yet to be. Besides, I was possibly in one of my temporary romances. Musicians weren't on my menu, and someone like Serge would have been in another stratosphere.

"Some of the guys and I used to stand out the front of the Mocambo. We listened to the musicians inside, but I felt that we weren't good enough yet to be playing in places like that. Imagine, a piddly joint like that, but then again, most jazz joints are piddly places.

"Desperate to play at the El Rocco, I kept pestering Arthur James, who owned the place to give me a gig. He kept ignoring me, but after I sat in one night with some musicians, I got a call from one of them, 'How would you like to play with our trio every Saturday night?' I nearly died! This was the top jazz joint in the country although it only crammed in about sixty-five people."

I added, "I remember the El Rocco. Carole and I went down there to listen to jazz because it was trendy. I remember the tiny street, more like a lane."

Not a good idea to interrupt a genius while telling you his life's saga, *"Okay Helene, whose life are we doing here? It was actually Brougham Street, just off William Street. It was a tiny cellar that got really stuffy, but it had a grand piano, and it was the home of jazz in Sydney back in the sixties."*

He tweaked his blonde moustache that drifted down into his beard, and continued. *"One night Dave Levy, the wonderful piano player, came in and said that we were the best-dressed group at the El Rocco, then added 'You shouldn't be playing here just yet Serge because you're not equipped enough musically.' He was right, but I had so much fuckin' balls to do it. I was practising my tits off twelve hours a day, every day.*

"After that, I played at the El Rocco for a number of years and hustled my way to play with Lenny Young. At the time he was the hottest drummer in the country, recording albums with Don Burrows and all of the top guys. Lenny invited me to join his band permanently. I noticed that he was an immaculate dresser, often wearing a neat dark jacket over a turtleneck sweater. Chicks used to say to me, 'You work with Lenny, so what's with him? He's odd, last night I was about to get into bed with him, and it took him ages taking off my clothes. He neatly folded each piece and carefully put it on a pile on a chair and did the same with his own clothes; it almost turned me off waiting for it to be over with.'

"Man, I've never seen anyone so fastidious. Sometimes when I picked him up for the gig, I'd be waiting for him to finish brushing and brushing his coat.

It was the same with his car. Rain was pelting down when he picked me up for a gig, and as soon as he opened the car door to let me in, he looked at my wet shoes, and immediately handed me a couple of plastic bags to put over them. I guess he didn't want me to ruin his precious Mini Minor.

"Lenny was one of my greatest teachers. He'd put on a record, play a couple of bars and then say, 'Now come on Serge, get that down,' and as I played a piece over and over again, he'd say that's not the chord, play it again, listen to it again. I don't think anyone else would have spent as much time as he did for me to learn. It helped me tremendously."

I interrupted, needing to clarify parts of his now rapidly firing dialogue and memories, "What do you mean, getting it down?"

"Gees Helene, I thought you knew music, learning the tunes, in my head, no reading charts, just getting all the notes into my memory. I was learning to play like the well-known piano players, Oscar Peterson, Bill Evans, Keith Jarrett and Herbie Hancock.

"I was screwing a country chick from Broken Hill; man, she was a real nympho, apart from playing with my dick, she was also a fine classical piano player. My best friend Al used to accompany her down to the El Rocco to hear me play; he'd screw her first and then bring her to me, (he laughed). *I was about seventeen then."*

"How awful that your best mate had sex with her too; couldn't he get one of his own?" I had never heard of such a thing.

Serge laughed again, *"That was the fun of it, sharing her. Hey, Helene, you can't put that in the book man! They'll have fucking contracts out for me."*

"Why? Screwing a chick is nothing to get killed for."

"No, but in Al's world it could happen."

"Why?"

"I'll tell you another time."

"So, you're telling me about your sex life instead."

"That'll keep you interested. For my first sexual experience, my friends in the neighbourhood took me to Crown Street Lane, near Palmer Street. I was at 16, still a little virgin boy and all the guys chipped in two pounds each. The chick was dark and thin, and after I screwed her, I realised that I didn't dig thin chicks. It was still a great excitement because you're not just fucking an ordinary woman. At that age, it's the greatest excitement you can possibly have because you're screwing a

woman who knows all about it, specialises in it. I remember saying to her, 'Aren't you going to take all your clothes off?' and she told me that it would cost me three pounds instead of two, so all she did was wash my dick with Dettol, lift her dress up, get on the bed and I got on top, and I blew my load in two seconds flat. I had to anyway, because if you didn't, they made you do it anyway saying, 'Come on, come on son, you haven't got all fucking night.

"*The worst of it was that the boys had got me drunk at the Criterion before another one of my stints with a pro, and who should turn up but Bumper Farrell, the infamous cop. He wanted to look good by showing that he was cleaning up the streets. I was still drunk and just happened to be going into one of the local brothels in the lane. He kicked and hit me in the gut a couple of times, telling me to 'get outa here and never come back, son'. Bumper Farrell then pissed off, but I went in for my screw anyway.*

"*I became a regular at that brothel, paying two pounds a week for one of the more voluptuous hookers that I preferred, until I met Geraldine with big tits, and I lived with her for a short while. She worked for the Rena Ware Saucepan Company, I cooled it with her when I found out that she was screwing her office manager as well.*"

"What a coincidence," I threw in. "For a while, I also worked in the office at Rena Ware. I wonder if your friend Geraldine was there when I was. Talk about serendipity."

I couldn't remember if I had a boyfriend at the time, and if sex was cooking in my saucepan.

Serge was so engrossed in his story, my moment of another almost crossover seemed irrelevant to him. He continued, *"By this time I was working six days a week at the El Rocco and Suzie Wong's on Monday nights in King Street."*

Unbelievable! But real life is odd, "That's where Carole and I won the talent quest that started the whole 'Barefoot Boy' recording in motion for me. Makes me wonder how many times you and I crossed paths back then, but somehow didn't connect."

I hadn't noticed the sky had changed colour. An early morning edge of a pale grey rose above the ocean in the distance beyond the balcony of my apartment. We packed it in for the night, and it wasn't until a few weeks later we continued with Serge's early life as a jazz musician.

"I knew that I had to go beyond the confines of Australia to get more experience, the pull was for New York and those iconic jazz joints. I sailed to London. All I wanted to do was play jazz and live the life.

"In London, I got a gig for an Italian guy who owned the Villa Cesare. The First night I played there, he rushed over to me, 'Please Sergio, you very good musician, I like you but please you no play jazz in my club.'

One night Shirley Bassey and Sean Connery were in the audience. The boss wanted me to accompany one of his Italian waiters who sang opera. 'Sergio, play for Julio, you gotta big ears you can play anything, accompany him for an opera piece.' I insisted that I couldn't, but nobody listened, and a grand piano was wheeled on the dance floor. Julio couldn't speak English, and all he could tell me was the name of some aria in C major.

"There was no way I could play a piece of opera, but it was my gig, I needed the money and I had to do something, maybe die

with my boots on as they say, so I played some big arpeggios in the key of B which was a hell of a key. Julio started to sing and I bull-shitted a bunch of notes up and down the piano. Everyone laughed, and Julio threw me murderous looks setting the whole audience rolling around laughing in hysterics.

"It was all too much for Julio who stormed off to huge applause; everyone thought that it had been some kind of comedy act. I didn't get fired; in fact, I landed more gigs at the Bull's Head, a prestige jazz place.

"I got to know the right musicians and people that got me Dudley Moore's piano gig with his trio. He was off to Hollywood to become a movie star, and I ended up staying in London for six years working both on radio and in clubs. I loved all of it, but it was time for me to return to Australia."

He became introspective, and I found it more difficult to extract the process of his thoughts as he dived into verbal improvisations, crossed the pathways of his mercurial moods, and demanded all my energy.

This is the point where my recording of Serge's life came to an abrupt end, it wasn't intentional; we had meant to continue with it, yet somehow never did. In those early years of our relationship, we had much more to deal with, many battles to win and lose, experiences to share, while the story of his life unfolded inside our joined history.

When I reflect on Serge's background, I can't help thinking although some of it had similarities with mine, migrants from war-torn countries, surviving the vagaries of childhood in a new environment, yet we were very different after all. It wasn't just the music, the family backgrounds or even the volatile nature of our individual personalities. Our values were vastly different, as well as the way we treated other people. As I got to know this man, there were many parts of his behaviour that screeched at things I believed in.

CHAPTER 12

Paddington Jazz Festival

"Humans are imperfect. That's one of the reasons that classical and jazz are in trouble. We're on the quest for the perfect performance and every note has to be right. Man, every note is not right in life"

– Branford Marsalis

Apart from my two-year banal marriage in my early twenties, I had not lived with anyone else since. Sharing space with Serge brought me a complex learning curve about adapting to someone new in my environment. Although generous, respecting someone else's space did not come easy for him, and added another log on the fuel of our bonfires.

Amidst this delicate balancing act, we had to bring in an income from our precarious industry.

The one-woman office was not equipped for a business partnership, let alone a larger-than-life individual with a booming voice. The desk, chair and files Serge brought into my office were the precursors of more to come. The ghastly wallpapered walls became full with the posters he had stuck on with 'Blu Tack'. At least there was less mustard-coloured patterned background to look at.

The corkboard with the photos of my actors and performers on the wall behind my desk, clashed with Serge's jazz mob on the opposite wall.

Serge's new phone line completely shattered what was left of the privacy of my second bedroom business place.

Maybe I had to learn to share, I rationalized. I had been running my solo race for too long, and if this arrangement were to work, I would have to adapt and use diplomacy with the ever-present temperamental outbursts from my new love interest.

"Darling, how am I going to manage running my business with yours on top of mine?" His response was a blend of verbal manipulation and loveable charm. Damn it, using 'darling' didn't work!

"Look, baby, I won't be in your way, I'll be out most of the time, seeing people." He folded me inside the cavern of his arms, kissed the top of my head and temporarily put my concerns to rest. Inside the big frame of his embrace, I felt safe from the harshness of the world. Lulled into believing this was like a bear's cave to keep out the winds of life's tempests.

The reassurance was transient; his presence dominated my entire space. His voice boomed through the room and down my phone line. I found it difficult to hear the chatter of my peach-faced lovebird sitting on its perch on a shelf above my desk.

Birdie was a Valentine's Day door prize my mother won at the Manly Pacific Hotel when she came to see me perform Madame Zelia. My poor mother! What I dragged her through. She could only assess my activities through her compact world and was either bemused or judgmental. She complained that my father, may he rest in peace, she'd say, would probably have been more accepting of my shenanigans.

Even during that early stage of us being together, Serge was not capable of holding his tantrums in check. Sometimes, a single comment from me, sent him off into another rage, another flow of aggressive language hurled at me, while I felt myself falling into a well full of tears, floundering in disbelief.

Tomorrow was always another day where a truce took us to the next situation.

I was about to step through a new portal of lunacy with a not-so gentle nudge into what Serge called, 'The real jazz scene.' "I received a royalty check for a few thousand dollars. It will come in handy for an International Jazz Festival I'm planning. How about you come in on it with me? You can do the promotion, you're so good at it, Boodgie girl."

Why didn't I say? "No, thanks, I'm too busy right now." But, of course I didn't, instead, I came up with lame responses. "I know little about jazz and besides, the biggest concert I organised was at the Bondi Pavilion for a few of my agency artists, and it didn't exactly set the world on fire. I hardly broke even so I don't think I'm up to this kind of thing. Where are you planning to have it?"

"Paddington Town Hall, I checked it out the other day. It's right on Oxford Street, between the city and the

Eastern Suburbs. It has a huge space and can hold a few hundred people and the acoustics are good."

A little itch made me want to scratch at something beginning to cause me some discomfort. His unpredictable moods concerned me as I was already experiencing the darker side of his personality. If I joined him and his idea didn't go according to plan, would I land at the slimy bottom of a discordant pile?

"I don't know, Serge, this is too big for me, and it sounds like it would need a massive budget to pull it off: the cost of the venue, musicians, promotion, sound-equipment. All you've got is your royalty cheque, which is not an awful lot for such a project."

"I'm selling advertising in a brochure, we'll sell ticket, and I'm getting a cut from the local paper. I've already spoken to them about it, and we'll sell more ads in the program. You worry too much."

Had I known the extent of his track record, I would have worried even more.

"What about sponsors? That's what concert promoters usually do." My trying to pull back from this was like stopping balloons from heading into the clouds.

My track record was not that luminous either, with only one stage show I produced years earlier, *The Mysterious Fireman's Bat*, based loosely on an innovative British film, *The Secret Policeman's Ball*.

Some of my cast had been delightful to work with, like the amazingly talented Keith Scott with his cartoon and impersonation voices, and my easy-going female vocalist. Dedicated and temperamental musician, Marty Shield fronted his band, Juggernaut. Although helpful with the staging, he was short on self-control. At one time, I had to hold him back by his shirttail to stop him from punching someone. Comedian George Smilovici had already made a name for himself with his "I'm Tough" routine. He provided the comedy for the show, but for me, too many headaches juggling his complicated love life. Also in the program I included a male singer who needed the proverbial nose and bum wiping attention to keep his high-octane vocals flowing.

Without planning to, I multi-tasked as: producer, director, administrator, wardrobe mistress, stage manager, publicity executive, cupid management, and panderer of whims.

Some people know how to get the best results from risk taking, but I recklessly dived into the unknown without thinking of the consequences. Why am I telling you this? So you can understand how much I was prepared to work my butt off to make things work, but was clueless about making a profit.

Why did I allow myself to be involved in a venture with this Serge person after such a new and tenuous relationship, and to be lured in with this barely conceived festival idea that could jeopardize my agency and state of mind? Was it commitment or a reckless sense of adventure?

Serge booked all the musicians, Australian or American, either living in Australia or visiting from overseas. He had an agenda, to get back into the swing of things, and I had a track record of unfounded curiosity.

Amongst the many tasks Serge gave himself, he organised a huge banner to be draped around the top of the town hall. And to draw more attention to the festival, he commissioned a huge three-sided signboard to sit precariously on the roof of his car, noticed everywhere he drove or parked.

Multi-tasking my newfound romance was also a challenge, but this was not the time to dwell on personal issues.

Getting media attention was important. Something we were both quite good at. We achieved a double-page spread in the local paper, and a mention on Channel 7 news. I also organised for Serge and his band to perform on *Good Morning Australia*.

We were like two maniacs on a mission to sell tickets, get bums on seats, and keep the whole thing moving smoothly. All the publicity, media attention, hard work, and the line-up of great musicians, generated a reasonable sized audience for the four nights of the festival, and fulfilled Serge's need to be noticed again in the jazz arena.

A few 'little' things had gone wrong – actually, not so little. First was the question of a liquor license.

"Leave my guys alone." I stood firmly in front of the inspector, protecting my two gay friends who had volunteered to help at the bar Serge had set up for the duration of the festival. I was completely unaware that he hadn't organised a liquor licence.

"Madam, they will have to go to court for selling illegal alcohol."

"My guys don't know about anything, and neither do I. They are just a couple of friends doing me a favour, and if you want to penalise anyone, it should be me because I am one of the organisers." I pulled up my five foot nothing almost landing my boobs on his chest.

It didn't work.

Serge started yelling at me, I got angry. Our security guy, a friend of Serge's, pulled him away and tried to reason with him. A crowd gathered for this extended entertainment. Weeks later we had to attend court. Luckily it was only a four hundred dollar fine.

Then came the mounting bills bringing me another mountain to climb: and debt collectors who were after the money for the large newspaper ads Serge had put in the Herald, the gigantic signs, and other expenses he hadn't informed me about. This was the first time in my life debt collectors appeared on my doorstep.

It finally dawned on me that my new partner had long ago misplaced his scruples and had a habit of avoiding paying bills. In the past, his father covered for him, saying his son was on tour, and he didn't know when he'd be back from the USA or England, or the North Pole.

This time, it was my problem. Faced with questions about the missing promoter, I could only answer, "I really don't know anything about a Mister Leo Ronin and I certainly didn't authorize any of these accounts."

"What about a Mister Serge Ermoll?"

"He's on tour with his band, and, I have no idea when they'll be back. You could check with his father who lives in Punchbowl."

I had dedicated too much time to the jazz festival and neglected my regular actors, one by one they moved to other agencies or gave up on their careers altogether. Some were not talented enough to sustain a long-term acting career. It takes talent, tenacity, and long-term commitment to an agent, especially one who goes chasing after the whims of a new boyfriend.

When the festival was over, the debt collectors and dust settled, my agency was left to hobble along and we continued with the chaos of our daily lives.

So who was this Leo Ronin character the debt collectors came for?

In the musical Cats, there is a puss called Macavity; who steals and disappears; this nefarious kitty could have been the blueprint for Leo Ronin. A smooth voice on the telephone giving a bogus name and address, it places newspaper ads, hires venues, books technical sound guys, using credit cards he rarely repays. Leo Ronin runs faster than a cat on a hot tin roof to disappear somewhere beyond the reach of his endless debt collectors.

I first heard his name after the Paddington Jazz Festival. People phoned about unpaid accounts. Seemed everyone was chasing this elusive jazz pimpernel.

Often broke, Serge always seemed to find unexplained sources of money. Although his financial track record was catastrophic, he managed to obtain a credit card with a twenty thousand dollar limit. Don't ask! I wouldn't have a clue where some of his cash flow came from. For instance, a man who hung out in Sydney's Italian district, was the angel who financed the *'Passion Dance'* album.

"Who is this guy, Serge, to fork out a few thousand dollars for an album that probably won't get him even half his money back?" I inquired timidly.

With a mischievous look on his face, the response was, "Better you don't know, just produce the album," while he mumbled something about laundry.

Angels were people who sometimes financed showbiz. They had to be angels, because if not for them, many movies, plays, musicals, and albums would not exist.

Money was mostly a hide-and-seek relationship for me. My exasperated mother often held her hand out, fingers spread wide and with the other hand, she poked her fingers through the spaces, saying that's the way I managed my finances. However, I had never developed any kind of door relationship with debt collectors, not until Serge came to live with me. I had a thing about my many parking fines; I wouldn't pay them, until a cop once turned up and threatened to put me away unless I paid up.

It was another one of those *'Oy vey'* situations. My mother paid, and I never heard the end of it.

Soul mates of a controversial kind, Serge and I had different agendas, and alternate routes to travel them.

Maybe if Serge had my mother as a conscience cop, there never would have been a Leo Ronin or the ashes of his exploits.

CHAPTER 13

Love And What Came With It

"Love can change a person the way a parent can change a baby: awkwardly, and often with a great deal of mess."

– Lemony Snicket

One of my very favourite books is Antoine de Saint-Exupery's *'The Little Prince.'* It taught me some of life's most valuable lessons. *'If someone loves a flower of which there is only one on the millions and millions of stars, it is enough to make him happy.'*

The Little Prince had a beautiful rose, which he nurtured lovingly. In return, the vain rose tormented him with unreasonable demands, until one day, she made him so angry he left the planet in search of how else he could make her happy.

On Earth, he discovered a garden with many roses; this made him sad because he believed his flower was unique and no other roses existed. The Little Prince befriended a fox who taught him some valuable life lessons, mainly, the rose on his planet WAS unique because she was his, he took care of her; watered, sheltered, killed caterpillars for her, listened to all her complaints, and most of all, loved her, The fox also taught him one can see only with the heart and what is really essential, is invisible to the eye.

When people asked me why I stayed and kept going down the rabbit hole with Serge, I could only answer from the perspective of The Little Prince. *"For what you have tamed, you become responsible forever."*

I loved him long before I met him because in all the relationships I ever had before Serge, I felt something was missing; the person wasn't interesting enough, masculine enough, didn't understand me enough, had peculiar mannerisms or had unacceptable views. My escapee boyfriends probably had similar reasons for my shortcomings.

So why did I settle for Serge? You may ask. It could be that he appeared in my life at the right time, a chunky teddy bear with thick fingers and stubby toes, and lots of facial hair, that his chin rested on top of my head, and I lost myself in his chest. There was always the pull of his incredible talent.

In our years together, I never saw him beardless; at times his beard became so thick and bushy, he could have got a job as Santa Claus. When he cropped his beard and gained weight, he looked like a chipmunk. On the rare occasion he wore a suit and shirt, it seemed as if the collar held his neck imprisoned, straining to escape into freedom.

These were the things that endeared him to me. The other side of him kept me on the seesaw of questioning my feelings, wanting to retreat from him, think of him with disdain, and sometimes, I even thought enemy forces with a grudge, had sent him to me.

His parents lived in a fibro housing commission home in Punchbowl. The front and back yards had large plum trees yielding masses of plums every year. His father gathered bags full for me and I made jars and jars of jam for my friends and me. To be honest, it was bloody good jam.

My first visit to the Ermoll's cluttered house initially made me want to rush out to the fresh air. The old furniture had a strong, rank smell of decay that clung to my nostrils. I stayed, and went on his father's guided tour. It included the music room with an upright piano, masses of posters, album covers, and newspaper clippings cluttering the walls with yellowing sticky tape. I listened to his proud commentaries about the highlights of his fame. My image of him had been different from this wizened, bald gentleman with a clipped breathless Russian accent.

The first time I met the old man, he kissed my hand with a grand flourish. I liked it. "I am so pleased to meet you Eliena, Sergei tell me much of you." He was beautifully polite and charming.

I succumbed and smiled. "I am pleased to meet you too. I hear you were very famous in Shanghai."

The way to a good relationship with an ego-centred person is flattery, and I was used to it. Besides, I really liked Serge's dad and enjoyed hearing his anecdotes about his past, his music and fame as a bandleader.

Clashes of ego often pushed conflict between father and son, "Dad, you look like a Papugay in that bright shirt, tie and crazy clothes," Serge chastised him for the way he dressed when we picked him up to go for an outing.

"What's a Papugay?" I innocently asked, amused at father's zany outfit.

He snorted back at me, "It's Russian for parrot, that's what dad looks like, a fucking parrot."

When I first met Xenia, Serge's mother, I was struck by the quiet gentleness of this once beautiful woman. She was a broken soul who had retreated into her inner world of silence. When I made attempts to communicate with her, I felt I was pulling her away from a far away horizon she seemed focused on. I knew she cared because she'd suddenly look at me, give me a few responsive words and hold my hand for as long as we both wanted the connection.

Her English was as broken as she was. Her dignified, silent bearing carried her aristocratic Russian background Serge had told me about. Photographs of her showed a beautiful, elegant dark – haired woman wearing fashionable twenties-style clothes making her look like a movie star. After all, she had led an exotic lifestyle as the wife of a famous bandleader, left behind when they migrated to Australia.

Some migrants adjust better to a new environment than others. Xenia couldn't. She was ill equipped for it, I can only imagine how she felt working as a factory hand. The loss of dignity, and having to deal with her husband's increased drinking and abuse of Serge, their young son.

Pushed further and further away from reality by being prescribed heavy anti-psychotic drugs that affected her mental state, she retreated into a silent world of her own.

Serge told me how much he grappled with the agony of his lost mother. I saw the pain in him when he talked about it.

I could only imagine the double pain of not having either parent give him love and acceptance. His father, protector when Serge had been a little boy in Shanghai, had turned into an abusive parent. The loss of fame, fortune, accolades, stepped up drinking, may all have been the excuse for Serge Senior to belt his son mercilessly. Child abuse has no place, ever. All it did was leave horrendous internal scars leaving young Serge with unresolved anger, aggression and emotional agony.

When my own father died, I was much younger, a ten-year old little girl in a strange land, living with a grieving mother doing her best to cope. With no extended family and no father figure in sight, I spent a whole lifetime needing my dad's approval; his attention and most of all, love.

♪♪

"Dad!" excitement brimming with exuberant pride, Serge phoned his father to share the news about the album that the questionable angel had paid for, "My new album *'Passion Dance'* has just been released."

The response from his father was shocking; "Yes, I remember when I released my record…" In one moment I watched Serge crumple like a deflated tent, his excitement killed. I saw the emotional kaleidoscope instantly cross his face until tears made their slow descent.

Protective anger emerged from me, and I took the phone from Serge's hand, "Dad, you dreadful man," I yelled into the little holes "How could you? Your son phones you to share this wonderful moment, and all you can do is you, you, you. Can't you say how proud you are of him, how wonderful? Congratulations, you selfish self-centred man," I blasted louder and louder with indignation.

Both father and son knew how to cry. Next to me Serge's tears rolled out, and at the other end of the phone line, I heard his father siphoning all the wet stuff up his nose, watery words came out, "Sorry, sorry, you're right, yes, I'm proud of my son." Crying, crying.

It would have been easy to burst out laughing, instead, I contained myself and shouted, 'So tell him,' I almost threw the phone to a now stunned Serge.

In a rare moment of unity and shelved egos, the phones were awash with their teary floods, and momentarily repaired some of the damage.

Ironically, I got on very well with Serge Senior. He told me I was the best woman his son ever had.

"Don't get me wrong Helene, I love my dad, well, I hate him as well, he's always so competitive with me, he never tells me I'm good but always shows off how much he's done, how he was a great band leader and all the people he got to know in Sydney's showbiz."

"So why do you bother to compete with him, just leave it alone, you know it's a lost cause trying to impress your father," were practical things I said. I forgot how much pedalling I often did to gain my mother's approval.

Serge absentmindedly ran his fingers into the edges of his beard, "I can accept he risked his life for me in China and worked hard for us when we came here. Honestly I appreciate that."

Love and hate live on the same floor and we can summon them equally. Situations and experience can throw us into either place.

It is not recommended to conduct therapy sessions with our partners; leave it to the professionals. Then again, how can we understand another human being as much as the one we live with, share a pillow with and talk with. Serge always talked his heart out to me, and I listened.

"Although I'm not drinking anymore, I'm still a dry drunk."

"I've never heard of such a thing. How can that be?" I responded to him.

"I told you, I haven't had a drink for two years, but now I have nothing to drown my feelings in, and that's why I sometimes lash out and get uncontrollably angry over very little."

Knowing little about alcoholism, I had trouble understanding his unpredictable rages, and sometimes wondered how I could love this person who was so aggressive, who could put a fist through a door, dash off into the night to return the next day full of remorse and a handful of flowers.

On the flip side of the coin, I loved him because of his kindness, generosity, suddenly jumping out of the car to help someone when the flotsam of humanity couldn't be bothered. I loved him for his undisputed genius, creativity and endless support of mine, for the many hours of spreading our histories and souls to each other with unguarded honesty. I ultimately recognised a large portion of what we both considered the great love for each other, was born from the hollow places in our souls desperately needing a sense of belonging to survive the kinds of childhoods we had both lived through.

I'm not even going to attempt to describe my version of love, except to tell you that there were other people I have loved in my life, and I had felt the pain of it running marathons through my body.

♪♪

We had been living together for about a year, when a musician friend and his girlfriend became engaged which was the catalyst for us to talk engagement and getting married. Serge gave me his mother's engagement ring, which he had inscribed with the words, *'Into the Sunset'*. A beautiful image I never lost sight of, shelved during the in-between times when Serge and I danced through our complicated relationship.

"You know boodgie girl, I love you so much; I would kill for you."

"There's no need for killing, darling, only your demons."

Whatever my apprehensions were about the relationship, the idea of getting married again distracted me, and I nursed the notion that the rituals involved could magically dissolve our difficult challenges.

Once engaged, we planned a jazz wedding to include an any-excuse-is-a-good-one-for a jam session.

My mother was flabbergasted, my friends confused, Serge's dad was delighted and his musician friends non-committal.

My close friend, Peter, didn't quite know what to make of it. He couldn't see me as a domesticated married lady. We had shared so many zany times together, from joking around about who could get the cute guy on the motorbike riding in front of us, to late suppers of Crepe Suzette and drinking Dom Perignon Champagne at the restaurant he part owned in a swish nightclub called Pips.

A few years later, Peter died of aids, and once in a while, I look upwards with dialogue about the queerness of my life and what I am supposed to do next.

By this stage, Peter owned a restaurant overlooking the river at Berowra Waters. This was a perfect place to marry my great teddy bear, and during lunch of lobster and seafood, Peter suggested that "We can have the tables in the round, pure white tablecloths, with a subtle trim décor, small clusters of flowers, and…"

"Where can we put our instruments for our jam, man?" Serge cut in.

"We can clear that corner near the window overlooking the water."

"What about a piano? I don't see one here."

"You can bring in a keyboard or I can organise one, will that do?" Peter could handle anything regarding restaurants and keeping customers happy, especially me.

A marriage celebrant seemed the best choice. Religions notwithstanding, synagogues, cathedrals or churches were out for both of us. Barefoot in the park could have worked.

I began to have misgivings about this committed long-term plan with my unpredictable fiancée, and kept postponing the wedding date. Serge, who had been looking forward to it, petulantly said, "You don't love me enough."

"What's Love Got to Do with It." Tina Turner sings. We rationalised a wedding is only a ritual to keep many people who don't give a damn, in business. Although it kept cropping up, we never got married.

People with challenging partners have all kinds of histories, walking a precarious tightrope to make the relationship work.

Serge and I dragged large chests of baggage into the complexity of our relationship, fuelled by childhoods we had not quite left behind, and parents that continued to impact on our lives.

According to John Bradshaw, an American psychologist, 'when people first fall in love, they are so besotted with the new partner, and the rush of hormones, they initially consider their beloved to be a super being. About six months later, our true nature reveals itself, and we either work it through, leave, or continue the struggle.'

We both carried the seeds of anger making us dance to the tune of our troubled backgrounds. The battlegrounds of words were familiar territory for me. I had fought many of them with my mother; in three languages, Yiddish, French, English, and a fourth one, silence – coupled with loud puffs of breathing, dragon to dragon.

With Serge, it was a relentless, emotional punishment leaving me confused, angry and helpless. I was crying more often than ever before. A single word from me could unleash a tirade of angry accusations pouring out of his internal well of long-held anger and misogyny. Initially, my response was to stand frozen in disbelief like a mesmerised chook, until my inner warrior finally found the weapons of retaliation.

We had found the perfect dance partner to externalise all our pent-up angers. The most potent weapon either of us wielded was the threat of the end, "That's it Serge, I've had it, we're finished, you can get out."

"You're like all the other controlling bitches, Helene. I'm leaving."

They were like scenes from a movie.

New dawns broke when we entered fresh dances, moving yet again to the tune of reconciliation, apology, eternal love, allegiance and bursts of, "I didn't mean it" "Sorry, I can't help myself" and "we'll have to try harder to make this work." Once these emotional devouring feasts were over and our energies depleted, we reconnected with the core of our love for each other and temporarily healed our wounds.

Years later, when I finally understood these issues, I relinquished my lengthy tirades. However, his anger was too deeply entrenched to change them, and his attempts to reinstate that dance no longer worked for me. I was ashamed to have participated in these scenes, determined never to return to the sick scenarios that had corroded my self-esteem. It took me many years to understand his hell, fuelled by his nature, childhood and the addictions that wove themselves in his life.

Other people found it incomprehensible that I willingly remained in this alien landscape, yet, that's what The Little Prince did: returned to his beloved, complicated rose.

CHAPTER 14

George Cables Tour

"Jazz is about being in the moment"
– Herbie Hancock

An old Errol Flynn movie portrays a swashbuckling Robin Hood, full of heroic action, as he dashes through Sherwood Forest, his well-aimed arrows slicing through the air. Further into the movie, inside an old castle, sword in hand, he makes a daring jump from a wide staircase onto a chandelier, then onto a wall hanging, and with energetic enthusiasm fights the nasty enemy of the kingdom.

I saw this kind of boyish eagerness on Serge's face, when he coerced a mate or colleague in yet another one of his ventures. I can't imagine a latter-day Serge, riddled with arthritis, in excruciating knee and hip pain, body depleted by years of karate and alcohol, to be a physical replica of the boisterous Errol Flynn. As we know, Errol ended in a mess of drugs and alcohol and a wicked, wicked life wasted.

Maybe mine was partly a life wasted, as a bumpy adventure punctuated by weak moments of coerced action.

"This is going to be a piece of cake, Helene."

Before I was aware of how it happened, I was involved in another of Serge's entrepreneurial activities, pulled further into his world of jazz and his precarious lifestyle.

"We've got to tour George Cables while he's in Australia."

"Stop right here, who is George Cables, what does he do, where is he from, and why should WE do anything about it?" Seemed like a stream of logical questions.

"You really don't know anything, Helene! He's a black American jazz pianist."

"So, why should we be involved?"

"Because," he puffed at his latest fad, a cigar, "it will be another feather in my cap to organise a successful tour for him."

"That sounds good, for you, why should I be involved in this? I know little about touring, it's an expensive exercise and too much money to lose if it goes arse-up."

"Fuck man, George Cables is well known on the jazz scene. The airfares and the Sydney accommodation won't cost us anything because he's coming to Australia just to visit his wife's parents. I figure it will be easy to organise a three major city tour with no trouble. I've already talked to a few people who are interested."

"You didn't tell me about it."

"I'm doing it now. I'll make you a cup of tea while you think about it."

"Please put that cigar out, Serge. It's stinking up the whole flat."

For the small things he did what I asked.

Of course I had no way of knowing then that George Cables had helped to define modern mainstream jazz piano in the 1980's and 1990's. He had played and recorded many albums with some of the jazz greats, Art Blakey, Freddie Hubbard, Art Pepper, Sonny Rollins, Dexter Gordon and many, many others.

Again, Serge coerced me into another situation. It would seem bizarre that after the whole Paddington Jazz Festival drama a few years earlier and now knowing the nature of the beast, I could be dragged in again. Surely you must be thinking, this woman is either too weak to say no or is insane.

Audiences at entertainment events can't begin to imagine the amount of work it takes to bring all of it to fruition. The many interminable hours of planning, convincing managements they would make a profit, and gain kudos from the success of the venture. One avoids mentioning potential failures.

Dealing directly with promoters and venues, Serge arranged for fifty percent to be paid upfront, providing us with the initial fees for George and the band.

The first performance was to be held at the elegant Don Burrows Supper Club in the Regent Hotel at The Rocks in Sydney.

Gremlins that cause things to go wrong must have a lot of fun meddling in my best-laid plans to bring me undone. Serge was home making phone calls and I went to the bank to withdraw the money to pay the musicians that night. Still at the counter, I rolled up the fifteen hundred dollars, put it in the back of my wallet and went shopping. Somewhere between the vegetables and the chops, I discovered gremlin beasties had caused the money to fall out of my wallet. Don't be silly – I hadn't been careless not burying the money in the bottom of my bag.

Panic didn't help; self-recrimination did nothing for me either, and if I had a tail, I would have gone home with it curled well under me, and if Serge might have had a degree of self-control, people might not have heard him screaming when they walked down the long stretch of Avoca Street.

If the situation had been reversed and Serge had lost the money, I too would have huffed and puffed, and accused him of either clowning around or doing something thoroughly dishonest again.

"It was the gremlins," my attempts at humour didn't work. "I'm going back to the bank to see if I can get an overdraft and sort it all out; it's my responsibility, so I'll deal with it." Luckily, my bank manager immediately sorted out the finances for me. I was so grateful I started crying, until I realised I was being girly and the bank was not the place for tears.

This time, when I arrived home with the cash, my satisfied partner praised me, "See Boodgie girl, you know how to fix things, I knew I could trust you."

"But there go the profits, and all that work for nothing."

"It's not nothing, that's jazz."

Of course, everyone was very sympathetic that night, but why wouldn't they be? They were paid and I was stuck with the overdraft.

The loud applause after the encore was a good sign that all had gone well.

The following day, George and the band flew out to Melbourne while Serge drove the two of us straight to Adelaide.

Australia is magnificent, and I love it. Country drives are pleasurable, particularly when they are unhurried, and you take time to enjoy the scenery, have leisurely pit stops with stays at comfortable motels by the end of the day. It's not the same when your budget is too tight for flights. Considering the cost of petrol and other expenses, the long drive is false economy. My mother would have called it picking up a feather and throwing away the eiderdown.

We envisaged another great night in Adelaide before continuing to Canberra and back to Sydney. Following the band, we covered thousands of kilometres across this vast country.

'Nothing behind me, everything ahead of me, as is ever so on the road,' wrote Jack Kerouac in his iconic novel, *On the Road*.

The scenic route between Melbourne and Adelaide takes in some of Australia's best beaches, greenest forests, amazing parks and dramatic cliffs. I saw little of it; Serge just kept driving taking us a couple of days to get there. The band had a one-hour flight.

We arrived in Adelaide and stayed with Serge's musician friend and his wife. The boys had a great time: talking music, past experiences together, and about their fellow musicians.

For me, it wasn't much fun – I had nothing in common with the wife, an avid horticulturalist and difficult to communicate with. Ah well, only for a couple of days.

The plan almost worked – The adequate venue was dimly lit with good acoustics. A crowded, eager audience lined the bar and filled all the seating, everyone ready to hear the music.

At the end of a great performance the audience applauded enthusiastically, and everyone was happy. At last, Serge and I had achieved an excellent result together bringing us a delicious sense of euphoria, and pride in something well done.

In my world with Serge, anything could take a sudden nosedive. It did.

Booked for the tour was Ed Gaston, one of Serge's favourite bass players, Ed was a quiet man who had played and recorded with many Australian and American musicians. Ed's wife, Di, the Sydney Jazz Action coordinator, included herself in the trip, as this was an opportunity for her to catch up with her Adelaide counterpart.

Most wives or girlfriends like coming to their men's gigs to enjoy the music, socialise with the other partners, and keep an eye out in case some hottie fan offers sex.

Performance over, people sat around drinking and talking. Late-night voices mingled with the recorded music. Suddenly, loud, angry shouting cut across the hubbub in the room, "You fuck, how dare you?" It became evident these words, together with a string of angry accusations coming from Serge, were aimed at Di. He got louder and louder while she helplessly tried to defend herself, "But, I…. thought…."

"You should have come to us. It's our gig, and you had no right to go behind our backs to organise another concert for George."

Serge had just learnt Di had booked George for an additional Sydney concert without consulting us first, big no-no.

The background noise subsided. Serge stood his ground, like a peacock on heat, emitting an even louder frustrated yell, and searching for the right words, he blurted out, "I'm … I'm … going to cut your tits off, Di."

It was all too much for Ed, the indignant husband, "If you don't apologise to my wife, Serge, I'm not performing with the band anymore. You can go and find another bass player to continue the tour." He was so angry his toupee almost slipped off his head, harsh words for a normally placid man.

The other band members were trying to stop themselves from laughing, and all I could do was pull at Serge's arm for him to stop his rant.

Eventually, everything calmed and settled down. They reached a compromise; we convinced Ed to stay and continue with the tour. Not only that, Di's tits stayed intact. Back at the house, the post mortem of the evening's event went on into the night with Serge and his friends. I had enough of it and went to bed. It took me ages to fall asleep. I was in a strange environment where the bed was seriously uncomfortable and I felt overloaded with apprehension.

Facing a long, boring drive through the middle of Australia, we set off for Canberra the next morning. I hoped we had finished with the incident of the night before.

No! Not Serge, he was still brooding about it, "That fucking Di, she had no right, you know."

"I really don't think you should have threatened to cut Di's tits off last night." I naively said. It would have been easier to climb naked over a barbed wire fence. He responded with a loud, animal-like roar; thumped the steering wheel viciously making the car swerve all over the road, then revved the engine to its full capacity and drove at a reckless speed across the highway.

Surely by now, and with Serge's unpredictable track record, I could have found a better way to pick my battles, particularly when I was in an eight-cylinder car with a lunatic at the steering wheel, driving at over a hundred and forty kilometres an hour.

This was the most terrifying road trip I had ever been on, at least, not until years later, when I drove across Tasmania with a girlfriend, manoeuvring our hire car downwards around a hundred hairpin bends over a fenceless narrow road towards Queenstown. My friend continually asked me to slow down my five kilometres an hour and keep to the middle of the road. "Do you want to live?" I shouted. My hands were shaking in a tight grip on the steering wheel, "So, shut up!" Ah, the luxury of telling someone to shut up, something I didn't have as the passenger of a raving out-of-control musician on the way out of Adelaide.

One thousand, one hundred and seventy-one kilometres between Adelaide and Canberra became a journey of horror. At first, Serge kept screaming, threatening, and speeding across the barren landscape. This was followed by hours of angry silence through the treeless landscape, dreary and devoid of any remarkable landmarks.

Worst of all, I felt trapped in this nightmare; I couldn't get out of the car and leave. There was nothing more for me to say, and I knew if I did, another angry tirade and dangerous driving would confront me. The only consolation was there was no traffic on the road.

Uninterrupted sullen silence was marginally better than angry screams or hours of nothing; no sound, no music, no people, nothing but relentless scorching heat. All I could see out of the car window was sparse nothingness as we almost flew through towns; Mount Barker, Pinnaroo, Ouyen, Underbool, Hay, Narandera, Wagga Wagga and Gundagai, where the dog sits on the Tucker Box. By then I hadn't even sat on a toilet, too afraid if I got out of the car, he might suddenly go off without me, and leave me in a town boasting of an iconic doggy landmark.

After the interminable unfriendly silence spilled into nightfall, I tentatively suggested we stay in a motel for the night. We still had a long way to go; I was hungry, thirsty and emotionally exhausted. I don't remember what country town we were in, only the gargantuan relief I felt when he finally relinquished his gruelling punishment of screams or heavily laden silence.

We booked in at a motel, had a meal, and he finally spoke to me. I knew I had to walk a tightrope of reconciliation and leave any comments on the long dusty road behind us. I don't think fear motivated me; it was more the need for emotional self-preservation.

The way ahead had a more interesting landscape, a respite from the harsh road of the day before. No more tits under threat, we continued peacefully to Canberra and a concert that went smoothly. I don't remember a thing about it, probably because nothing went wrong.

A person with a greater sense of self-preservation might have arrived back in the safety of their own city and home, and decided she had enough of this Mister Serge Ermoll, super pianist-composer, great talker and exciting individual, not bad looking either and the best hugger. The person would have decided that these things were not enough to make her happy, nor give her a sense of equilibrium, nor continue with the fantasy of reaching towards a rainbow coloured future, interspersed with great dives into turbulent oceans. No! A sensible person may just have decided that this was the last egg in the carton of their love adventure, the last song on this recording, and decide to turn off the sound system of the relationship.

Of course, a blinkered Helene Grover didn't do that. Not this time.

CHAPTER 15

Woman Of Mystery

"There is something else that is trying to come through – that lure of becoming – and it does come from the realm of spirit, it does come from the quantum universe, it does come from the great spark that is the threshold of time and history trying to emerge and electrify us."

– Jean Houston.

I survived Adelaide after all. Yet, I was still on the road of what the hell was I doing and where the heck I was heading? And would any of this bring me what I really didn't know I wanted?

Although my actors and I had abandoned each other, I kept my agency going, and diversified into live entertainment.

Punters in ordinary land, have a limited understanding of the entertainment industry. Many people want to be performers and when overnight success doesn't happen, it's got to be the agent's fault for not trying hard enough.

As an agent, no matter how much you try, or how many phone calls you make on behalf of your client, if they haven't got whatever it takes, they remain in obscurity and eventually settle into a day gig.

I admire show people who have paid their dues with years of training; sitting in with other musicians in dingy, smoky venues, little money, sparse audiences, chasing one potential gig after another, and taking years to achieve any kind of success. Maree Montgomery is such a person. Although not a household name, she has paid her dues working through live performances, recordings, fashion shows, tours, large club stages, obscure joints, and plush hotels.

"You know, Helene, Serge bullied the best singing out of me," she told me. "I recorded a couple of tracks on one of his earlier albums and it was an absolute nightmare, I almost quit because it was such a tough gig. All the guys were smoking dope in the small studio, and I didn't, the smoke got in my eyes and throat and I couldn't stop coughing but Serge made me go over and over the notes until it was the way he wanted the song to sound. It was the first time I had done heavy jazz, and I learnt so much from him."

I could understand how difficult it must have been for her to deal with that kind of situation.

Maree was planning to record a new album, and wanted Serge to be her musical director, and to write all the arrangements. This was a welcome catalyst to rejuvenate his flailing career.

The mammoth task kept them busy for months.

Papers, files, mementos, bed linen, and towels live on different shelves in dark spaces of my wardrobe. Cream-coloured folders, full of my song writing, hold all the bursts of my creative moments. Pieces of paper with lyrics written on them, some in pencil; others, typed on the old clacketty-clack Underwood I used to own, and now regret having tossed away. On those sheets, are many songs I wrote a long time ago; about love, loss, or subjects that caught my attention.

Bob Dylan wrote his politically driven song, *'Blowin' in the Wind'*, and I wrote *'Child of Abraham'*. The lyrics came from one of the deepest places of my heart, the land of my roots, Israel: *'At the edge of the sea with a gun in my hand, where mingles the blood and fruit of my land, I grew a tree on hot barren sands, and built cities with my hands.'*

Many of my songs were the sleeping beauties of my creative moments, waiting to be woken up by the kiss of voice. The Prince who rescued them was Serge who suggested we include three of them on Maree's album. 'Barefoot Boy', already a hit, plus the other two, *'Money Man'* which I wrote as a sequel to Barefoot Boy, and *'I found You'*, I've lost the reason why I wrote this song. All the arrangements are fabulous.

Amongst all the stuff Serge moved in with, I was surprised and a little disappointed that a piano wasn't part of his treasured possessions. He said he had pawned his keyboard for much needed cash. I wondered, how he would write all the charts for the album without an instrument, and didn't have to wait long for an answer.

I came home one evening to find him sitting at my dining room table engrossed in moving his fingers across the tabletop. Every now and then he leaned over to write on sheets of music paper. He was naked except for a tight pair of navy blue underpants; his bare fleshy toes beat the rhythm on the carpeted floor.

I was confused. "What are you doing?"

"I'm writing the charts for the *Woman of Mystery* album and if you'll be quiet, I'll get on with it."

"Without a piano!"

"Yes, I can see and hear the notes in my head." And he continued with his task.

Later that night, during dinner at the same dining room table, he explained, "I visualise and hear the notes in my head, that's why I can structure charts for each piece I write. It's like having an invisible piano in my brain."

Years later, when I was chasing ways to unearth the workings of my bellybutton in the many workshops I attended, I discovered a book called *"The Possible Human"* written by Jean Houston. In it, she wrote about the flexibility of the brain, and how we can expand our skills by visualising whatever we aim to achieve, and to quote her, *'You are not an encapsulated bag of skin dragging around a dreary little ego. You are an evolutionary wonder, a trillion cells singing together in a vast chorale, an organism – environment, a symbiosis of cell and soul.'*

Out of Serge's masterful original soundless notes, emerged all the tracks for the album.

Some of Australia's greatest jazz musicians were hired for the recording. Ed Gaston, Alan Turnbull, David Jones, Andrew Oh, Steve McKenna, Steve Giordano, Peter Cross, Warwick Alder and James Morrison. I was impressed that the album included these great jazz musicians playing from charts born on my dining room table. Ah well, if I could write a hit song on top of a ladder, why not a genius composer, on a tabletop?

As musical director, Serge once again coerced the best out of Maree, making her go over and over one single note of the song, 'God Bless the Child', until it was perfect.

A glass panel divided the recording studio: One side for the musicians with their instruments, as well as the vocalist. The other side, for the huge panel-board with countless sliding recording buttons. The man operating all the equipment was the expert recording engineer, Wyn Wynyard. I sat next to him, watched, listened and sketched.

The hours in the studio were peaceful and creative with friendly chitchat. At home, the storms brewed intermittently.

Ultimately, the album went through its metamorphosis: mastering, cover artwork, pressing of the many copies, and finally, promotion and airplay.

'Woman of Mystery' went on the Larrikin label, owned by Warren Fahey who had formed the company and its label in 1974. Warren contributed a great deal to the Australian recording industry. Eventually, he sold the publishing side of the business to a multinational company, and was dragged into a convoluted court case, when Men at Work front man, Colin Hay accused him of stealing a part of the music of '*Kookaburra Sits on the Old Gum Tree*'. This was eventually settled, and of course, the winners were the lawyers. Mercifully, Warren still brings Australia's great larrikin sentiments to stage with his actor partner, Max Cullen in a two-man show, '*Dead Men Talking*,' about

Henry Lawson and Banjo Patterson. It resonates with my great love of Australia and its artistic creators.

The transition between a plan and its fruition can take a long time. This one took over a year and by the time of the album's release Serge and I were living elsewhere.

Released in April 1986, '*Woman of Mystery*' was nominated for an Aria music award. One critic wrote that Serge's arrangements were reminiscent of Oscar Peterson and the whole album was a work of art. We celebrated the news with a banquet Chinese dinner at the Emperor's Garden.

We were all invited to attend the Sydney Aria awards night. As you know, the Oscar awards we see on television brings us movie stars decked out in fabulous evening wear, long dresses and men in tuxedos. I wanted to make sure that my man, formerly of the black leather jacket, would be dressed appropriately for the occasion in a dinner suit with matching bow tie and cumberbund. I dragged him to a hire place where they found him a tuxedo large enough to fit his bulky frame, "Shit man, I look like a stuffed penguin with a butterfly around my neck, I'm not wearing this shit," he complained.

"Yes, you are, you look magnificent in it. Let me trim your hair and beard. Imagine, if you win the best jazz album of the year, you and Maree are going to have to go onstage to collect your award, you'll look fabulous." Flattery is magic on a Leo; I should know, I am one.

My outfit for the night was a dress I hired from a bridal shop, so you can imagine the kitsch affair I squeezed myself into, a soft butter-coloured silk fabric, large puffy off the shoulder sleeves, V shaped tight-fitting bodice with a wide billowing skirt. Very Hollywood, I thought.

The hairdresser piled my long hair in a curly affair on top of my head made stiff with most of the contents of a can of hair lacquer, and to make sure everything stayed firmly in place, what must have been a tin shed's worth of bobby bins inserted on my head. I looked like a cross between the fairy on top of the Christmas tree, and a custard-coloured snowman.

Maree went for a sparkle glamour look, after all, she was often the fashion compere in shopping malls. For this occasion, she put herself in a flowing shimmering evening dress with long glittering earrings that reached down her slim neck.

"Remember that night, Helene." Maree and I were in hysterics years later, reminiscing about our outfits. "We were the only ones dressed up to the nines and looked like a pair of idiots."

I continued our memory session, "I still want to run off and hide somewhere when I think about it. All the other women wore short dresses, and some were even in denim."

Our little group had been seated at a table too far from all the celebrities, and as much as I would have loved it, nobody introduced us to the guests of honour, Elton John and Cliff Richard.

Although the album didn't win the prized award, the nomination was an honour, and a proud creative achievement. I still get royalties for my songs, and sometimes they get played on international flights or on the radio.

There were more dreams to chase, and events to create. Much later, Maree performed at the opening of the Beijing Olympics

CHAPTER 16

A Few Drops Of Sherry

"And if the wine you drink, the lip you press end in the Nothing all things end in – Thou shalt not be less."

– The Rubaiyat of Omar Khayyam

Short spaces of peacetime and break-up times with Serge gave me the chance to reclaim parts of my life, to heal the emotional bruises from his verbal battering. When alcohol entered the arena, it became worse.

My peach-faced lovebird was in my life before Serge entered it. I put her cage on a shelf in my office where she was the overseer of all my casting calls. She fluttered in her confinement gibbering wordless noises. Sometimes she sat on my head or engaged in an ongoing love affair with my bedroom mirror.

Birdie was witness to the ongoing dramas with Serge.

♪♪

The first time I attended a Russian funeral was when his mother died. I came home from visiting friends to find him sitting at my desk, distraught, crying, and sipping burgundy liquid from a liqueur glass. I rushed over to him and swept my fingers over his wet face. "What's up, darling? It can't be that bad."

"My father rang to tell me my mother died."

I put my arm around his broad shoulders. "I'm so sorry; we knew this would come when we saw her in hospital the other day. She won't be suffering anymore."

My big teddy bear wound his arms around my waist, buried his head in my body, and poured the pain of his loss in a tearful tsunami.

Holding him close, a faint smell of alcohol reached me. In almost two years of living together, all I ever saw him drink was Coca-Cola or lemonade.

"What are you drinking?" I didn't mean to sound accusing.

Immediately, he went on the defensive, "Just some sherry I found in your liquor cabinet. It's lolly water. I needed something, don't worry about it."

I comforted him about the loss of his mother, but wasn't aware yet about the ramifications of that small glass of sherry.

When I was a child in Paris, a glass of wine with dinner had been part of our evening family meal, and never a problem for any of us. I couldn't begin to understand the devastation of alcohol and what it brings into relationship dynamics, or its impact on society in general.

Many of the great jazz people of the sixties travelled through dark shadows of addiction until their early death: musicians like John Coltrane, Charlie (Bird) Parker, Chet Baker, as well as the controversial comedian Lenny Bruce and many others. Maybe their choice of departing from an ordinary life, coupled with an insatiable need for acceptance of their creativity, brought them substance dependence as the price that they had to pay.

Entertainers may claim drugs, alcohol or other diversions enhance their performance, or they may be looking for ways to escape mundane reality. In truth, addiction may inflict itself onto anyone, regardless of age, social or creative standing. The havoc it unleashes on them and those around them is hell in any environment.

During my twenties, I spent some marihuana filled nights with my long-time mate, Pete; we played endless games of backgammon, discussed philosophy, current books we were reading, or had fits of the munchies and ate anything we could find in the fridge. Some days we talked and laughed until almost morning. Our conversations were probably rubbish, but in our doped state we believed we were utterly brilliant. Pete moved to Western Australia a long time ago. Occasionally, we have lengthy coast-to-coast phone conversations.

When I gave up smoking sixty cigarettes a day, I gave up the green weed, too. I found I needed a clear head to deal with the vagaries of Serge's temperament. A hazy brain was not the most practical way to cope.

That innocent glass of sherry when his mother died was the return to Serge's alcohol addiction, and like all addicts, he was secretive. I took a long time to discover the enormous quantities of booze he had built up to, and even longer for me to learn about the pills. I was aware that alcoholism is nasty, not only the addict suffers but those close to them are also caught in its vicious dance.

Addiction inevitably took its toll, both on my fractured genius and on my own mental state.

   I got my wish. Life wasn't boring. It hurt.

CHAPTER 17

Dizzy Gillespie Concerts

"Some days you get up and put the horn to your chops, it sounds pretty good and you win. Some days you try, and nothing works and the horn wins. This goes on and on and then you die and the horn wins"

– Dizzy Gillespie

Whenever I found a piece of music that appealed to me, I played it over and over and over, until it spun around in my head and interfered with other thoughts – and for a while, the singer or band was my favourite –Until they were replaced. These days, I return to old favourites and love them just as much.

For Serge, his approach to music had been much more significant. "Dizzy Gillespie was my first musician hero. I listened endlessly to one of his albums when I was a kid. This was a way for me to learn; get the feel of 'real' jazz and master those intricate 'chops'. I was never, never bored to hear the same record over and over? I was gaining an insight into how much dedication it takes for a musician to get to the heart of his craft, know how jazz is played and what makes it great."

As I listened to the origins of Serge's attachment to music, I began to understand the basis of his prolific career, and what it took for him to develop his skills. After all, my one hit rock and roll single, '*Barefoot Boy*' was not the result of knowing the construct of music. I couldn't even read or write it. I just let the melody escape me from who knows where, and for lyrics to manifest themselves through my fingers onto paper. Compared to my puny contribution, the years of focus Serge had put into his music, humbled me.

Around the late eighties, Dizzy was coming down under for an Australian tour, starting in Sydney, at The Entertainment Centre, followed by a night at the Basement.

The Musician's Union had become strict about having Australian content as support for overseas artists.

Does a bird think about why it stretches its feathers to leap into the sky and ride the currents to its destination? Could I help myself from picking up the phone to follow another opportunity for my brightly plumed musician? I felt compelled to do as much as I could to include Serge and his band for those Dizzy Gillespie Sydney concerts.

I began by bulldozing my way through the support bands booking hierarchy, and as my mother would say, stayed on it like a dog on a bone, making one call after another, and talking my brains out until I nailed it.

"Serge, I've got you the Dizzy Gillespie support gig for Sydney."

As usual, he was sceptical. "I appreciate your trying but, me on the same program with the great Dizzy Gillespie?

I tell you, they'll just pull my band out for better known Aussie guys."

"No, it's settled, we're signing the contracts this week and locking it in, and then you can start rehearsing. By the way, they really want a vocalist."

"Shit, man," came the response. "I'm not having any chick singers. Not for this one."

"How about a male singer?"

"Not many on the jazz scene, they're probably not available."

Something else to deflate my excitement after I felt as if I had achieved something akin to climbing Mount Everest, I was not in a frame of mind to give up easily. If a magician can pull out a fluffy bunny from a hat, I could pull out a male singer from somewhere. Actually, I was the bunny who hopped to it.

Where and how could we find a male vocalist to sing jazz and deal with Serge's temperament? He was determined to include a couple of his own compositions, which would also need time for anyone to learn. I had enough experience by now to know the various musicians he worked with, their personalities and the way he interacted with them.

Being the support band for the great Dizzy Gillespie was far too important to just throw in anybody to be front man. The band members he chose for the two concerts were: Steve McKenna, guitar, Dale Barlow, sax, Jonathon Swartz, bass, and Steve Marksell, drums.

We were faced with finding a singer. "There's not enough time, Helene, it's useless."

"Don't be so quick with the useless. Trust me, I'll figure it out."

What was I saying? Could I bridge what seemed almost impossible?

Think woman! There just has to be someone, maybe from my world and not Serge's. Thinking not only gives you a headache, but it has potential to find the solution. And finally it did, pouring out of me in one stream of dialogue. "I've got it, how about my mate Graham Lowndes, he's a great singer, has worked on big concert stages, toured with Jeanie Lewis and Margaret Roadnight. He knows your music and is a fan of yours. By the way, he's a terrific vocal improviser and can scat. You've met him already when he came over. How about it? If he'll agree to it, that is."

"Mmm … Do you know what you are doing, Helene?"

"I think so."

"Think so? Graham is a flake with all his peculiar Hindu shit."

"That's irrelevant. He's a devotee of Osho."

"That's right, I remember, he's got a peculiar name." Serge's scepticism could not put me off.

"Devaprem, that's his Sanyasen name. He became involved with the Orange people when he had to give up playing and doing concerts because he got R.S.I. in his hands and extremely bad backaches."

"There you go, an invalid."

"That's shit, Serge; I hate this mentality, and he's not. He writes a lot of music."

Handling Serge and his objections called for the best of my capabilities. After all, way back in my career explorations, I was a sales person. No, not behind some counter, that would have been too static for me. I drove around Sydney and the countryside, selling greeting cards, and later, leather and suede jackets and vests. Just say, I had gained enough sales techniques to convince Serge.

I won, or was it a miracle he gave in?

Graham was thrilled to be asked, and here they were, two tormented musicians with completely different backgrounds and musical styles. Although Graham had studied and followed jazz, he was a blues and folk-rock musician.

The Jewish matchmaker in me put these two diverse characters together. Luckily they respected each other enough to make it work. I found it fascinating that apart from their music discussions, they explored their spiritual and religious diversities. Graham had abandoned his Jewish roots years before and dedicated himself to soul searching, and meditation. Serge couldn't be bothered with his Russian Orthodox background. Instead, he conglomerated a blend of God, Jesus Christ, bits of Judaism, some spiritual writings of Joseph Murphy with other esoteric and Zen teaching he learnt from his years as a Karate student.

Sometimes they had a convergence of ideals, although Graham felt that Serge still held a lot of anger, and he thought that Graham was off with the fairies. However, they worked happily together, rehearsing and writing music for the upcoming concert.

Sadly, they didn't continue composing together, however, the result of their initial collaboration was fabulous. I kept a fifteen-minute tape bearing witness to the extraordinary music they could have produced. In the ethers of modern technology, you can find a Channel Nine performance of theirs on YouTube, as part of the promotion I had arranged for them.

Did I mention temperamental? On the day of the concert, it looked as if Serge was not going to perform, "I feel sick, Helene, it's not going to work, it was a stupid idea. Besides, I don't need vocals."

"Just nerves, you've both worked very hard. You'll be great. Do you want some chicken soup?" I made a pot the night before because I knew how much Serge loved it.

"Are you crazy, I couldn't hold anything down. Thank you, thank you." But he ate it anyway.

"Take it easy, you have hours to go and one more rehearsal; I know you will feel better once it's all happening."

"You will come, won't you?"

"Don't be silly, a runaway tram couldn't stop me. Don't forget to take a change of clothes with you."

When I think about it in retrospect, I was putting my life on a distant back burner to make him happy. During his lucid, rational times, he greatly appreciated what I was doing for him, telling me that no woman had ever done this much for him, and that he loved me all the more for it. He often articulated this to his colleagues, friends and the world at large about Helene, his wonderful lady, and was excessively proud of my achievements. That was during the good times.

Under different influences, I felt indignant when the ABC conducted a program in my house, about his life and career. Throughout the interview he forgot to mention how I had reshaped his career from the earliest days of our relationship.

In the end, it didn't matter. I had enough memories to soothe my temporarily bruised ego, and enough pride in knowing I was the person who had pulled up his waning career out of the darkest corners of his self-sabotage.

The lavish applause at the Entertainment Centre said it all. Serge and his band won the audience over.

Afterwards, when performers and audience dissolved into their own spaces, I sat backstage in Dizzy's dressing room. We talked for a while, about his home, wife and family, as if we were old friends catching up. He wasn't a young man anymore, yet he still had great presence and a cheeky sparkle. I wish I could have got to know this wonderful man better and consider it a privilege to have had this tiny piece of time with him.

The next night, in a small narrow street at Circular Quay where boats and tourists share the Sydney Harbour, a buzz of human activity milled around Sydney's iconic landmarks: the Opera House, Harbour Bridge and the historic Rocks. In a narrow laneway nearby, music spilled out of the open doorway of the Basement. It would have been quite a challenge to fit one more human in the packed jazz club, hot, oppressive and filled with a smoke-filled haze.

Serge had performed at the Basement before. This night, part of the Dizzy Gillespie concert tour was exceptional. Hunched over the keyboard, he played with enormous intensity, whilst making strange vocal sounds.

Once, I had asked him, "Why do you make those sounds when you play?"

"I don't know. I wasn't even aware I make them."

"You sound like a bumble bee in agony." He laughed at my odd comment.

During interval, hot and sticky from all the body heat and music fuel, I squeezed my way to the club's entrance to get some fresh air and found Dizzy, looking uncomfortable and disoriented. "Are you okay, Diz, can I get you anything?" He stared at my chest.

I was concerned that being a diabetic, he might be about to have a hypo. My mother was diabetic, and I was familiar with that blank look.

"Can I get you an orange juice, a chair or something?" I asked him.

He continued focusing intently at my chest and I panicked, thinking he may conk out any moment. But no, he kept staring until he quietly pronounced, "I can't decide if I prefer your right tit or your left one better!"

What a crazy anecdotal memory about my brief time with the late great Dizzy Gillespie and his admiration for my boobs, which were always too big, and too challenging to keep comfortably housed in a bra.

Twenty-years later, my boobs received a different kind of attention. I was diagnosed with breast cancer, from which I was treated and recovered.

Sharing a few successful nights with the American jazzmen, Serge was in his element and he found a close kinship with John Lee, the American bass player. I invited him and some of our 'boys' home for dinner. I loved sitting at the table with a bunch of creative men who all enjoyed my cooking, and I their company.

For small pockets of life, we are delivered these magical moments, and if we can hold them inside memory's pleasures, they are investments towards our happiness.

My work was done; this project was a satisfying one for us.

By everyday standards, I had achieved quite a feat. Certainly much more exciting than the office jobs and boredom I had worked on so hard to escape. Yet, I am left to wonder whose life was I enhancing? This was work done for my relationship, to boost my clever man, give him joy and purpose and achievement, as well as adding one more impressing activity to his CV. Of course, it added something of value to mine. However, it had been about Serge's career, not mine. Somewhere inside the creative bubble of who I was, were still chunks of unfulfilled pieces.

CHAPTER 18

Joe (Bebop) Lane

'The only people for me are the mad ones, the ones who are mad to live, mad to talk, mad to be saved, desirous of everything at the same time, the ones who never yawn or say a commonplace thing, but burn, burn, burn like fabulous yellow roman candles exploding like spiders across the stars!'

– Jack Kerouac "On the Road."

If I had chosen to be a good little housewife, I would most likely not have met the amazing people I did. And, if my *zeida* (grandpa) had wheels, he would have been a bicycle. This old Jewish piece of wisdom considers the "what ifs" of life, and the potential for different outcomes. If I had done what my mother wanted from me, by now, I might have had a couple of kids, beautifully washed and starched sheets, and know how to make cabbage rolls, one of my favourite foods.

Instead, I came across a character called Joe Lane, a rebel of his own kind, and a much-loved singer-musician of the Australian jazz world.

Serge hired Joe for a gig at the Basement.

About to start, Serge counted the band in. Joe nonchalantly walked onto the stage and plonked his old battered suitcase on the piano, opened it, fumbled inside it, pulled out charts, moved them around, looked at them, oblivious that the set had started and the audience were waiting. Serge and the other musicians yelled at him. "Leave it Joe, get on with it."

Joe ignored Serge and the audience and calmly answered, "What are we doing guys?" Obviously he'd forgotten the repertoire from rehearsal.

In the moment, it looked as if this was part of the act because people chuckled. It really didn't matter about the charts anyway. Joe had a way of doing songs his way, his raspy voice accompanied by jerky up and down hand movements.

During the break between sets, and after introductions, Joe chatted with my friend Jeanie. He seemed quite smitten with her. "Are you hungry love?" He fished in his pocket and pulled out a crumpled serviette, carefully unwrapped it to reveal a cold piece of grey coloured steak, a leftover saved from a previous meal. He generously offered it to Jeanie who gave him a beautiful, enigmatic smile, gracefully thanked him and declined. "Thanks Joe, I'll order something from the waitress."

He seemed disappointed that the object of his amorous attention had other food plans, "Are you staying for the gig? I'm doing another set."

"Yes, I'll be here."

In his mid-sixties, Joe vaguely dressed like Colonel Sanders of Kentucky Fried Chicken. He sometimes rinsed his hair and pointy beard with orange henna and looked like a cheerful pixie or a garden gnome without the pointy hat.

His clothes were often crumpled, sometimes stained, a fancy belt buckle made vague attempts to hold in his escaping belly. He occasionally wore a black string tie under his collar, held together by an American Indian type jewelled ornament. Joe Lane was a uniquely recognizable individual.

Initially, I thought: what's the big fuss all the jazz guys are making of this man? His voice is shocking. He's half singing and scooby-doing all over the place. His gravelly voice sounded more like a string of mumbles and jumbles to me. He could almost be mistaken for his idol, Jo Cocker, with his jittery, awkward hand movements.

Surely these musicians knew something I didn't.

They did.

The first time I had heard him sing, was at the Burdekin Hotel, on the edge of Oxford Street's gay strip.

The pub was a popular place for jazz musicians to sit in with their colleagues, play, improvise and generally catch up. I had heard so much talk about Joe's amazing ability to scat and sing jazz lines. Don't ask me what that means; it's impressive for the people who know. Sometimes the fabulous Australian actor, Tony Barry would come and listen for a while, and catch up with his jazz musician buddies. Many years later, Tony was pivotal in helping Serge with his alcohol addiction.

Drummer, John Pochee often helped Joe out of his financial messes.

After a fall landed Joe in hospital and his finances were a disaster again, Serge and I organised a benefit to raise some cash towards his rent. We booked The British Ex-Servicemen's club and packed it with many of the jazz guys and friends who all came to play or listen, for the love and respect of Joe.

They donated money as well as their talents, and created an afternoon of great jazz, which included James Morrison, a long-time friend of Joe's.

We were all happy with the event and the anecdotes that made us laugh. Afterwards, I presented Joe with several hundred dollars we had collected for him.

Everyone had packed their gear, lugged drum kits and double basses back to cars and while waiting for the lift, Joe shouted, "Hey guys, let's go to the Malay for a feed, the treat's on me." His spontaneous generosity was delightful and childlike.

We explained the money was not to feed the troops, but for his rent, and that we would pay for our own meals. That night, the Malay was filled with discussions dissecting the afternoon music of who did what, and how they had played.

Overriding my objections, Serge decided Joe would be an interesting front man for an upcoming gig in a ritzy Melbourne nightclub. To be honest, I felt that Joe and class was not exactly a perfect match.

You would think after the catastrophic trip across Australia, I should have known better than to take another long car trip with the same lunatic at the wheel, although, under normal circumstances, he was a good driver.

The long grey ribbon of road between Sydney and Melbourne slipped away from us while Joe's chatter in the back seat kept us entertained with muso gossip. After a few hours, he announced, "Hey guys, I cooked us some lamb's fry for the road. Here have some." He leaned over to the front seat offering us a container with an unappetising looking concoction.

He was such a sweet man, it was difficult to reject his offer, but I did find a way out, "That's so nice of you, but we need plates and spoons to eat this. How about we have some sandwiches I made before leaving home."

"I suppose I'd better feed the animals then." Joe tossed his offerings out the window and happily tucked into my substitute.

Kilometres disappeared, until he hit us with an unexpected comment, "I thought I'd make some extra cash, so I've brought along some really great hashish to sell to the guys at the venue."

"Absolutely not, Joe, don't even think it. The boss is in enough questionable trouble with the cops about his wife's death," Serge threatened him. "Forget it."

"Okay, okay, dear boy. Point taken." Joe often addressed some of his mates as 'dear boy'. With me, it was "dear girl."

The point may have been taken, but we had barely stepped into the venue, when Joe exclaimed, "Anyone interested in some great hash?"

Other than our Adelaide expedition about eighteen months earlier, car trips with Serge were always mystery journeys where anything could happen, and mostly did. Spaceships could have landed with lesser impact.

Initially, the drive through New South Wales was peaceful. Only after we had crossed the Victorian border, did things change.

Heading towards Glen Rowan, we were stopped by two young cops on motorbikes. Maybe this was the spot where the ghost of Ned Kelly, famous Australian bushranger, was hovering to protect his home territory.

Serge was asked to pull over, step out of the car and show his driver's license.

All of this should have been easy, a speeding ticket, a warning, and continue on our way. No! The circus began. Serge and the cops moved out of earshot and engaged in what looked like a friendly, jovial conversation, as if they were long time buddies.

Bemused, Joe and I sat in the car until one of the cops came over, leaned in the window, and commanded me, "Give me your name and address, madam."

"What for, officer? There's been no accident, no other car involved, only that my guy drove too fast."

He kept insisting, "I need your name, address and a driver's license, if you have one."

"Hang on officer, I don't see the point."

It became a battle of wits, the more he insisted I give him my name and address; the more I was determined not to be bullied into something that didn't make sense.

Being a cop, he had leverage, "If you don't give me your details miss, I'll have to take you into Glen Rowan police station."

"Fine," and almost added, 'make my day,' but instead said, "I will have some complaining to do to your superiors if you do, so let's go."

Instead of backing me up, Serge, in a blaze of bravado and masculine bullshit came over to my side of the car shouted at me and pulled my door open, "Helene, give him your details, or I'll throw you and your luggage out, and you can make your own way back to Sydney."

Joe was silent in the back seat. The cop stood back seemly enjoying this new twist. I felt utterly squashed. My sudden rebellion lost its fire, and I resentfully gave the cop my name and address. I could barely hold back the anger churning in my gut. Serge started the engine, waved at his allies and drove off.

Fire bolts of anger tore out of my mouth, "How could you, Serge? That cop was utterly out of line. Why didn't you back me up and what was all the buddy, buddy stuff?"

"He was a Vietnam vet and showed me his tattoo when I told him I had been in 'Nam' as a muso, he loves jazz. You could have just given him your details without your usual anti-cop bullshit, Helene."

"I don't have anti-cop bullshit, I hate unfair things, and power games, just because someone wears a uniform."

We still had a long drive to Melbourne, and for endless hours, Serge and I screamed at each other. He carried on with the list of his perceived views of my anti-cop attitude. "What about when you took on that policeman in George Street, and that time you had the cop car chase you all over Randwick with their siren on?"

"I shouldn't tell you anything," I screamed back.

I was so embroiled in this shouting match I didn't understand he was subjecting me to another chunk of bullying.

Many years later, I wonder if confronted by this kind of interaction, I would still be hanging in there. Again, don't ask. At the time I guess I moved to the sound of a different drum and had a load of learning to do about the odd dances people engage in to fuel a dysfunctional relationship.

Sitting silently in the back seat, either asleep or looking out at the Victorian scenery, Joe's scratchy voice suddenly floated out, "Even score, you two," silencing us all the way to Melbourne.

When I think of Joe Lane, I remember a character that could have been at home in an "Alice in Wonderland" setting, and I smile in loving memory of the only musician who ever sent me Christmas cards.

♪♪

I look back on an unploughed field of lost friends who, for whatever time or reason, lived in the spaces of shared activities, and then retreated into unknown places.

I wonder what makes some friendships go the life distance, while others, like burnt buildings, become the ashes of yesterday.

Serge had entirely different relationships with his buddies, from intense to toxic.

I was sitting at the back of the ABC rehearsal studio in Harris Street, listening to Serge's band preparing for an upcoming recording, and wondered how I was going to survive hours of doing nothing, keeping quiet, watching the fiddling about with instruments and musicians going through the paces of rehearsal.

The long night loomed, interrupted by a lightly built young man in a tight red and black leather bikers' outfit. He came in, stood quietly listening to the music, and seemed to devour every note.

Serge came over. "Good, you could make it. Adam, this is my lady Helene."

Troubled eyes focused on my face. "Good to meet you, Serge told me about you."

I knew he was one of Serge's piano students and a friend, "You ride a motor bike, what kind?"

"A Harley."

"I'm impressed." The band resumed their rehearsal and we stopped talking.

Adam was a sad, morose man stifled by his loveless, boring marriage. Disenchanted with life in general. Serge told me that the bond between them was not only because of the love of jazz, but their similar histories of child abuse by their fathers.

Eventually Adam relinquished his café, trained at the Police Academy, became a policeman, and was assigned to a local station. Nothing ever went right for him. At first, he was shot while on duty, followed by an attack by a knife-wielding intruder outside his home.

A few months later, the Six-O'clock news on television, reported an off-duty policeman had been shot in the stomach while he was in a local park. Serge and I rushed off to the hospital to see him and found the place overrun with police.

"The police are checking all visitors," the receptionist on the floor said, and added casually, "If you have any weapons, leave them here at the desk."

"I'd better come clean then." Serge unclipped his flick knife hanging off his bunch of keys hooked on the back of his jeans and handed this weapon to the receptionist, "You can come and get it back when you leave." She responded quietly.

Although the doctors had removed the bullet, Adam never fully recovered from the shot and became an invalid. Like so many crimes, this one went unsolved.

Dodgy cops, colourful musos, controversial friends and acquaintances were part of Serge's entourage. It included one friend he claimed was a mafia boss.

"This man has been my best friend for a very long time, his name is Alberto but we call him Al." I wondered if the 'boys' called him Big Al. I couldn't imagine this charming, dapper gentleman being a mafia heavy. He always dressed impeccably in a tailored suit, crisp white shirt, tie, and crinkled leather Italian shoes. Al, a quietly spoken gentleman had a slight accent and a reticent smile. I liked him a lot. Occasionally Serge brought us together, either at my place or in an Italian Restaurant in Norton Street, maybe it was his nefarious turf, but then again, location doesn't make one a crim.

I enjoyed our discussions. Al was passionate about philosophy and told me, "Schopenhauer held the belief that individual morality could be determined by society."

When conversations moved around my dining room table, Al also talked about his early family life, and the reason for his sadness. I found it difficult to accept that this quiet, gentle, angst-ridden man was anything other than a restaurant manager, and perhaps Serge had over-stretched his imagination about being buddies with an underbelly chief.

"Don't tell him you know, Helene, Al likes you, and it's not a good idea to discuss that part of his life with him."

"So how come you know about it?"

"He's my best friend and I did him some 'favours,' of course I know things. Anyway, I can't talk about it."

"So why are you telling me then, if you don't want to talk about it?"

Caught in his flight of I-don't-know-what, all he could say was, "I tell you, it's true."

"Bullshit," and after that, all I got out of him was a Cheshire like smile.

Al's first wife had complained to me about him being out gambling most nights; maybe there was 'something else?'

All the years of my tumultuous relationship with Serge, our 'forever' breakups sometimes lasting weeks or months, Al was the go-between, coming over to pick up clothes, and other bits and pieces. "Helene, Serge is suffering badly without you, you know, he loves you more than he has anyone else in his life, believe me I know him long enough, he's got a good heart you know."

"Yes, I know he's got a good heart, and he's caring, loving, loves me, will do anything for me, but I can't handle his behaviour anymore. No! You have to take his stuff to him. Oh, and give him this letter from me please."

"I'm so sorry Helene, I know, he's difficult."

Ceaseless long letters and emails followed the breakups. I replied with detailed farewell letters. Serge sent me back pages of hand-printed ones full of raw emotion. Sometimes, it was about his pain regarding his music and his anger about being overlooked by everyone in the jazz industry. At other times, he wrote about his deep, limitless love for me, or a volatile litany of my many wrong doings.

There were long poems of eternal love, and I wrote back my poems of love gone wrong. You may laugh or think, isn't that sweet. Those two are like Elizabeth Barrett and Robert Browning of the modern world, except ours was born out of the fractures of our histories and dramatic breakups.

Walking out of my front door with a green plastic bag of Serge's clothes, Al looked like a dejected Santa on his way to the flea market.

The biggest surprise was after his wife divorced him, Al hooked up with a plain, Australian woman he married when she got pregnant. He bought a house in the suburbs and led a boring life. He never lost that sad face that lit up when he saw Serge, and the two of them chatted like crazy over the backyard barbeque, while I listened to an agonisingly boring saga about knitted tea cosies from the new Missus Alberto.

No matter what, I would never knit tea cosies in the suburbs.

CHAPTER 19

Jungle Juice

"Try to understand man, if you understand each other, you will be kind to each other. Knowing a man well never leads to hate and nearly always leads to love"

– John Steinbeck, Of Mice and Men.

Kids will say, 'I'm bored' and wait for a grown-up to provide amusement. When adults get bored, we have to find our own way out. Although life with Serge was always difficult, it was never boring.

Not sure if it was boredom, curiosity, or just the need for distraction which made me renege on not getting involved with any more of Serge's projects, I was tempted by an unexpected proposal, and grabbed the opportunity to showcase his amazing talent once again.

Imagine, back in the days of no mobiles or Internet, how anyone could find and contact another person. Miraculously they did. Serge received a phone call from a long-ago friend, John Howell, the newest catalyst for the merry-go-round to spin again.

John had sold up his little jazz joint in Adelaide and moved to the far north Queensland minuscule town of

Kuranda, set on the edges of the rainforest. He became the local real estate man and half owner of the new Noctarium.

I hadn't heard about this man before, not until Serge's excitement, "Helene, there was a call at my dad's place from an old music buddy who wants me to go up to Cairns with my band and do a couple of concerts. It's too far so I can't go."

"What do you mean too far, just a flight, and if this guy pays all expenses, why can't you go?"

"Oh, it's a long way to drive."

"Have you heard of planes?"

"I don't go on them."

"What do you mean, never?"

"No! Never."

"How come?" It seemed strange, a grown man who had toured Australia and travelled to England, had never been on a plane.

Reluctantly he admitted he had a fear of flying and his trips were by car, ship or bus.

"Well, it's too far to drive to Cairns. What if I came with you and held your hand."

He laughed, "I can just see this, how long is the flight?"

"It's a lot further than the Gold Coast, and I've only been up north as far as Surfers, which I hated."

I was reminded of the brawny B.A. Baracus from the A Team TV series, and had no intention of drugging Serge to get him on a plane.

Several phone conversations with John, mildly reassured Serge it was a smooth, safe, four-hour flight if we didn't stop in Brisbane.

We persuaded Serge the benefits would be worth it, and he agreed to the flight. John paid all expenses, fees, and provided a large house in the rainforest for us to stay.

Adding class to the band, Maree Montgomery was the perfect choice, so were Steve McKenna, guitarist, and Steve Elphick, double bass player.

My big, burly, blustery man sat nervously in his plane seat. I held his hand, talked, asked him to breathe, close his eyes, and listen to music on his earphone. It all helped. We arrived safely in Cairns and were met at the airport by John, a gentle, quietly spoken man with unruly silver hair.

Many kilometres north of Sydney's winter weather, Cairns temperature was well over thirty degrees, becoming much cooler as we drove up the winding road to Kuranda. I had the unexpected pleasure of seeing a part of Australia I hadn't been to before as the road twisted its way through a thick jungle, scenic lookouts, rocky waterfalls, and into the heart of the rainforest.

In the late nineteen eighties, Kuranda was still under-developed. I felt as if I had come to a tropical kind of Brigadoon where the rainforest with its unique flora and fauna crept in on this dormant, one-street village, and the home for a large indigenous community.

I had never been that far north before, and was surprised to see small groups of Aboriginal people sitting around on the ground, drinking.

The pace was slower than in the big smoke. It may have been the heat of the jungle that made the inhabitants and John move around at a lethargic pace. It wasn't passion he lacked, just speed. He established his real estate home-office in the middle of Kuranda, pursued a rustic lifestyle and became a respected member of the local community.

The house he had arranged for us was a big old place on the edge of the jungle with non-human residents of crickets, frogs, spiders and crawlies providing us with a nightly nocturnal symphony.

Frogs Restaurant, where Serge and the band performed for two nights, had a large open veranda backing onto the jungle. Close to our living quarters, the cosy bar and eatery became our dining and hanging out nook. In all, this was an easy laid-back gig where audience, musicians, John and even me, were happy. Phew!

We extended our trip for a little holiday with John as our tour guide. I had never been this close to Australian nocturnal wildlife, and felt disoriented when we entered John's Noctarium. The dark, barely lit interior hit my nostrils with the pungent smells of fruit bats, sugar gliders and other nocturnal species, normally difficult to encounter in their natural habitats.

John organised a riverboat ride for us. The still, dark, muddy crocodile-infested river of tropical North Queensland concerned me – what if our little boat capsized? I could become the potential handbag's lunch.

The cloying heat through the rainforest slowed us down. Serge held my hand until the moisture of the tropics invaded our joined palms and we had to let go. Every now and again, a kookaburra laughed at us from the treetops.

Of course, I had a wild shopping spree at Kuranda markets. Stalls full of locally produced arts, crafts and 'stuff'. Luckily the items were small enough not to have a great impact on the weight of my luggage, unlike other trips I took overseas, where suitcases ended up bulging and zips broke with my over-zealous souvenir collections.

During our five-day we were there, John's girlfriend Joanne invited us for dinner and an overnight stay in the mud brick cottage she had built, way up in the rainforest. I had never been in such a fascinating rustic home before. It had raw tree beams, and odd shelves jutting out of the brickwork. I loved the three-walled bathroom with a bathtub set into the ground facing nature, open to the elements and any local critters that might want to share bath-time. I imagined lying in the warm water, looking out into the vista of greenery, lush trees with noises of animals and birds.

Relaxing in the lounge after dinner, I noticed something strange happening in the kitchen. "I've only had one glass of wine Joanne, but I think your kitchen floor is moving."

She laughed, "It's the frogs, they pop in at night, I'll shoo them out before we go to bed."

"Oh!" Frogs weren't the only creatures to share the house. Just before Serge and I settled for the night in the visitor's room, John said, "Don't mind the snake, he's harmless, he might slide over the bed to the side table, he usually likes to sleep there."

Snakes? Where I was going to sleep? Mon Dieu! The curled up reptile lying so close to me was completely oblivious to my hot-bodied panic. By the time I woke up the next morning, it had slithered away and I was still alive.

After the success of our first venture together, John and I agreed to produce an album with Serge and his band recorded live at Frogs Restaurant.

A great plan, but the best-laid plans of mice and men often go astray.

What could go wrong?

I did say I didn't want a mundane existence.

♪♪

I was mostly focused on Serge's progress during the eighties and believed recording an album in the Jungle of Kuranda would be a significant boost to his career.

The tropical monsoon season happens early in the year, so we planned for the project to get under way a few months later: giving John time to organise the funding, for Serge to create new compositions, put a band together, and for me, to glue all the pieces together.

Assembling the best jazz musicians for this tour was easy: Steve McKenna guitarist, Jonathan Zwartz, bass player, a fairly unknown but talented young drummer, Steve Marksell, and Mark Simmonds, tenor sax player, whose music pulled at the deepest core of one's soul. Bobby Scott, a seasoned jazz singer was also Serge's choice.

At this stage, we weren't aware of Bobby's out-of-town antics.

The months of preparation were a time of peace and creativity for the three of us. Serge wrote the music and arrangements, including his composition 'Rainforest Blues', while Bobby and I were happily writing lyrics about the Kuranda flora and fauna: sugar gliders, kuss-kuss, and koalas.

In these early days of computer technology, all I had was a typewriter and a telephone. So I roughed together a promotion booklet. At the time it looked great. Now, when I look at the last remaining copy, it reminds me of a school project.

Hindsight is magic, it provides everything you need to know to avoid some disastrous pitfalls. If I had known how things would turn out, I'd have made better choices. Instead, I gave in to my adventurous spirit, leading me to juggle with unwanted consequences.

My bags were packed for a morning flight to Cairns. I was leaving a few days ahead of the band to help John with the preliminary organising.

I had to rush out to shop for last minute items. Any trip I ever take, means packing items that God forbid, I will desperately need. Just in case stuff: just in case the weather changes, just in case the dress code varies, just in case different comfortable shoes are needed, or just in case I'll regret I forgot 'something'.

While I was out, something changed dramatically. As soon as I walked in the front door, I was confronted by a very pissed off Serge. "I've had it, I'm pulling the plug on the whole thing."

"Honestly! I go out for a little while, and come home to what sounds like impending doom." A string of thoughts ran inside my head. Why doesn't anything ever go smoothly with this man? "What is going on? I won't allow plug pulling." Though it was out of character for me to stay calm, I did and went straight into Miss Fixit.

"Okay darling, tell me what's gone wrong, and why you want to stop the whole thing?"

"Mark rang and said he wouldn't come because he found out he couldn't get his methadone program transferred to Cairns hospital."

Methadone! That meant a heroin habit. It's all I needed. "Bloody hell, why didn't you tell me he was a heroin addict? There are other great sax players."

"When I booked him, he told me he was clean."

"You knew about his habit in the first place?" It was no use going into the blame game, so I calmly continued, "Yes, well, methadone does indicate he's trying to get clean, but that doesn't solve our immediate problem. We have to do something about it!" I believe there is always a solution even if one doesn't have a fairy godmother.

"What I don't get, darling," moving into damage control to calm the beast waiting to pounce out of Serge, "Is why he waited until the last day to tell you? Never mind. Let's work on trying to get someone else."

Finding another sax player at such short notice presented a problem. Dale Barlow, the first choice, was unavailable, he was booked for another gig – the best ones usually are. Paul Andrews, another great sax player who had done a lot of gigs with Serge, was clean from his habit, but living in Western Australia.

"I told you Helene, it's impossible. I am going to kill that arsehole."

"Murder won't solve anything, I promise, but it might be possible to organise the methadone transfer if we get hold of Mark's doctor, and the hospital." I looked for alternate solutions.

Leaving John out of this new development was not practical, so we called to let him know the situation. It didn't phase him because his usual phlegmatic self didn't allow anything to derail him, "Let me see what I can do, I'll talk to my local doctor, he's a friend." He rang back with what he believed was good news, "I've sorted it out. My doc friend is going to give Mark all the heroin he needs to get through the concerts. See, easily fixed."

Serge was happy, I was furious.

"Not in my name. There has to be another way because I will not be responsible for getting Mark hooked on shit again. I am not the kind of promoter to fuel a drug habit just to get my plans fulfilled. There must be other doctors to transfer the program to Cairns Base Hospital, or else Mark isn't going, and we'll make the album without a saxophone player."

More phone calls between the two States finally got us authorisation for the transfer. Problem one sorted, now on to problem number two, how to get Mark to Cairns hospital from Kuranda at eight o'clock every morning for his methadone. I'd work it out when I got there.

I flew out on schedule the next morning.

Out of town gigs are great. Not this time! The elements were all there; super musicians, leisurely holiday atmosphere, arranged rustic accommodation, a congenial easy-going promoter, and mama Helene running around like a blue arsed fly.

Forever the media animal, I organised a local TV crew to film the band arriving at Cairns airport, screened that night on the seven o'clock news. All I had left to do was make sure everyone would be where they were meant to be: play music and entertain the audience. Oh yes and behave! What do you want out of my life? You can lead a horse to the trough but …

John allocated us the same house as for the previous trip, big enough for six musicians and me. What the hell was a nice Jewish girl born in Paris doing in an insane environment with musicians, spiders, frogs, crawlies, reptiles and unbearable humidity?

The boys didn't want to share the only double bed in the house, so Serge and I scored a kind of attic crawl space where the heat soared by a lot of uncomfortable degrees.

At first, all was well in paradise; everyone slipped into light clothes and a slower tropical mood. During lunch at Frogs, John magnanimously handed the guys a large bag of marihuana. "Okay fellers, I hope this will do you all, give us a shout when you run out."

No, no, no, bad move, an alcoholic, a drug addict, and a general taste for good dope. We had just arrived, and there was a lot to do: rehearsals, sound checks, and instruments to be sorted. Drugs were an overkill.

"What about after the concert? At least let's get the first night under the belt, John, I don't want anyone bombed out for it."

"It's cool Helene, chill out, they're all used to dope; you should know that."

There was a lot I hadn't bargained for. Starting with Bobby.

After lunch, the engineers and technicians arrived for the first rehearsal and brought with them a new set of problems: egos and more egos. Prima donna musicians and technical staff; all embroiled with tempers; shouting, threats to leave, not to play or set up. Man, it was a mess.

Taking a stance between anger management and parental discipline, John and I managed to calm them down. It would have been great to give them all a good spanking. Then again, not knowing anything about their private lives, some might have enjoyed it. They were grown men and eventually understood that co-operation was vital from everyone and together they would create great music.

For my sanity, I needed to be on my own for a while so I hired a car and drove up the coast to Port Douglas.

Classical music on the radio, gorgeous scenery, lunch in a quaint café, a leisurely drive back to Kuranda, delicious peace and quiet. No craziness! That came later.

The next morning, Serge hijacked my freedom machine to take Mark to Cairns hospital, so my new wheels became a horse-drawn tourist buggy taking me through the rainforest.

What else could I do in this minuscule town? I would have liked to spend some time learning about Aboriginal culture and sit on the ground with a local group I spotted, but, they were passing a bottle around, and I'm not a great drinker. Nor would I consider joining koalas getting out of it on eucalyptus leaves.

Frogs Restaurant and bar was ready for the first night of incredible music. Nervous tension wove around the musicians propelling them into an energetic start. The notes tumbled out from Serge's intricate and fabulous compositions, together with inspired solos from the other band members.

Something wasn't right. Normally, a singer stands in front of a microphone and sings. Bobby Scott was standing behind a music stand holding up sheet music.

No singer ever performs in front of an audience with a music stand between them. Adding to this crime, Bobby was attempting our *Rainforest Blues* song. And, horrors! He started whistling and making peculiar bird-warbling noises. A few lines from the song, and again, strangulated bird sounds came out of his mouth. I suppose this was Bobby's idea of rainforest noises. Confused and angry, I was close to dragging him off his perch. The audience were oblivious.

Bent over the keyboard, Serge was engrossed in playing, and only turned around when Bobby's warbling grabbed his attention. Who knows, he might have exploded there and then, if Steve, the guitarist hadn't shouted, "Keep going man" and an intricate drum solo distracted the audience.

As long they are entertained, audiences rarely notice when things go wrong, unless someone dies on stage. During my theatre days, the public sat quietly through improvised dialogue when an actor forgot his lines. Once when a large backdrop got stuck on the stage curtain and started to topple over, did the audience jump out of their seats to avoid being squashed under a make believe dining room.

Serge contained his rage until the next day when he threw all Bobby's charts, lyrics and music stand into the jungle. Bobby hunted all day for them like a lost puppy sniffing around looking for the comfort of his security blanket. I guess animals, weather and the jungle eventually chewed up all the missing music notes. The second concert night, Bobby resorted to some scooby-doobee-doo vocal nonsense, and the band played on.

We had almost reached the end of the tour and apart from Bobby's digression; all had gone relatively well, until the third and final night.

Mark showed signs of restlessness and petulance. The heat, humidity and nightly playing to a tight crowded audience all culminated in a rancid cloying smell of accumulated perspiration floating out of him, making its way to our agonised nostrils. It was likely he hadn't washed the whole time we were in Kuranda.

"Mark, will you hurry up and get ready. You've been wearing the same clothes for days." I wanted to drag him to the shower but didn't see myself pulling a grown man in a druggy mood to the bathroom. We'd just have to put up with the smell. At this point personal hygiene was secondary. Mark was more concerned about getting his early morning dose of methadone because we were booked to head back to Sydney early in the morning, on the only flight that day.

Serge, aggravated beyond his flimsy tolerance level, threatened to kill Mark, almost dragged him from our jungle house to Frogs.

The audience wasn't aware of any problem, bad smells or that the statue-like figure sitting propped against the piano with a saxophone on his knees was in a rebellious mood.

At interval, when the lights came on, Mark wandered off towards the exit and I called out, "Serge, can you make sure he won't disappear in the jungle and please try to convince him to play in the next set. Otherwise, he'll look like the Mexican under a cactus."

"He can get fucked, I've had enough." Serge wandered off as well.

Please, don't ask where I found the agility of an Olympian sprinter to rush off after Mark, grab the back of his pants with one hand, and with the other hand pull Serge towards him and stop the two of them from going off in opposite directions. I yelled, "You're both selfish fuckwits! Others are relying on you, I went through so much work for you, and you can't even finish the set. How dare you? It's the last night, now you get in there and play, both of you."

A puny woman with a good Jewish guilt trip yelling in a loud, angry voice had punch. They went back into Frogs and played the shit out of it for the second set.

In the end, the audience was happy. John was thrilled. The technicians packed up their gear and said they would come by the house later with the heavy reels of recorded tape needing to be mixed in a studio in Sydney.

Later when Serge saw the tapes, he shouted, "You can chuck them out in the jungle, it's all shit, I played like shit, Mark didn't play, it's all shit." I took no notice and kept the tapes in safety all the way home.

Back at the house for our last night in Kuranda, Bobby walked up to me with a bizarre look on his face and mumbled, "I paid eighty cents and lost my soul."

My insides were depleted and I felt utterly alone, with no female buddy to stand beside me in sisterly solidarity. John was safely in his house while I floundered in this temperamental bullshit. I couldn't hold it together anymore and snapped. I grabbed a nearby kitchen knife shouting, "If you don't get out of my face Bobby, so help me, I will stick this thing into you."

Reason had left me, it would have been easy to let my arm drop and plunge the sharp metal into this human being. See how crimes of passion happen? Lucky, Jonathon or one of the Steve's took my arm and slowly released the knife from my hand, "Calm down Helene, I'll make you a cup of tea, you go and relax in the lounge." I was relieved to have someone else take charge and make me a cup of tea.

I felt as if I was in a fantasy kingdom where a series of events were moving from one thing to another. Still not done with lala land, I heard voices galloping down from the attic room, 'I'm going to kill you, you motherfucker.'

"Get fucked. What do you know?"

"You piece of shit, you screwed up the whole recording, you're dead."

Coming from upstairs, two voices yelling at each other about killing and getting fucked overshadowed my own wanting to kill someone.

I had exhausted all my powers of reason and didn't really care what was about to take place up there, I was going to sit where I was and enjoy my cup of tea.

They can both get fucked, I thought. The screaming suddenly stopped. The silence was more ominous than the loud vocals. I thought this is it, it finally happened, all that tension and one of them is dead up there. Serge has probably done a karate chop on Mark, and now we'll have the police join the circus. I better go and have a look.

I did not expect to walk into the attic and see two lunatic musicians hugging each other and mumbling, "You're my favourite player, you're great man." "I love you man, you are a motherfucka player."

"Jesus man, you played the hell out it."

"You're a legend."

Nauseating! Unpredictable, talented musicians behaving like grown babies, hugging, crying. Repeatedly, they chucked in 'man' into this love-in. The only thing I could do was to stand there and lamely say, "MAN! I feel like killing the both of you."

The sky had turned into a soft tangerine colour. The early morning found us all in various states of half sleep. Serge had got up early and drove Mark down to the hospital for one last sip of methadone and to drop my hire car off. John drove the rest of us to the airport.

♪♪

Weeks later, Serge and I were in the studio to mix the tapes I had rescued from his destructive moment and hauled out our verbal boxing gloves to argue all night about which of his compositions to leave out. I wanted to leave in my favourite track, 'To Hell and Back', Serge wanted to cut it from the album.

I knew it was one of the best compositions he had ever written and played. Even though I loved 'Helene's Song' he had written for me. Exhaustion from an all-nighter in the studio made us compromise, and 'To Hell and Back' was kept in the final mix. It turned out to be one of his most successful compositions.

'Rainforest Blues' that Bobby and I wrote, was not included, his attempt at bird impersonation didn't cut it either. Nor did the other noises he had made. My fantasy chooses to think the song could have become an iconic Australiana chart topper. Instead, it's buried in the undergrowth of the jungle, our words swallowed by nature's whims.

Finding a recording company to release the album was another challenge, together with Serge's apprehension and negativity, "You don't know what you're doing Helene. Nobody wants my music. There's no money in jazz."

You must be wondering by now, how did she put up with all that, what made her keep going, why didn't she tell him to go suck eggs? For some insane reason I did keep going, I think it was a combination of tenacity and belief in the music.

Jungle Juice had just about squeezed all the juice out of me.

Warren Fay from Larrikin records signed up the album on his prestigious label, The Cornerstones of Australian Jazz and *Jungle Juice* was released in 1987, and nominated for an Aria Award. There was a certain degree of kudos to have an album I was the executive producer for, reach the place of nomination for an Aria.

We received an invite for the Aria award night, and unlike my last time outfit catastrophe, I didn't run around looking for a flash outfit. I fished out something appropriate from my wardrobe, black satin pants, a white chiffon blouse and stiletto shoes. My hair was cut very short. Serge wore one of his dated suits, shirt and tie. For a man with a thick neck, the tie was more like a constricting hanging rope. His premonition that he wouldn't win was confirmed, and the award went to Vince Jones.

A camel ride might have been less bumpy. *Jungle Juice* had delivered me much more than music. It also highlighted for me how much I could cope with under the most difficult conditions. Even though it was my choice to be involved with it, it was MY choice and I was responsible for the outcomes.

I realised how much I was prepared to do for someone else, whilst abandoning my own needs and ego that also needed to be nourished with recognition.

None of this would have happened if I had listened to the wisdom of my mother and opted to be a suburban missus housewife.

CHAPTER 20

My Mother And My Russian

"When you take the hand of someone you love, what happens to those hands? Your darling comes, and you ask, how can I help? Come here."

– Rumi

My mother and Serge had a love-hate relationship; he loved my mother and she hated him. In fact, she never warmed to the dysfunctional men I dragged up.

The relationship between Serge and my mother was precarious from the beginning. Knowing that he was a white Russian, her first remarks to me were, "You know the Cossacks killed many Jewish people in Russia."

She had a point. During the early nineteen hundreds, Russian Cossacks took part in pogroms, killing or displacing hundreds of Jews from their small communities in Russia and the Ukraine. This was an important reason why many Jews migrated to the safety of other countries during this period. Who knows, maybe Serge's great grandfather killed some of my ancestors. Maybe, that kind of history stays in a person's DNA. I don't know. I'm not an expert.

I was caught in the crossroads of history, my mother, my father, and my Russian.

"He told me he was more Tartar, Mum, and he had nothing to do with his ancestors or family, he is a musician."

"Musician, schmusician, dey anti-Semitic."

"You can't say that of all non-Jewish Russians, Mum, that's not fair. You've met my friend George Nicholl. You said he was a very nice man?"

Her unequivocal response was, "I no remember."

"Of course you do, Mum. Remember when he first came to our place and you opened the door for him, you said, 'Ah *broch* is giant man with a horse coming for you,' because he was so tall and came to visit with his Great Dane dog."

"Ah zo, he different."

"So is my new boyfriend Serge, mum. He's different too, loves me, and is not anti-Semitic. His father told me a Jewish woman brought him up, and not only that, mum, he speaks a few words of Yiddish!"

Determined to hold on to her point of view, she ended the conversation with, "Dey all Cossacks."

On the other side of their relationship, Serge tried so hard with her, always polite. He called her Babushka, an endearing Russian term for grandma. Ironically, she sometimes told her friends, "You know, Helene's friend Serge would go through fire for me, I know dis." That was true; he did his best to please her. Knowing how much she loved Chinese food, he included her in our outings to Chinese restaurants. His first order was sweet and sour pork because she loved it. I know, what's a nice little

Jewish lady doing eating pork? Well, she never pretended to be kosher.

Serge and I often talked about his hunger for his father's approval. I witnessed his struggle between love and resentment, made all the more poignant when it was constantly wrapped in disappointment, like a demon snapping at his love.

I guessed the larger part of his suppressed anger was with his mother. Her absence, both physical and mental, had haunted him since his childhood in Shanghai when he was five and needed his mummy who was busy chasing her socialite life. In Australia, she deserted him again when she walked in the shadows of her mental disorder. Although his parents loved him in their own way, they were not equipped to fill his empty emotional spaces.

Physical or mental absence from a parent to any child carries years-long consequences of who we become. Serge had a mentally distant mother, and I had a dead father, both of us lived with the seeds of our losses. This could have been part of our mutual attraction. Although we both had experiences of previous liaisons, they didn't contain as much of the glue that pulled us together.

When I think about the relationships I had with my mother and with Serge, I realise my escape from one set of constraints and expectations, led me to another.

My connection with my mother was entirely different from Serge's with his. No matter where the messes of my life took me, I always returned to my mother's bosom to cry on. Later, when I was grown up, she became the little human for me to take care of.

In the dreary city of Warsaw it was impossible for my mother to have a childhood. Without enough food to feed a family of eight children, my grandfather gathered the two youngest, my mother and her brother Herman, and went looking for work in Germany. The only work available for a nine-year old girl was to look after geese.

Her memory was hazy but she recalled doing chores and helping with the children when she worked for a wealthy family. I always saw her mouth lift and her tiny eyes sparkle when she described her days off to attend operas, which she loved, but could barely afford standing room.

Having lived through two world wars, she became a resilient survivor with a wonky optimism overshadowed by fear from whatever life dished out.

Our communication consisted of Yiddish, German, bits of French, all glued together with made-up words and, when confronted by confused responses, she'd laughingly say, "Ferry sorry, I no schpeaking zo good English, you understanding me, no?" Yiddish curses were monumental, *'Ich ob zei a misse meshine,'* meaning she wished someone to have an ugly fit.

One time, my mother invited Serge's parents for Christmas lunch, and it turned out to be a strange mix of Russian Orthodox, Jewish Chanukah, and the general Christmas celebrations we all know. All coincide around a similar time of year so we opted for a conglomeration meal of them. We even created a weird type of Christmas tree. Mum cooked the traditional turkey, with little baked potatoes, pumpkin and carrots. The rest of the meal had Jewish/Russian chopped chicken livers, potato salad, and a Russian eggplant mix. For dessert, my mother insisted on the real pudding, bought at Coles. Jewish and Russian traditions are similar when it comes to massive quantities of food.

The language was also a verbal menu – fractured English, chunks of Russian, pieces of Yiddish, much hands and arms waving, strung together with monosyllables, and accompanied by laughter. Watching their attempts to communicate with each other, our parents looked like they were all playing after lunch charades.

It was poignant to see my mother and Serge's mother hold hands on the back seat of the car when he drove his parents home to Punchbowl. This had been a beautiful Christmas; full of food, warmth and for once, family unity.

Mum might have taken more kindly to Serge if I had not continuously gone crying and complaining to her about his erratic behaviour. Years later, when illness and dementia diminished her, she was confused about his presence in my life.

Extremely supportive, Serge always drove me to visit mum in the nursing home and push her wheelchair around the garden. "Are you okay, Babushka?" He pulled the blanket up on her knees.

I almost laughed when she responded to him in Yiddish, *"Gey in dreyd arain, shtick nevayle."* This was a particularly nasty curse sending a person to hell. Then again, during some of our previous heated arguments, my mother had hurled these same fireballs at me. I guess, it was her own 'get fucked' kind of expression. However, in this context, all I could think of was, just as well she doesn't speak Russian and he doesn't understand Yiddish.

I had to improvise when he asked me to translate what mum said, he wanted so much for her to love him, "Oh, she thinks you are a wonderful boy, to look after her so nicely."

"She really loves me, doesn't she?"

"You'll never know how much." There was no way on earth I would have wanted to burst his bubble because I knew that his connection with my mother made him happy, and his support during this one of my most difficult times of my life, was a gigantic lifeline.

CHAPTER 21

Moving To Woop-Woop

"And the danger is that in this move toward new horizons and far directions, that I may lose what I have now, and not find anything except loneliness."

– Sylvia Plath, The Unabridged Journals

Some city folk develop a yearning for the quiet of the countryside. They imagine a vista of green and sky, maybe a lake or river. Traffic a distant memory. The idea sometimes embeds itself in a person when things don't go quite right, with the belief that a move to the great outdoors will fix everything.

Somewhere over the rainbow is the illusion someone created to give us hope, so that we can play out our lives with a sense of direction, where dark shadows fall away, and you live in the glow of perfection. However, Dante had another vision when he wrote: "Abandon all hope ye who enter here". I wonder if he really meant the gates of hell or the life we are delivered as the consequence of bad choices.

My fantasies of the good life included a house with a fireplace, a dog and a beautiful garden to sit and meditate in. This ideal tableau would include Serge being sober.

The view of an ocean horizon, the menagerie of a bird, a cat and man, living a chaotic life on the third floor of my apartment in Randwick, were not enough. I developed a yearning for gum trees and a bush setting, but hadn't foreseen a place where I couldn't even buy a potato after five pm.

Twenty odd years had seen a diverse décor metamorphosis to my average two-bedroom flat – from what my gay friends called Jewish colonial, to hippy phase in the lounge room of eye shattering emerald green walls and low-slung cushion seats. By the time Serge came along, my bad-taste décor had matured to a peach-coloured modular lounge matched by my peach-faced lovebird. You see, I was a crazy bird, owned a pretty bird, and lived with a boozy genius – A pot-pouri of loony diversity.

Along came Spencer the Cat, bequeathed to us when his owner, Ken James moved with his girlfriend from a house to a flat. Hello! Why was kitty going to another flat?

Challenging interactions were rampant in our household, not just between humans, but puss and birdie were going through their own Sylvester and Tweedy bird scenarios of, "I think I saw a putty cat, I did, I did." Serge often mimicked Sylvester the cat with his funny outbursts of, "Thuckering Thuckotash." Don't ask!

The vet told me the bird suffered from stress while the cat needed feline company and sprayed everywhere.

My escape to the office in the other room was futile. Two phones and a clash of personalities did not provide a quiet haven.

We finally let Spencer out, and to call him back home, I stood on the balcony screaming out across the neighbourhood, "Spencer, Spencer, Speee-e-enn-enn-eeence."

Neighbours could easily have believed insane people lived on the third floor from where they could hear frequent shouting, yelling, loud aerobics music or jazz from Coltrane or Parker, Ravel's Bolero, John Denver singing about Rocky Mountains High, and that crazy woman standing on the balcony yelling at all hours for her cat to come home. Altogether, it must have sounded like the general chaos of our insane lifestyle.

Money tight, jazz gigs scarce, made Serge look for alternatives.

"Helene, I'm going to call Marie Montgomery's husband, Jim, to see if he can give me a job as a salesman in the security company where he's the manager. You know I'm a great salesman."

He got the job, and enjoyed the selling game with its perks and benefits including a new company car, regular money, and talking to people. The fees Serge charged a client for security depended on how much of a schmuck the owner of a business was. His most fanciful sales pitch convinced his client there was an overhead security blimp flying nightly over the area to ensure no break-ins.

It didn't take long for Serge to become one of the top salesmen for the company and to earn high commissions.

"I'm taking you and Babushka for a Sunday drive so you can see my sales territory." The freeway hadn't been built yet, so it took us over an hour to reach Campbelltown.

The sprawling suburb was free of high-rise buildings and there was little traffic. The surrounding lush greenery with its abundance of eucalyptus trees had a rural town feel. What an idyllic place to live in, I thought, far enough away from the madness of Sydney.

Sometimes, overloaded with too many pressures, our minds create escapes.

For one reason or another, I often checked out properties in real estate windows. This time, you could say I had valid reasons to look at places for sale in the Campbelltown area where big houses with large front and back gardens cost less than one hundred thousand dollars. I was impressed and Serge even more so, "Think about it Boodgie girl, if we moved out here, it's only an hour's drive. We could have a lovely big house; a dog, I'd love a German Shepherd, an extra room for a little recording studio, and we'd be really happy."

"Mum will have a fit if I move away this far." Luckily she wasn't tuned into our conversation.

"Let's drive out again tomorrow and get a better feel of the place."

By that stage, my brain was not operating on all cylinders. We returned to Campbelltown the next day, went into a real estate agency and bought a house; it had three big-bedrooms, split-level front and back yards, trees everywhere, two bathrooms and a double carport.

It was located in a suburb called Ruse, claimed to be the upmarket Vaucluse of Campbelltown.

The house cost eighty three thousand dollars. I signed the papers and paid the deposit. It was that simple. The rest was much more complicated.

We had an argument the first night in our dream home, and then we unpacked our stuff.

Some people wrap their lives in emotional cotton wool, while others are impulsive sentiment warriors racing into situations, ignoring any signals of ultimate reckoning. You couldn't possibly call me a warrior, yet there I was heading for a new battle territory, already wearing too many emotional wounds.

So what could be risky moving to a house surrounded with lots of gum trees, plenty of space for an office and music room? I even painted some rooms while Serge was in bed with the flu.

What I hadn't taken into consideration was Serge's increasing battle with alcohol. It took the move and change of environment to hit me with it's full blast and for me to arrive at a place where it tore me apart.

♪♪

Our life was playing out like a movie. We had met, got together, fought, made up, hit the road, made music, and then a real movie came along – A phone call from someone making a documentary about the early jazz scene in Sydney, *"Beyond El Rocco."*

The producer wanted a film crew to come and interview Serge at home. Yes, of course.

The day of the film shoot I prepared a lavish lunch for the crew who were busy setting up the recording and filming equipment. Tony Barry, the actor, narrated the documentary at a later time.

Relaxed, sitting close to the kitchen window, Serge talked about his time at the El Rocco while the cameraman and sound guy were recording him. Right in that moment, Spencer the cat got it in his kitty-brain to come in from the great outdoors and grab a moment of fame. My handsome puss walked on the window ledge right behind Serge, boldly swished his tail across Serge's face and meowed, nonchalantly disrupting the interview. Even the cat had an ego in my household. Filming stopped, the crew laughed; Serge was furious and yelled at me. "Get rid of the fucking cat, Helene." The roar of the lion outranked the meow of the puss.

♪♪

I found it difficult to reconcile the gigantic gap of living on the outer fringes of Sydney, and although everyone spoke English here, it sounded different. Salesgirls asked, "Watchawannna?" and greetings were conveyed as, "ow yer goin'?" I felt like an alien in this unknown universe.

My theatrical agency had lost its impetus, and I discontinued Helene Grover Enterprises. I had to do something, so I opened a local drama school. Not an easy task trying to bring culture to local yokels. Some of them had never travelled further than the edges of the train line.

♪♪

Home is the space for your treasured mementos to surround you with their familiarity. It's part of your comfort-zone holding everything you are accustomed to. Home is where you know the streets and where they criss-cross each other. You are familiar with the houses, buildings, and your favourite shops. This knowing is like a safe cocoon from the vagaries of the unknown.

Pieces of furniture, trinkets, and mementos occupy corridors and rooms of my house. I make throw out plans, and my heart breaks at almost every piece I get rid of. Don't get me wrong, I am not a chronic hoarder, my house isn't buried under a pile of 'stuff', but the objects I find difficult to relinquish still lurk in my forgotten spaces.

Years earlier, I travelled with a girlfriend to London where we lived in temporary digs in a belowground studio in Kensington gardens. It had the basics – two small beds, table, two chairs, a tiny cooktop and narrow wardrobe.

In order to make our bed-sit feel homely, we added large travel posters, crepe paper flowers, and matching cushion covers we fabricated with sticky tape and placed candles around the room. We created a warm place to come home to after our day's explorations. And to give us a sense of something alive, we included in our temporary home sweet home a goldfish we exercised in the bathtub, and gave it to our landlady when we left for a three months car-trip through Europe.

The place in Ruse was never my comfort zone. No matter what I did to it, I never felt this was my home, my sanctuary.

Serge and I loved dogs. I had in mind a cute, small one, and he hankered for a German shepherd, so we got a German shepherd, he named Tooska. The toilet and puppy training, vet visits, and walkies were left up to me. Hugs, licks, pats, and putting down the food bowl were Serge's territory.

I was hopeless at training both dog and man; one pulled me around posts in the street, and the other pulled me up and down an emotional roller coaster.

Serge went to work, and almost every day he came home drunk. The drunker he was, the more verbally abusive he became. As a salesman, he was in his element with the company's enormous drinking culture, long, expensive lunches in Chinese restaurants with an open-ended booze tab. My life was unravelling more than ever. I had nowhere to turn. I couldn't run to my mother anymore. I was too embarrassed to tell my friends. I only had two friends I had made locally and those ladies understood too well the demons of the alcoholic.

Yet, in the midst of all this, I engaged in the folly of accepting an invitation to join Serge for five-days at Jupiter's Casino on the Gold Coast, courtesy of the company rewarding their top salesmen.

I hated the claustrophobic gaudy atmosphere of the Casino, operating twenty-four hours a day with masses of people milling across those giant rooms. I was more than uncomfortable with the endless boozing of Serge's bosses, sales colleagues and wives.

It was almost a relief to get back home to Ruse, where I also felt I didn't belong.

CHAPTER 22

Trying To Adapt In Suburbia

*"In an expanding universe, time is on the side of the outcast. Those who once inhabited the suburbs of human contempt find that without changing their address they eventually live
in the metropolis."*

– *Quentin Crisp – English writer, raconteur.*

The horse paddock at the end of my street was a big deal for a city girl, and knowing bugger all about horses, I kindly offered a horse an apple. The gentle looking animal not only took the fruit in its mouth but half my hand as well and wouldn't let go. I extricated myself, drove to town with swollen fingers and in a lot of pain. The local doctor was amused when I told him what happened. "I've never treated someone with horse bitten fingers before."

Bored, I drove around the countryside looking at green hills, sparse houses, pockets of local shops, and cows. I liked the tranquillity of cows, but not as a regular activity.

I felt cornered with few choices and wanting more.

With problems at home escalating, this was not a period of music.

Serge's sales pitch got wilder, the drinking outcomes rougher and although initially he had been the company's golden boy, he became an out-of-control drunk. Client complaints and arguments with people at work finally got him fired, ending his free booze and being a top salesman kingpin.

His escalated drinking and no job inevitably had an impact on me, pushing me closer to an emotional crisis. However, projects were a way to regenerate me, and as long as I was involved with 'something', I could distract myself, for a while at least.

Desperate for something to catch my attention, I discovered that Campbelltown was a historic area where convicts were sent during the eighteen hundreds. Frederick Fisher, a former convict had become a local landowner but was murdered around 1816 by George Worrell, later executed for the crime.

My interest was further aroused when I learnt that in 1836 the local newspaper published an article reporting that the ghost of Frederick Fisher was often seen sitting on a rail post near his home. This became the legend leading to the Fisher's Ghost festival, celebrated every November.

Ha-ha something to get my teeth into, I grabbed the opportunity to showcase my drama students and enter a float in the festival.

Someone provided us with a large tabletop truck and I scrounged through the Reverse Garbage place in Marrickville where I found a delicious haven of industrial waste including bags of leftover fabrics, and stuff. Out of those discarded treasures I created a float that became our truck's eerie graveyard. My 'ghosts', dressed in shredded outfits, looked like Michael Jackson's 'Thriller' zombies.

I marched in the grand parade down the main Street of Campbelltown in front of our graveyard-decorated truck, and we won best theme award for our efforts. The local paper published a photo of us, which gained me a few more students, making my local drama studio marginally more productive.

Teaching drama a few days a week still left me with too much empty time to ruminate about my situation. Who the hell had I become? A woman sitting on the fringes of her man's life to shop, cook, and listen to kookaburras laughing in gum trees.

Tooska's training was a disaster. Puppy school was full of adept owners, and I was the embarrassed owner of a renegade canine. He got tangled in my legs, moved when told to sit, and dragged me through rain-soaked mud. At least we entertained the successful puppy owners.

Over the years, I witnessed the rise and fall, and rise again of Serge's battle with alcohol.

For him, no more the exotic salesman life, and with no gigs in sight, he went back to driving taxis, coming home angry after his night shifts, complaining about the drunks in his cab. How hypocritical was this? Considering he was still drinking.

Fundamentally, Serge was capable of adapting, creating music or anything else to earn money, by most means necessary. He had started a Karate school, driven taxis and being a sales rep. He was particularly talented at hustling dollars from mates. Sometimes he paid them back.

Serge desperately needed to play music while I was wilting in suburbia. We were both stuck in a way of life neither of us was comfortable with.

A return to music brought in some fresh notes.

♪♪

Wedged between the flamboyant Les Girls drag queen venue in narrow Roslyn Street, Kings Cross and the popular Piccolo Bar coffee shop, Round Midnight, emerged as a new jazz venue, a smart environment with comfortable seats, lounge nooks, a bar, dim lighting and a busy buzz.

Finally, Serge launched himself out of the suburban doldrums with intermittent taxi driving and a regular gig at Round Midnight.

Occasionally a great musician from the States turned up and 'sat-in'. Sometimes, I went along; what else was I supposed to do? Watch hair fall out of the dog or listen to nocturnal bush noises?

We were leaving the club at two one morning and found two drunks bent over his car, dicks in hand peeing on his car. Even after a four-hour gig, Serge found enough energetic fuel to grab each one by their clothes and yell, "Get off, you motherfuckers, I'll teach you to piss on my car." and threw them both across the bonnet. They were mid-piss with their dicks still sticking out as they went sailing on to the hard pavement. I stood speechless on the footpath as he got applause from startled passers-by.

Round Midnight was building up as the 'in' jazz place.

Life dives into the directions it chooses to take us. Most times we have little control, and for Serge, it had even less. This occasion brought the well-known bandleader Warren Daly to the Club. The jazz guys mostly all know each other, from playing in bands together, jam sessions, going to listen to each other play, and generally gossip. I tell you, I've heard some doozy stories, and no, I will not divulge them here. Then again, I later heard some delicious stuff regarding my own colleagues.

I wasn't in the conversation between Serge and Warren at the Round Midnight bar. Later, on the way back to Ruse, Serge told me about it, and his ambivalence about joining the band. But he did.

It was a welcome change. For almost a year, there were regular well-paid gigs, concert tours and the extra pleasure for me was to be a part of the social side of the Warren Daly family. All lasting long enough for two delightful Christmas band picnics at Lane Cove National Park. Stability, good times, convivial people, a well-organised bandleader, were great criteria for me. However, Serge always had his own agenda and although it all started smoothly, too soon came his criticisms and complaints. I'm up there with the best of them, but when it came to nit picking, competing with Serge, I was in kindergarten. He found a litany of reasons, including the claim that other people were coo-coo.

"Considering you were off your rocker for two years, I don't think you can judge others."

"Shit, Helene, you sure can come in for the kill. Still, I guess you're right."

There were situations where he'd get himself worked up about the consequences of some of his activities, and I announced, "Darling, I'm about to give you a reality check. Are you up for it or would you rather I shut up?"

With an impatient flick of his hand he'd say, "Okay, get on with it, let's hear it." He accepted that until the next time when he sounded off about the many gigs he'd given other musos, and they never asked him to join theirs.

"They love playing with you and think you are a great musician but you have to admit, your verbal outbursts and unpredictability freaks them out."

"But only when I get drunk."

"Duh!"

"I've given the guys so many gigs, but when it comes to the crunch, they leave me out, they'd rather book Liberace."

"See what I mean? Calling one of your colleague's names doesn't help. You frighten them as well."

"What, because of my karate and the gun, that's stupid. I wouldn't hurt anyone, but I'd kill somebody if they hurt you."

"Not only that, your drunken phone calls, swearing at them and behaving like a Yachne."

"A what?"

"It's Yiddish it means a gossip.

We had these conversations in times of peace and his favourite foods.

There were a lot of gigs with Warren Daly's Big Band: Sydney, Canberra, country areas, and several festivals.

Eventually, the elements that drove Serge's personality and perception, such as the discipline, not being in charge nor curbing his drinking, gave him enough excuses to leave the band.

All my attempts to normalise his perception had failed.

The good year once again became the deflated place of discontent, for both of us.

♪♪

The suburbia I had run away from all my life became an uncomfortable reality I had been unprepared for. Here I was, in a place where mundane existence played out daily.

After all, the house amongst the gum trees had temporarily delivered my fantasies and I was again left with the dog, cat and an out of work musician heading towards his nemesis.

Grey days engulfed me in a cloak of ominous darkness with the needle on my emotional compass bouncing around from the perpetual instability.

You might wonder what kept me going – What keeps anyone going? Birds in the trees, phone calls with friends, overnight stays at my mum's, going to see 'Dirty Dancing' at the local with a friend, and reading. Somehow, I held myself together for a while longer.

CHAPTER 23

Jamming With Branford Marsalis

The whole point is, give me a break with the standards. You go to the average jazz label and suggest a record and they want to know which standards you're going to play. I'm saying break the formula

– Branford Marsalis

Spencer the cat was busy exploring his surroundings, including the wildlife close to our backyard. He meowed to come in when it was dinnertime or curled himself up in the sun in a large flowerpot on a wall outside our front door. At night, he made himself comfortable on my lap, oblivious to the disruptions going on around him.

The human leonine cat in the house was verbose, louder and more demanding.

I know the gurus of whatsits keep lecturing us about living in the moment. But, how can we discern when that exact time happens? – You know, the one that changes everything or brings us a platform for an incredible event. I found one of those moments.

The media announced Sting was coming to Australia for a national tour and bringing with him his new band of great jazz players he had recorded with: Branford Marsalis on sax, Darryl Jones, bass, Kenny Kirkland, keyboard, and Omar Hakim on drums. I am a long time fan of Sting, from his "Walking on the Moon" days when he was with the *Police*, and years later, I played to death 'An Englishman in New York' track from his album, *Nothing Like the Sun*.

I heard that while in Australia with Sting, Branford Marsalis wanted to jam with some local jazz musos, and when I talked about it with Serge, I got a bitter response: "I guess he'll be playing with other local hot shots. Sure wouldn't be me."

Nothing happens if you don't try. So I did. I rekindled my inner fire, jumped back into the chase of the hustle, and found the way to revitalise Serge. I started with a phone call to the Musicians Union, which led to a string of other phone calls, until I located the hotel where Sting and the band were staying. Miraculously I reached Branford Marsalis on the phone, told him I was a musician's agent and managed one of the best jazz pianists in the country. Our conversation led us to agree on a place, time and venue for when he returned from his Australian tour.

It had been a delicate balancing act for Branford to agree to play with Serge, and the Basement manager to allow the place to stay open for an after-midnight jam session. The proviso excluded fees for everyone. Serge invited his best jazz colleagues for the late-night freebie.

Because of his contractual agreement, Branford made it clear it was imperative for us not to contact any media. The

Basement management and I complied. However, It took a chain of phone calls and word of mouth to materialise a packed audience.

"I'm driving Serge, just relax." He was understandably nervous while I drove my little red Laser through the sleepy darkness. I felt as if I was a foreigner from the West, heading towards the big City, an hour from our suburban greenery.

"You set me up Helene. I'm going to look like a schmuck. Branford won't turn up. Why should he play with me, he's got his own great pianist, Kenny Kirkland."

I just kept driving and repeated calmly, "I promise it will be fine."

In spite of no media, the Basement was packed, hot, buzzing with anticipation, drinks filling up the glasses, and a smoky haze spread over the dimly lit jazz club.

Close to one in the morning I felt nervous. Serge seemed to be shrinking. Maybe he was right; maybe Branford Marsalis wouldn't show after all. My eyes vacillated between Serge and the entrance.

Right on time, the American saxophone player walked into The Basement carrying his instrument case. I went over to him and introduced myself. He smiled warmly, we shook hands and I introduced him to Serge, "Here's the man, Serge Ermoll." Underneath all the bluster, a pussycat lurked in Serge, "Man ... Are you sure you want to play with me, haven't you brought Kenny with you?"

"I heard a lot about you, man," a small smile spread across Branford's dark face, "and I want to play with you, let's go."

Both walked on stage followed by the rest of the musicians.

For the next two hours, the music sounded as if they had been playing together for a long time, the notes drifting through the atmosphere in a dance of exploration. There is a strange love affair that happens when musicians share an exchange of creativity. Although they are lost in their own world, the audience feels it.

The only way to stretch these emotionally charged times is to return to their memory of them, ghostlike and slightly distorted by the games of the mind. We revisited that memory many times.

A few years later, Branford Marsalis returned to Australia and contacted Serge for another impromptu jam session. But by then, I was no longer involved in Serge's career moves.

Despite being told not to contact media, Serge passed the information on to a jazz PR person, resulting in a radio announcement and a newspaper mention.

Sadly, this backfired and put an end to the planned jam session between Serge and Branford. Consequently, there was no more music magic between them.

I wasted a lot of time trying to repair the damage but nothing helped, and Branford's manager cancelled the session.

The Basement had to cope with a huge line of people waiting to get in for a performance that never happened. The fallout devastated Serge, and his only way to cope was to find solace in bottles of vodka. My coping mechanisms didn't have substance escapes. Instead I ended up with an accumulation of more emotional baggage.

CHAPTER 24

Pentridge Prison

"I'm not intelligent. I'm not arrogant. I'm just like the people who read my books. I used to have a jazz club, and I made the cocktails and I made the sandwiches. I didn't want to become a writer – it just happened"

– Haruki Murakami

Living in Ruse was a kind of gaol sentence for me. I couldn't relate to the people around me. My emotions for the local greenery were past their use by date. I felt the creeping boredom of living in a place lacking the busy maelstrom of city life. I had little to do but dust another piece of furniture or go look at contented cows.

Serge grappled with booze, disappeared to unknown places and came home for meals and to watch television.

Imagine, life with a brilliant, intelligent, creative musician and a neurotic, creative Jewish woman; a match made in the twilight zone. Our most frequent entertainment was watching Tooska, the dog, and Spencer, the cat, staring at each other from either side of the screen door. We were so dysfunctional we kept the cat in, and the dog out.

Justifying why he hadn't won a recent Aria Award, Serge explained, "You see Helene, my music is too out. I told you they wouldn't let me win the Aria. See, Vince Jones is so much more commercial, and he sings."

"You don't do commercial jazz, Serge. It's great you were nominated for an Aria, how about we aim for next year's awards? Are you prepared to compromise a little, with some funk, commercial musicians, a hot young horn player, and how about some tracks with a great vocalist?"

These discussions went round and round, coming back to lack of funds and the difficulties of getting a recording deal. When daylight flowed into his mental comfort zone, he argued, "I've thought about this, Helene, I'm not selling out. I play the real jazz and am not going to dilute what I do into commercialism for the sake of maybe winning an award."

"So how about expanding your horizon and tackling more accessible music?" I suggested naively.

"No Helene. I'm not selling out." And that was that.

"Do you have to be so hard-nosed about your convictions Serge? Times change, you were the great innovator with Free Kata, can't you find a contemporary way to rejuvenate your career?"

"Charlie Parker and John Coltrane wouldn't sell out like that."

"We will never know. Early death stops change."

"Very cute, Helene, I'm not doing it."

I could see there was no way around Serge's attitude regarding his music; it was his way or no way. Bloody convictions! Tick, tick, tick went my over-active thinking as I dived headlong into an idea of behind bars… if I could produce an album in the jungle, why not in a gaol? At least, wayward musicians would stay put. Not like that disaster up in Kuranda. You would think after my previous experience of producing the Jungle Juice album, I would have learnt to leave well enough alone, a prison could present more challenges than spiders and frogs.

I wonder if my thought processes were impaired by emotional amnesia about things that go horribly wrong.

Serge had convictions about not selling out to commercialism, and yet yearned for accolades, and I seemed to have a kind of psychotic need to bash my head against the wall.

Michael Yabsley, the then Liberal Federal minister for Corrective Services, rejected my request to record the album in Sydney's Long Bay Prison. Determined to achieve what I set out to do, one way or another, I miraculously found another Michael, Michael Knight, the local Labor Party member.

I met Michael's wife at a function. See! My being a cheeky bugger helped. Michael connected me with John Griffin, the Victorian Minister for Corrective Services, who gave me the go-ahead to organise my project in Pentridge Prison, Melbourne. Years later, Michael Knight became the big chief of the Sydney Olympic Games in 2000.

Ah well, not the home State I was planning, but I went ahead with it anyway and flew to Melbourne to meet with a parole officer woman delegated to conduct me around Pentridge Prison.

Not having any family in Australia has always been tough for me. I had considered moving to Melbourne at various times where my close friend Hazel and her family lived in Caulfield. It was a joy for me to stay with them whenever I went to Melbourne. I always hug this relationship in my heart – It goes back a long way to when they lived in Sydney, and when the first child, Allan was born, my mother was honoured to be his godmother. When she died, I inherited him as my godson. Allan is a delight and the relationship is a rich rewarding one for us all. They are my surrogate family.

♪♪

"You're not serious, Helene. You're not going into a prison, are you?" Hazel was incredulous.

"Yes, I am, you know me."

"I do, but it's dangerous."

"This is the most crazy of anything you've done before." Hazel was used to my goings on. The more concerned she was for me, the braver I felt.

I learnt about the grim and colourful history of Pentridge, which was associated with crime during the Victorian gold rush of the 1800's.

In 1850 Coburg established a number of penal stockades where prisoners had to break up the bluestone to build the Sydney Road. They worked, slept, and ate in chains. Eventually, the stockade was transformed into a proper prison, and the last man executed there was Robert Ryan. Serge's latter day hero, Mark 'Chopper' Read had been the notorious houseguest that became the ghost who was heard bellowing through his cell. According to rumours, faint torturous screams were also heard from other dead inmates who had been hung within these walls.

I had chosen a dark place where crumbling walls surrounded by barbed wire held such a grim history, and ignored the prospect that in this environment anything, besides music, could happen, particularly with my lot.

I was thrilled Geoff Kluke, the brilliant bass player, and Keith Stirling, trumpet player, agreed to be included for this project.

Pentridge had a beautiful chapel, and the prison warden suggested we hold the concert there. But I wanted the band to perform in a tougher environment where there would be a greater visual impact for a doco. Consequently, the warden offered me Division D, the toughest part of the goal: Steel bars and tight security for the worst criminals housed there.

There were things I did in those days that I wouldn't do now, even if you held a gun to my head.

"Can I look inside this security section to see if it's the right location?" I asked my guide.

"I can't go in with you, because I was the arresting officer of the screwdriver rapist, and he's in there, so best you go in with the guard. You'll be okay." She handed me over to one of the guards who took me through an imposing security gate.

I suppose by now, you might believe I had misplaced bravado, cloudy judgement and would do almost anything to take an idea to the end.

My next trip to Melbourne and Pentridge gaol didn't run so smoothly. Serge, Geoff and Keith were first timers to the place, they had come to check out where the band could set up and if it was safe enough for them.

Just as we were about to go through the gates, I remembered a teeny little thing: "Serge darling, where is your gun?" (I'll tell you more about the famous gun later.)

"Where it always is, why?"

"We are going into a high-security area, and will be searched, so where is your gun?"

"In my back pocket."

Panic!

"Take it back to Geoff's car and leave it there. Is that okay, with you, Geoff?"

Nothing about Serge ever surprised anyone, "Sure. We'll put it in the boot."

A veteran of one visit, I showed off, "Great choice, hey! It's going to be really exciting."

"Are you expecting us to perform in there, right in front of all those hardened criminals and killers? I thought you said the warden suggested the chapel."

I was having fun. "He did, but I feel this area will have a better visual impact for the documentary, besides, it will be heavily guarded."

"What if these guys hate jazz? Why don't you get them a heavy metal band instead?"

"Don't be a wuss, Serge, you're just trying to get out of it."

Without a fairy godmother or benevolent benefactors, I had to find ways to finance expenses, so to cover costs I booked the boys for a few gigs in a Lygon Street restaurant.

Unforseen situations had a way of manifesting themselves with Serge. He ran up a large bar tab, which used up the three nights fees. Once again, I was left holding the hassles baby – it had a heavy nappy full with out of pocket expenses.

That was it! I had enough of being in the shit over Serge. I killed the whole 'music in Pentridge Prison' idea, and retreated from anything more to do with managing his career.

Of course, there was regret for what could have been if we had completed the 'Convictions' project. Would it have become an Aria winner album? And would I have remained sane?

Like many things in life, we will never know.

In the process of writing this book, I contacted Geoff Kluke to get his take about the project. This is an extract of what he wrote back to me:

Hi Helene. Yep I can remember Serge calling around to our house and pick me up to take me out to Pentridge, which was just off of Bell Street, the main road that went out there. This would have been around 1988. A warder gave us a tour around the jail. It took about half an hour or so. I can remember the warder telling us that there was a big problem with drugs in the jail and that none of the prisoners were doing rehab, or learning skills. Pentridge has since closed down as a jail. Part of it has been turned into a museum I think, and other parts redeveloped. The Album was going to be called "Convictions" a great name I thought.

The Serge Ermoll quartet live from Pentridge but sadly it never happened.

Geoff
GEOFF KLUKE

I wasn't sure yet how to exit the Mad Hatter's tea party. Get out of the rabbit hole and dive into other ways to indulge my insanities. My inner Alice was getting tired of chasing elusive fantasies that did little to justify my own creativity.

CHAPTER 25

Lost Laughter

"Are you bored with 'nice guys' who are open, honest and dependable?

Many women find themselves drawn into unhappy and destructive relationships with men. They then struggle to make these doomed relationships work, and often don't realize how powerfully addictive these unhealthy relationships are."

– Robin Norwood – *Women who Love too much*

There wasn't much left after the abandoned gaol project.

Isolation, boredom, failed album attempt and Serge's increase of alcohol, all pushed me into a prison of self-doubt and confusion about what to do next, or dive into a pool of inertia.

My stress had to have an outlet, and without thinking anything through, I decided to build a swimming pool to replace the double carport. In that state of mind, I entered into my very first ever building-project and had an above ground pool built in-ground. How was I to know the site was on a rock ledge where it took four days for a huge jackhammer to dig a big pool hole?

Eventually I achieved my longed-for pool and spent the summer swimming around like a trapped goldfish in a bowl.

I now had a house, a dog, a cat, a mini pool, and a man.

My man was doing intermittent taxi driving and stepping up the alcohol.

In exile and unable to see my options, I was spinning around on an out-of-control merry-go-round, flying past a blurry countryside, unable to decipher warning signposts.

Isolated from the life that once was, I felt like a prisoner in a thorny world, asleep in a glass coffin with the ogre crashing about shouting, screaming, staggering, threatening, complaining and finally falling into deep drunken sleep, snoring and muttering.

Living in Ruse, I became an emotional mess trying to cope with Serge, his alcohol, pills, and mood swings. A hellish cloak of helplessness wrapped itself around me and continuously brought me to the edge of tears.

Serge and I were at a function, someone at our table told a joke and everyone laughed, I opened my mouth; my lips started to move but somehow didn't connect to that place inside that feels so good that a joyful sound comes out. Instead, the joke hit my pain button and activated an unspeakable sadness. All my body could respond with were tears, and for the first time I realised I couldn't laugh at something funny anymore.

I felt embarrassed that anyone would see me cry and hurried to the toilets to let my flood of tears run dry.

Depression is such a private thing.

I had lost my laughter! It was blocked by shame and self-hate for the situation I allowed myself to be trapped in, swinging up and down like an emotional yoyo from my tortured relationship with Serge. One moment, he was effusive with his praise and undying love, and the next, put-downs, ugly criticisms, loud and aggressive language. He was never physically abusive except for an occasional fist through a door or flimsy wall.

After another depleting screaming episode, he staggered drunkenly to bed.

I followed him to our bedroom and watched him snore. Grappling with the monstrosity of it all, I suffered his demons as much as he did. In that distorted moment, I took out his gun that I knew was in the bedside drawer, and aimed it at his head. The loaded weapon felt heavy in my hand.

I stood there for a long time debating with myself, if I shot him, he would be dead, and it would be the end of allowing him to plunder my life. Reason returned and with it, understanding the futility of becoming a murderer. Going into a prison for a music project was one thing, but as a long time resident, utterly careless.

I put the gun back in the drawer.

Not long after, I began to have panic attacks. I was in a video shop in Campbelltown looking for a movie to rent. An odd sensation suddenly went through me, I felt as if my head was spinning, I lost my bearings and almost passed out. It lasted a moment, until everything returned to normal.

I forgot about it until a few weeks later when I drove across the Harbour Bridge and without warning, I experienced the same sensation, only this time I was behind the wheel of a moving car and could have gone crashing down into the charcoal waters near the laughing mouth of Luna Park.

Next time, in the home of a musician friend of Serge, I was again confronted with this kind of disconnect. Panic attacks are terrifying; they invade your sense of self and become more intense as they keep happening. The room began to spin, I couldn't breathe, gasped for air, became confused, lost awareness of where I was, and reached the brink of passing out.

Lucky for me, the musician's girlfriend, a nurse, took my arm and pulled me to the divan, "Helene, take deep breaths, close your eyes, and breathe slowly." She brought me some water, and I gradually got my bearings back.

She sent the guys out of the room and gave me the space for the words to gush out of me, and I told her about my recent panic attacks.

"They're probably stress related. I know you have a handful of a man to deal with, so I suggest you go and see a therapist and get professional help." I was frightened enough to take her advice.

Therapy brought my world back to a stable axis. I had finally reached a safe haven where I unlocked the origins of my old wounds, dealt with the new ones and discovered the dance of bottled-up anger.

Every week, I drove to Balmain for my one-hour session with Jenny, my genius therapist. Jenny had a generous pile of cushions of various sizes and colours, where I tossed myself down, clutched a huge stuffed gorilla to my chest, almost squeezing the stuffing out of it, and poured out the genesis of my life's struggles. Three years, on and off the pile of cushions, included bashing the shit out of a blue pillow that symbolised my mother, and a black pillow, Serge.

Sometimes massaging my feet, Jenny pulled out my memories; the war, losing my father, grappling with my mother, and growing up before my time. She helped me work through the debris of my life.

I was doing therapy, and Serge was doing alcohol.

♪♪

You know, when you make yourself a coffee and absent-mindedly keep pouring in that extra amount of water, it overflows into a mess? My overflow happened when one of Serge's muso friend and his wife stayed with us for what was to be a couple of weeks. They parked their caravan in the driveway and slept in it.

Initially, the days were filled with food and memories of the 'old days'. Two weeks stretched into more than a month and evolved into nightly dope and alcohol fuelled reminiscences.

I felt like a stranger in my own home, left out of the buddy-buddy reunion, as well as out of sync with the wife. Hugging the cat and patting the dog consoled me marginally. The only respite came from my weekly trip to Balmain to see my therapist.

Late one afternoon, refreshed from a productive pillow bashing session guided by my therapist, I headed back home, leaving the clutter of city buildings for the wide-open spaces of my almost rural suburb. All the local critters had gone to rest in their nooks and treetops. I reached home to find Serge and his friends waiting for dinner – I begrudgingly prepared a meal wishing I had something nasty to sprinkle on it. Pity, because Serge began to hurl mouthfuls of alcohol-driven venom at me.

Making no attempt to intervene on my behalf, the couple continued eating until they finished and silently slunk out to their caravan.

The cesspool in me bubbled and boiled with the remnants of that afternoon's pillow bashing session making my anger spill over the rim of my endurance. Demons of resentments, regrets, sadness, all poured out of me, I screamed out all of it through echoes of frustration, "That's it, I've had enough, Serge, just get out."

"I'm taking Tooska with me. Where is he? Tooska, Tooska." Serge staggered around looking for our canine surrogate child.

"No, you don't, I'm the one who took him to puppy school, walked him every day, fed him, you can't have him."

"Tough shit, baby, I'm taking him."

"Don't you dare? I'll fight you in court if I have to." We had reached a place of fighting for doggy custody. I found a hiding place for the dog in the back shed. Serge left, alone with a few of his belongings. The visitors disappeared too.

We had reached the nineteen nineties, the last time Serge and I lived together full time. I didn't have his career in my hands anymore, nor did I have anything of a career left of mine either. All I had; was this big house with a pool that was useless in winter, a couple of local friends, and the bulk of my mates in Sydney.

Unwelcome ear bashings waited for me when I drove to Sydney once a week to stay with my mother. She made incessant complaints about my living somewhere at the other end of the universe, and a lot of uncomplimentary dialogue about Serge. Yet, pleased that he finally was out of my life. My feisty little mother was never lost for either words of wisdom or fiery judgements.

Not knowing how short-lived her happiness at my newfound freedom was, she was happily singing as she cooked my favourite meals, always perfect.

CHAPTER 26

Move To Coogee

"What is that feeling when you're driving away from people and they recede on the plain till you see their specks dispersing? It's the too-huge world vaulting us, and it's goodbye. But we lean forward to the next crazy venture beneath the skies."

– Jack Kerouac – *On the Road.*

I went through a slow recovery period shifting coo-coo gear into a world of the New Age where Balmain was the epicentre of it all: my therapist's office, alternative lifestyle shops, Tibetan clothes, incense wafting out of the odd shop, a café or two with tarot readers in corners. I immersed myself in it, chanted many 'Om's' and drank herbal teas.

A heart-shaped rainbow-coloured cassette tape cover delivered me life-changing messages. The voice of Louise Hay telling me I am special, I am the only thinker in my mind, and to repeat 'I love and approve of myself' three hundred times a day. So, what did I have to lose? My sanity was already in question. I played the tape of "You

Can Heal Your Life," over and over repeating, 'I love and approve of myself' every day for weeks.

I returned to my Transcendental Meditation twice daily, and even had an attempted love affair with my reflection in the mirror, although I felt like an idiot telling my image how much I loved it.

At the many self-development seminars, I met other people also stumbling around looking for themselves.

New age people embraced Rebirthing, a trendy type of therapy. Naturally, one couldn't start from the womb again, so the method was to lie on the floor, breathe in and out quickly. I don't know if it was the power of suggestion, the overload of oxygen to the brain, but here I was with another bunch of lost souls lying on the floor, encouraged by facilitators until we howled and cried like a nursery full of newborn babies. Lucky no one went looking for a bare boob.

Lighter by many dollars, I felt better. Amazing what an hour of heavy breathing on the floor could do to help you cope with the mess of your life.

I still had to figure out my reasons for hanging onto a use-by-date relationship, with one UGG boot foot in suburbia. Graduation from the University of Dysfunction was still quite a way off.

Living alone in a big house with two bathrooms and a man-empty bedroom, impacted on my sense of isolation, made all the more poignant by the leftover remnants of Serge's possessions: his clothes, a second-hand keyboard and an echo of his energy clung inside the molecules of my existence.

At night, I heard creaks of shrubbery and noisy nocturnal critters.

As a child survivor of the Holocaust, I lived with night fears all my life, and my present solitary existence brought them to the surface. I couldn't sleep alone in the dark because I dreamed about armies of jack-booted Nazis, and woke up screaming in terror. Then, during the day, when I walked the dog through deserted tree-filled streets, I felt overwhelmed with the realization that no matter what, I didn't belong here.

The great leap to change my situation was to sell the house and return to where I felt I belonged. I found a cute semi in Coogee with a small garden and a hills hoist in its centre.

My mother had a green thumb, I didn't. I remember when we lived in Erskineville, armed with a scoop and broom, she charged after a horse-and-cart delivering milk or ice to get fresh horseshit for her tiny garden. She had to beat the other neighbours to get there first.

Maybe my questionable behaviours are a legacy from my mother.

I made my move back to the Eastern Suburbs after eighteen months living in Ruse.

My car packed to the roof with stuff left over from the removalists, I could hardly see the traffic behind me in the rear-view mirror.

On the floor in a cage, Spencer meowed incessantly while Tooska's snout, draped on my shoulder, made intermittent growls, punctuating their long-standing feud.

It was a miracle that we reached Coogee safely where the continuous buzz of traffic and a bustling nightlife were a vivid contrast to the cultural desert of Campbelltown. What a relief!

My exile in Woop-Woop was over: I was enchanted with the ocean being five minutes down the road, purple sunsets, a place to walk in the evening and look at slate-coloured waters disappearing into a never-ending horizon, I actually talked with people, locals and tourists who walked along the beachside promenade. Tooska found new enticing canine bottoms to entertain him.

As for Spencer, after a gaoled week of orientation in the new house, I spread butter on his paws (I don't know if it works or not, but he did come back home) and went off to discover what this new location would provide, hopefully, no birdies.

Unlike the quiet of my recent bush setting, the new unfamiliar external noises didn't disturb me. I found peace inside my house and myself. I played CDs of Miles Davis, Steely Dan, Edith Piaf or John Denver.

Deciding to make changes to my new house, I became busy directing workmen for the renovations, and like Ravel's Bolero, it all began slowly and picked up momentum surrounding me with the many activities. The friends I had left behind came more frequently than when they had to schlep out to Woop-Woop.

Happiest of all, my mother was thrilled my new house was within walking distance, and I went to visit her much more often. I was also enticed by the large outdoor swimming pool at her building, going everyday for a swim followed by afternoon tea, relishing my mum's unbelievably delicious nut and jam rolls she baked.

Serge kept away. He had his own life to either rebuild or continue to destroy.

Like a hunter on the prowl, I leaped into more personal growth. Simultaneously with a Science of Mind course, I signed up for psychodrama and psychology training. Anything to change the way I had tackled my life up to then – My reward was a fresh sense of delight and wonder.

The transition from briefly living out in the Western Suburbs and returning to the maelstrom of city living had nevertheless been valuable. I realised that changing location didn't make a great deal of difference but that I had sacrificed my own needs by trying to fulfil Serge's. Ruse had not been for nothing after all, it had given me time to experience my circumstances from a different perspective; I wasn't cut out to live in isolation and now was the time to look for what was going to fulfil me.

CHAPTER 27

Laughter Found

"Humor is an antidote to all ills. I believe that fun is as important as love. The bottom line, when you ask people what they like about life, its the fun they have, whether it's racing cars, dancing, gardening, golf, or writing books. Philosophically speaking, I'm surprised that anyone is ever serious. Life is such a miracle and it's so good to be alive that I wonder why anybody ever wastes a minute!"

– Dr Patch Adams – *from his book Gesundheit*

You may ask how on earth did I make the transition from music, theatre, making albums, having panic attacks, to doing laughter?

We are blessed with the physical capacity to laugh. How else would we cope with everything life throws at us? It's counterproductive to suppress the healing power of the "hahas", and ignore the methods that take us there. During the many interviews I had over the next few years, I was often asked, "What made you think of laughter as a career?"

"It's all very well to deal with the past, but my objective is for people to create a happier future for themselves."

In the early nineties, there was no such thing as laughter therapy in Australia. There was happiness training.

During the hunt for enlightenment and digging into my imagination, I inadvertently opened a box of emotional treasures, and unearthed gems to lighten other people's lives.

I found Feldenkrais, a type of exercise reconnecting the brain and body to improve movement. During the sessions with my practitioner Alexandra, we discussed teaming up to conduct a workshop together.

We had different approaches on how this could work. Alexandra's focus was about opening chakras, and bringing down dolphin energy. Me? I dug into my years of teaching drama improvisation, recent training programs I was attending, including psychodrama and incorporating fun activities. There would be more to it, but for the moment, the potential was there.

"We can run workshops on tapping into our chakras," my new age colleague suggested. She enlightened me about the seven chakras centres in our bodies where energy flows through. Never mind about all seven of them, it was the orange-coloured one a couple of inches below the belly button that caught my attention. It supposedly generates a sense of abundance, wellbeing, pleasure, sexuality, and … activates laughter. Hello! Apparently, only people with a special 'gift' can see it. I must have been missing that particular 'gift' because all I saw was a light bulb going off in my head, LAUGHTER!

This was the moment I gave birth to my new idea. This baby giggled in my head, and pushed out the words, "Why don't we do a Laughter Workshop?"

"A what?"

"A workshop including laughter." I plucked a concept out of nowhere allowing my inexperience to take me where this craziness would go.

"Never heard of such a thing. How do you propose we go about it?"

I added, "You jiggle the chakras, and I make with the laughter. It could work." I was warming up to this. Maybe the experience of rekindling my lost laughter from the pits of my emotional pain and learning to have real fun again, made me equipped enough to lead others down that road. It was somewhat impulsive to dive into a methodology of therapy I knew almost nothing about.

I had plenty of material from my years of conducting drama sessions. My colleague already had a successful practice with techniques that worked, so it seemed easy enough to combine the two into a one-day workshop.

Only after we started to structure the programme and booked the venue, we both realised our vastly different approaches towards the objective of getting people to sign up: She relied on the universe and dolphin energy, and I was entrenched in the practicalities of brochures, media and legwork. So, after a friendly tete-a-tete, we decided to dismantle our partnership.

The laughter baby still giggled in my psyche and I couldn't let it crawl away into nothing. I wasn't yet aware of any work done in that field anywhere else in the world, or that I would be breaking new ground in Australia.

It is said, there are none so foolish as those who think they know, but don't. Knowing bugger all, I plunged into an uncharted territory of humour, fun and laughter.

Subsequently, I took years of research, intense training, experimentation, shelves full of books on the subject, and attending conferences, for me to become part of a great movement which included the most incredible people I have ever met.

More than a year later, I met clinical psychologist Robert Holden who headed a laughter clinic in Birmingham, England. We spent hours in a posh tearoom in London discussing this new kind of therapy. Robert was just completing his book, "Laughter, the Best Therapy", and put my details in his referral pages. Several years later, he wrote the foreword for my book, "Laugh Aerobics". Robert Holden is one of my great heroes in the laughter and happiness movements. It was an absolute privilege for me to connect with this amazing and dedicated man.

Engrossed with the discoveries of our meeting, I almost missed the start of *Phantom of the Opera*, which I had booked to see that night. When I returned to my overly priced hotel, I sat on my uncomfortable bed, my thoughts filled with the music, the laughter and a maelstrom of new ideas. I spent the next few hours scribbling copious notes.

The long flight back to Sydney was another opportunity for me to make notes on how to expand my new concept, and as soon as I got over jet lag, I prepared for the launch of my Laughter Workshops.

Venues, locations, and bums on seats, especially when they are to be guinea pigs, are always a daunting part of the business, whether it involves music, launches or seminars. And don't let me get started about the finances, so I won't! Having jumped those barbed-wire walls, I test ran my first workshop. Somehow the fifteen or so people in the room responded well, They laughed, claimed to have had fun, and brought me some positive feedback, which gave me the impetus to continue with my new ha-ha career.

Life was good. My working fireplace threw sparks and flames up the chimney. Too big to sit on my lap, my dog made himself comfortable near the fire, but Spencer the cat was gallivanting around the neighbourhood. I needed puss to complete my domestic bliss. I hadn't seen it for a couple of days so I went to the front of my house and called him until panic made my voice rise to a screeching crescendo, "Spencer, Spencer, Speeeence." Nothing! No chubby grey and white furry feline of mine bounced over fences in response to my frantic calls.

A person, I mean, a mean, disgusting, horrible, vile creature of a neighbour came to tell me the cat had been run over. "Where is Spencer now?" I asked.

"I threw it in the bin."

My beloved kitty who had seen me through so much trauma, who had moved twice with me, slept on my bed and woke me up every morning with either a paw on my face or a whisker in my nostril, and had endured never-ending misunderstandings with the dog, now departed to pussy paradise.

Spencer was dead, thrown away in a bin by a cretin with no feelings.

♪♪

He stood on my doorstep, a bunch of flowers in his hand.

I stood on my doorstep, confused. I hadn't seen Serge for a long time and he looked good. A number two haircut, neatly trimmed beard and moustache, he had a lost boy look on his face.

For a moment, my brain didn't connect with words and I found myself standing there saying nothing.

"Why don't you ask me in, Helene, I just came by to say hello and give you a belated present for your new home."

Ah, the conundrum! Slam the door shut and keep him out of my life, or, be sociable with a long time friend I really had missed a lot, and still held residual feelings for?

Finally, some dialogue escaped me, "You can't stay long, Serge."

I let him come into my home and after I made us some tea, we talked. It was as simple as that. After all those workshops, all that therapy, all that new life, here he was, back in my life.

Talking together was always the best thing between us. Eating together brought us that sense of belonging we both craved.

However, I was determined we live in our own places, me in Coogee, and Serge in his studio in Parramatta. Eventually, our arrangement changed. He stayed for longer periods at my place. His clothes began to infiltrate my front room. Bits of music found their way into my

CD spaces. Trying to be a little more Jewish, I was going through a period of not eating pork or shellfish, so insisted he keep his ham sandwiches out of my fridge.

As long as he was sober, no booze or pills, he was a kind, interesting, intelligent man I loved being with.

♪♪

Noticing that the annual Festival of Sydney called for entries in their umbrella events, I entered my first Laughter Workshops as a part of the events. Always on the lookout for crazy adventurers willing to expose quirky ideas, the media responded to my ads by contacting me for an interview.

Although a veteran of my previous television Madame Zelia debacle, I still wasn't all too savvy with my answers when the reporter asked, "How do you make people laugh, Helene?"

I spontaneously responded: "Easy, I tell people to talk to the dishes, and sing to their garbage." Several people phoned the station to make comments about the crazy lady. One woman who rang said, "If my neighbours caught me singing to my garbage, they'd think I've lost my marbles."

Many interviews later, I developed better answers to explain how laughter interrupts painful brain patterns, and quoted research about how fun and frivolity that leads to laughing is therapeutic.

I still had a long way to go to legitimise the work and present this new kind of therapy into acceptable mainstream.

When my song Barefoot Boy had been on top of the charts, many years before, I had my first taste of media attention, television and newspaper articles, which I kept and stuck in my scrapbook.

By now, my hair was shorter, my boobs a little fuller, my experiences a lot more. Memories of my father still haunted me. My mother, living up the road, continually managed to frustrate me, while I was still trying to gain her approval. She did smile proudly however, when I showed her The Sunday Telegraph photo of me with a full-page story, I read to her. "See mum, I did it, I did it. The paper here says how wonderful it is I have found a way to make people laugh."

"Very good, boobale, but vat about married, und I no happy about him again."

It was no use trying to convince her otherwise, I just had to enjoy my achievements and leave it at that. The newspaper article helped to establish me as the first laughter therapist in Australia and gave me the impetus to continue.

At last, after floundering for so long through my many career changes, I finally discovered what my work would be when I grew up. I had found my niche where I could be passionate, express myself, and contribute something of value to my fellow earth dwellers.

As for my mother, she couldn't bring herself to tell me I was doing well, but her friends told me how proud she was of me.

Inevitably, Serge messed up, and we went through yet another break-up. I claimed this was the absolute end and couldn't endure anymore broken promises.

I gave him an ultimatum, stop the alcohol and learn to restrain your anger or … It's over … forever…

Sometimes forever, is not forever.

CHAPTER 28

PARIS

"A walk about Paris will provide lessons in history, beauty, and in the point of life."

– Thomas Jefferson

You could judge someone for what they do, be intrigued by their actions, and feel confident you would do better. No one really knows how he or she would act, until faced with a similar situation.

Have a cuppa tea or whatever else wet takes your fancy, while I continue to tell you about this life of mine.

The seesaw of my relationship with Serge constantly rose and fell through our separations: permanent, short-lived, long term, silence, and emails full of venom or endless love.

Sitting in dark places of my cupboards are his long letters and gut wrenching poems, decorated with pretty pictures and primitive hearts he had drawn like a diligent child. They are mementoes that make me wonder: how could he maintain being a decent person, yet live in a cave and behave like a barbarian?

♪♪

Two timely events helped me move on.

My beloved aunt Dora was turning one hundred and I received an invitation from my family in France to attend her birthday celebration. The Lord Mayor of Paris was to present her with a certificate and my whole family would be present, and they wanted me to be there too. About the same time, I learnt that three weeks later, in Santa Barbara, U.S.A., there would be a *Laughter for Health* training program conducted by a clinical therapist.

My mother had a saying; you can't dance with one bottom at two weddings. I gave my bum a double workout and managed to attend both.

I put my plan in action by first going to Paris for the birthday.

Long flights were a killer, and all the way to France those cramped seats felt like I was a bobby pin squeezed in a row on a card.

The first time I had returned to Paris, many years before, I visited my aunt, and as I stood on her doorstep wondering if we would recognise each other after seventeen years of separation. I heard the lock pull back, watched the handle turn and the door open slowly, a slice of light poured onto the landing. My aunt stood on the edge of her doorway, tears streaming down her face, she opened her opulent arms and pulled me tightly to her, "Ma petite Helene, ma petite Helene," and bathed me in a sea of emotion.

My life was full of returns. Here I was again, home in France, or was it still home? A hundred years had claimed my once robust Russian aunt leaving in their trail a frail old lady. I gently stroked the thin, pale skin of her hand, she covered mine with her other one, and with a quiet, slow breath, said in French, "After your father died, your mother should have come back to Paris to be with the family, and not be left alone so far away." After a few more minutes, she added, "I want you to get married, *ma petite*, you mustn't be alone." Not bad for a one-hundred-year old lady, hey!

Perhaps the reason for my aunt's longevity was her nightly supper of eating knobs of fresh garlic with a slice of buttered baguette. I stayed with her a couple of nights and suffered the consequences – Squashed on her bed with her, I turned my nose as far up the wall as I could squeeze myself, to escape the unbearable aroma of freshly eaten garlic.

I wonder how different my life would have been if my mother had chosen for us to return and live in France and be close to my *Tante* Dora.

Australia is home for me, and I love it with the passion of a totally devoted lover, but France holds all the people of my childhood.

This was a short stay. I savoured every ornate building, crooked narrow street, shop and museum. I drifted along the Seine and continued on to the magnificent Notre Dame Cathedral. The gods of music must have been on my side that day because they delivered me an unexpected performance by Carl Richter. The notes of the organ lifted through the intricate Gothic architecture and transported me into a euphoric state.

Discovering historical treasures is never enough. The gallery of my emotions put me on a platform where my experiences were intense, my brief visit to the Rodin Gallery made me yearn to touch the silky smoothness of his masterpieces and connect with the creative imagination of Rodin's sculptures.

Eagerly I accepted my cousin Alain's invitation to a 'Boite' in Saint-Michel to listen to some jazz. I should have known jazz would scratch some inner scars when the notes of a piano solo plunged me into the memory of the "Soup Plus" in George Street, where I heard Serge play many times.

Maybe that's why a few days later, I was prompted to buy him some black trouser braces decorated with John Coltrane playing his sax.

Why buy a present for a man you've broken up with?

My aunt died soon after her hundredth birthday. After the funeral, my family and I spent a few days in their holiday villa in the French countryside. We reflected on her life, leaving Russia with my father, her six children, and the death of her husband, my uncle David who never returned from the concentration camps. We all carried the warmth of her boundless love and generosity, and cloaked our grief with the memories, strengthened our family unit and for this short time, I was in my place of belonging.

Three weeks later I flew on to Santa Barbara to learn how to be a dedicated laughter trainer.

CHAPTER 29

Santa Barbara

"We keep moving forward, opening new doors, and doing new things, because we're curious and curiosity keeps leading us down new paths."

– Walt Disney.

I'm not a fan of Los Angeles although it was a landing point for me to reach Santa Barbara where fifteen of us were signed up to attend the Laughter Therapy training program with Doctor Annette Goodheart. Honest, that's her real name. We were there to learn as much about laughter and humour as was available at the time, as well as about the pioneers already doing significant work in the field.

We were shown how to develop therapeutic programs to take our clients out of their fearful thoughts, and teach them how to incorporate humour by using various techniques.

Along with tears and anger, laughter is also a cathartic process, and in Annette, we had a remarkable teacher who also helped us work through our own individual issues. It sure helped to dust away some of my old painful cobwebs.

I never owned any kind of teddy bear – plenty of dolls, but no bears – so I was excited to become the owner of a huge dark brown fur stuffed grizzly bear Annette gave all of us laughter students to take everywhere we went. I named my bear Booby, and for the next few years, Booby became part of my many laughter sessions and was passed around rooms for plentiful hugs.

Maybe the gods of 'sometimes good things happen,' were finally poised to reward me and Santa Barbara was the place of delivery. Tony, one of my course colleagues presented me with a special gift for my fiftieth birthday by driving me to the Santa Barbara Buddhist temple for an early evening meditation which became one of my most memorable and loved gifts.

Chanting ohm in the hills began my celebrations, followed by dinner in a restaurant with all of us laughter trainees clutching our stuffed bears, laughing and eating the large chocolate cake baked by Annette who had the best laugh ever.

I was completely happy and couldn't be in a better place.

Between training days, I explored my surroundings and found some interesting facts about Santa Barbara and its Spanish history. For instance, the local Mission was founded by Franciscan Friars in seventeen eighty-six. The world's first oil development area was established at Santa Barbara's Beach and the world's largest movie studio during the silent films era had been in Santa Barbara, until it moved to Hollywood.

Knowing I would probably never come this way again, I felt very sad to leave Annette and my fellow students at the end of our training days.

Being my first trip to the States, I booked a ten-day bus tour around the West Coast. I hated Las Vegas with its garish neon lights, ugly gambling dens, the whirring noise of roulette wheels and poker machines. I preferred the magnificent wide spaces of the American landscape, like a flight over the Grand Canyon in a four-seater plane, a walk through Yosemite National Park, a boat ride on Mammoth lakes, and a mock shootout on the Rawhide film set in Scottsdale Arizona were what fascinated me the most.

San Francisco gave me something else, not just a video camera purchase from a handsome rugged Israeli salesman I had dinner with that night, and don't ask about my encounter with him, I could tell you, but the outcome would surprise you.

During one stop after another, I bought stuff: mementoes from places I visited. I needed to hang on to the experiences that were the onset of such dramatic changes for me. Together with the new, there still were tenuous pieces clinging to the old. As much as I needed to move on from my tumultuous relationship, little cracks in my resolve, opened up. Why buy a large sized American Indian motif T-shirt as a gift for Serge, if I wasn't going to ever see him again?

When I unpacked the purchases from my trip, I came across two items I should never have bought, the Coltrane trouser braces from Paris, and the Indian head t-shirt from the United States. They jolted the longing in a dormant piece of my heart.

These two things of barely anything had the power to unnerve me. I chose the delusion of 'out of sight, out of mind' and hid those items in a drawer in the spare room where I couldn't see them. Foolish woman, I knew they were there.

Something drove me to pick up the phone. "Hello Serge, I'm back from my overseas trip and I have some presents for you. Don't think it means anything. I thought you might like them."

Was life so good I needed to challenge it with the rationale we could be friends?

This was the first time in all the years together I was the one to make the first move. His voice always triggered my emotions, especially when he sounded so happy to hear from me, and couldn't wait to come over and 'catch-up'.

Each return to the relationship was a renewal, excited to share the experiences we'd had during our break-up, so much to talk about, laugh, eat together, and be close, I felt like I had come home again.

He promised, "This time it will be better."

Again, I wrapped myself with hope and failed to consider that like many beginnings, the unresolved parts of our inner selves would inevitably bubble to the surface, although much of the glue holding us together was our continued support for each other. The other stuff, the dark part of our relationship, the side that kept tearing me apart, I pushed into the overly stuffed corners of my inner wardrobe and pretended the good parts would outweigh the bad ones.

We adapted to a workable arrangement. Serge lived in his studio in Parramatta and I lived in my house in Coogee, his regular visits often heralded with a bunch of flowers.

CHAPTER 30

Much Ado About Laughter

"There are only two ways to live your life. One is as though nothing is a miracle, the other is as though everything is a miracle"

– Albert Einstein.

Revitalised, and back on my own turf in Sydney, my head buzzed with all the ways I could develop my Laughter Workshops. By now, I had received quite a lot of media attention. Some reporters were keen to dismantle my credibility and others, to praise me for being inventive. All of it brought me unexpected bookings from all kinds of businesses; large corporations, hospitals and other government bodies. I didn't have to slog to promote my self-funded workshops anymore because someone else was paying me to do what I loved.

Suddenly the snowball rolled into a diversity of places and experiences; amongst them, it pulled me into the Mind, Body, Spirit festival at Sydney's Darling Harbour, and for the next few years at their Melbourne and Brisbane locations.

I believe that if you keep doing the same thing over and over, you become stale and what you deliver gets mouldy along with it. So, I kept changing and adding to my repertoire. Pity I didn't implement the idea in my personal life.

Along with all the activities to create laughter and fun for my workshop participants, I carried a large carpetbag with all kinds of silly items: A barking bone, a laughing bag, a whistling mirror that kept repeating, "You are so beautiful", a hammer making shattering glass sounds, juggling balls, and anything else I could produce to engage people with the idea that fun by any means, interrupts serious, stressful thinking. To quote a cliché, which by the way, I hate, 'we teach what we need to learn."

Eventually, my items ganged up on me. On my way to the Wayside Chapel to work with street people and addicts, I hurried through the seedy prostitute area of Kings Cross. I walked so quickly it caused the gizmos in my bag to go off: the bone barked, the mirror pronounced, "You are so beautiful", and my sweet little compact mirror wolf-whistled loudly. Can you image all those strange noises moving down the street alongside me? No wonder the men around there, who were looking for I don't what, gave me some very weird looks. I was mortified and slowed down to stop my wilful objects from their unwelcome sabotage.

Like the court jester, I was ready to do anything to amuse, delight, and influence the subjects of my life's castle.

♪♪

Intrigued with my new career, Serge suggested, "How about we pool our resources, Helene, create a package to include your laughter workshop followed by a Free Kata concert."

Knowing my experiences with him, I was tentative, "How do you figure, a laughter workshop and the chaos of Free Kata?"

He still was a great salesman, "Both are cathartic, yours, brings laughter – mine through music and sound." The idea made sense so I went along with it. Our participants played and laughed in the afternoon, and listened to the chaos and redemption of the Free Kata music at night. It worked for the small amount of people who attended.

♪♪

I didn't have to carry my bagful of tricks for the next Mind, Body, Spirit Festival at Darling Harbour; Serge did it for me. I felt like a school kid having her books carried by the 'boyfriend'. Going past the New Age stalls he blurted out, "What a bunch of whackos, this is Lala-land."

"Shush, don't embarrass me. I'm part of all this today."

He couldn't help himself, "Fucking idiots, what a rip-off."

"Shush!"

"Yeah, yeah, okay Helene."

I expanded my laughter work and Serge became my occasional chauffeur, cheering squad and debriefing personnel, "How did you go, Boodgie?"

"They were an odd bunch today, they sat there like stunned mullets." I appreciated having someone on my side to listen, encourage me, tell me my work was worthwhile, and that I made a difference in people's lives.

A government community service in Wollongong booked me to conduct a couple of workshops for parents whose children had severe mental health behaviours. How could I possibly bring fun and laughter to people who were on the verge of breakdowns?

Here are some comments from those overstretched parents; "I couldn't possibly laugh or have any fun," "I'd feel guilty if I did," or "There's no way I can enjoy myself seeing my child in their condition," "I don't know how I can go on."

Instinct told me to sit with them and listen. The best I could do, was help these parents diminish their guilt about having time out, give them a few practical ideas to create some fun for themselves and, for them to know it's okay to be a little frivolous.

Just when you think you know it all, you know nothing. I couldn't just stand there and deliver a prepared session. It's not in my nature to be deaf to other people's pains. I also learnt that the work of laughter is not nonsense. If done properly, it is invaluable.

"I'm taking you to Chinatown for Yum Cha, Helene, and you can tell me all about how the session went." Serge was genuinely interested in what I did, and I was keen to have my beloved braised tripe, chicken feet, grilled octopus, fish topped tofu, and mango pudding.

♪♪

Much of my work evolved from word of mouth, for example, the Vietnam Veterans Association invited me to be guest speaker at their conference in Canberra and after that, for regular retreats in Berrima for the vets and their wives.

During the week's retreat, the two-hours I was allocated to provide them with coping strategies, could not possibly be enough to reach the core of what these vets had gone through and what they were still experiencing. The thing is, the work of humour and laughter is not that simple; it is a delicate balance requiring respectful understanding. Fun stuff isn't always the answer.

"What are you going to do with us tomorrow? It says on the program something about laughter. Are you going to tell us jokes?" One of the vets asked while we were relaxing after dinner in the lounge room. This informal socialising gave me the opportunity to connect with them.

"I don't do comedy. The session will be about how laughter, humour and fun helps us to cope." I had no way of knowing how that would impact on them, but just like that, it came; the first story tumbled out like juicy gossip running through a village, gathering momentum. One humour filled anecdote after another surfaced from memories of the war zone. In humour, they had found the respite they desperately needed.

"We were filthy and caked with mud after our trek through the jungle, so I threw my trousers in the bog hole, our temporary dunny, and suddenly it dawned on me I had left my wallet in the pocket and had to go down there and get my pants back. Gees, me mates and me had such a laugh when I came back up stinkin' to high heaven."

"I nearly fell out of the tree trying to make a bed for the night, and ended up hanging like a gorilla from the branches, I laughed so hard I nearly lost my grip."

One story after another generated streams of spontaneous laughter. Afterwards, the wives told me, this was the first time their husbands had talked about their experiences in the Vietnam War.

I felt this gave me the rare privilege to hear what Australian soldiers experienced trudging through steamy jungles laboriously making their way through swamps, rain, mosquitos, predators – human and other, fearful of an unseen enemy lurking behind trees and undergrowth.

Separated by tables and chairs in a U-shape was not the most conducive atmosphere to relax these men, and I knew it would take a lot more than two hours the next morning to provide them with some real help, and give them respite from their nightmares. Times like this made me realize that I could do my best, but the magic wand I carried in my bag of tricks was just another tool to provide a small moment of respite. After all, I explained, the real magic for all of us, is to find whatever way we can with the choices we make. And although a little tentative at first, some did laugh and join in. I did get a lot of chortling from them by getting down on one knee, clutching my hands together, and with a ridiculously melodramatic lament, beg them to "Please, please, you guys, for heaven's sake, be silly, have fun, do your best to laugh, even if it means changing your trousers." My zany performance did make them laugh. You see! By any means I could.

On one occasion, when Serge came with me, he commented, "Did you see that idiot therapist woman in charge, pouring the guys wine with their dinner and offering them more booze in the lounge afterwards, knowing so many are battling alcohol problems. What a fucking unaware bitch." Earlier that evening he had talked to the guys about his experience as a muso in Vietnam and played them some jazz on a battle-scarred piano.

♪♪

Gigs were not often close to home and during my twenty-odd years as a trainer, I covered endless miles meeting people from diverse backgrounds and cultures.

Serge and I had never heard of one suburb where we stopped for lunch and explored the area, "Maybe we could move here, it's lovely," he offered.

"Don't even go there, I mean here, I'm not moving to any Woop-Woop ever again".

Later, after a challenging workshop, I told him, "You won't believe this, in today's session for women social workers, I mentioned I was Jewish, and a woman who sat in the front, suddenly shouted, "You killed Jesus Christ."

"Nobody talks to my baby like that. Let me get in there." Here was my knight ready to come to the rescue.

"It's okay, I just looked at her and said, 'I didn't kill Jesus Christ, I promise. A nice Jewish bloke though.' Everyone cracked up and the woman later apologised."

"You see Boodgie, you have such amazing stage presence, I told you, and you can handle anything."

Not always fun with this mercurial man, especially the times he was taciturn, moody, and argumentative; yelling obscenities at other drivers and by the time I faced a group, I had to pull out my inner resources, smile, and launch into, "Hello haha everyone, let's get laughing."

Serge drove me to my next series of workshops in Gilgandra. We stayed in the area for another mini holiday visiting Dubbo Zoo and Parks Observatory.

♪♪

The more I travelled through the Australian landscape, the more I fell in love with this country. My accommodations varied from basic places to luxury motels, resorts, and people's homes.

I often stayed in unknown locations with total strangers to deliver laughter for whatever reasons I had been summoned. An invitation to the Atherton Tablelands had all these elements, including a category three cyclone, announced on the news.

Familiar with fear, I took the flight to Cairns anyway. As the wings wobbled upwards, panic kicked in: What if the cyclone causes the plane to crash in the coffee fields? I love my coffee but not as a final resting place.

Sticky heat clung to my skin as soon as I walked away from the plane. Dark clouds did nothing to diminish the heavy humidity of Far North Queensland, and I wondered how I was going to survive the next few days, and if I had enough light clothing.

The Business Women's Network had invited me to "Lighten Up" a hundred women from the local farming community and the weather was behaving like a delinquent teenager. About half an hour into my first session, a noisy downpour played a symphony on the roof of the venue competing with every word I delivered.

What a time for the microphone to break down. "Okay everyone, come closer to the front," I shouted "Now, just for fun, stick your fingers in your nose. Good. Now, face each other and point your fingers in each other's belly buttons." The rain pounded the roof, and laughter filled the room.

During lunch, I was told stories of abusive alcohol driven husbands, and how these women's low self-esteem had corroded the joy of their lives. Most, had 'escaped' and entrenched themselves in alternative lifestyles with supportive friends.

No matter where I go, what I do, and whom I meet, I find there are always new things to learn and understand how other people deal with their lives. They inspire me.

I hired an old Holden and mooched around the country roads until I discovered a local coffee plantation that had once been banana fields. Once inside the slick tourist shed filled with everything coffee, my nose bombarded with the delicious, powerful aroma of hundreds of roasted fresh coffee beans, I tasted different coffees, explored the history of machines and bought a couple of kilos of coffees beans. If I can wear it, look at it or taste it – I buy it.

Driving in the middle of nowhere, I felt like a grownup doing what I pleased until charcoal clouds rose up from the distance, crashes of thunder invaded the peace of the countryside, giant streaks of lightning threw light across the sky, and finally, the tropical rain unfurled its opaque curtain and forced me to pull up on the side of the road.

The heavy load of rain relinquished its tantrum into a steady drizzle. I turned on the engine and drove to Toga, a small pretty country town where I scurried into the nearest café, ordered a large coffee and apple pie, and settled near a partially open window.

The pungent aroma of the tropical rain-drenched earth, mixed with the smell of various woods, reached my nostrils while I watched the slow descent of raindrops landing on the greenery outside.

I relished this newfound solitude, so different from all the dramas surrounding the jazz events. This storm brought me a deep sense of peace and fulfilment, knowing my laughter work meant so much more to me than just a career change.

♪♪

A phone call from Malaysia brought me a sales conference in Kuala Lumpur. I was told it would be somewhere in the Genting Highlands, and assumed it would be the flash resort at the top of the mountain. The actual location turned out to be a huge let down from my idea of a luxurious working environment.

My contact at the Malaysian high Commissioner's office in Canberra, assured me my programme would not be offensive to the diverse male delegates at the conference, however, learning the details of my session, they suggested

I don't ask anyone to poke their fingers in each other's belly buttons.

Why don't things turn out as expected? The conference venue and my accommodation were in a plain concrete building – The place didn't have an inch of garden, not one coffee shop, nowhere near the top of the mount, and I was to stay here from Thursday when I arrived, to Sunday afternoon for my session. What the bloody hell was I going to do? Fate stretched her crappy wings and found something to occupy me.

Helene in 'I-can't-believe-this-is real land', was led into an apartment to share with a couple of the lady conference organisers, and what really freaked me out were a bunch of men watching television in the lounge area, right outside my allocated bedroom. I immediately imagined the slave market.

"What are all these men doing here?" I asked one of the girls. "I can't stay here with them." While the men were being cleared out, I rang my best friend Hazel in Melbourne. "If you don't hear from me in the next few days, please contact the Australian Embassy. By the way, I don't have a clue where I am. Its somewhere in Kuala Lumpur." I could imagine the family conversation, "She's done it again, gone somewhere crazy." and sweet young Sarah saying "Aunty Helene, Meshuggah. (nuts)"

For some reason, drama still followed me. One of the ladies had overflowed the bathroom sink leaving something like a mini swimming pool on the floor; I walked in, slipped, crash-landed on my knees, and lay there screaming until someone rushed in, and sent for the only other Australian; Graham, a blind physiotherapist. He made sure nothing was broken and insisted they send me to a doctor.

The old rickety ambulance wound its way up to the top of the mountain sending me into excruciating pain every time it made another turn.

"What does the scenery look like?" Graham, tried to distract me.

"Beautiful palm trees, Ouch ... Lovely sloping hills ... Woo." Alternating between painful screams and describing the scenery, we finally made it to the resort's doctor. He gave me painkillers and installed me in a wheelchair.

During the Saturday night conference dinner, a floorshow of drag queens pranced about the audience. I thought that dragging their fake tits across some of the delegate's heads was a lot more intrusive than my asking them to put fingers in each other's belly buttons. Maybe if I hadn't checked with the Malaysian embassy person in Canberra before leaving, I might have instructed all these men to do that and who knows if I may have ended up somewhere more uncomfortable than a wheel chair.

Sunday afternoon, I delivered part of my session from the wheel chair. "Okay gentlemen, let's see how humour and play can help your sales and the stresses of your work." I stood up to juggle three balls, which I dropped, I was a klutz juggler but this time it worked in my favour, "In sales, you can't always keep the momentum up, but a sense of humour helps you to pick up your balls and keep going." Mercifully, my balls comment didn't offend anyone, and the roomful of men of all colours and religions, actually laughed.

Graham and I were sent to Jakarta for two days, to showcase our seminars for potential clients. I wobbled along on my bung knee and steered Graham around with his white stick. Talk about the lame leading the blind.

I realised through my laughter seminars, I didn't need to trail after someone else's career to find my own self worth, and that I had enough drama to keep life exciting.

CHAPTER 31

A Gun – A Festival

"Miles Davis was shot and wounded in the hip by unknown assailants in the early morning of October 9 in New York's East Village. The injury was not serious,. The trumpeter, who was appearing at the Blue Coronet in Brooklyn, told police that he had been warned not to appear at the club, unless he paid part of his salary to the unidentified man making the threats.."

– Down Beat magazine, November 13, 1969

Serge loved guns. "You've got to protect yourself, you never know."

No, you never know when lunacy or other elements are in play and you go down the hole.

The alcoholic in your life gives you half a life. You drift in and out of optimism, hope and despair, after many, many times of busting, recovering, AA meetings, redemption and hope this time it will be better, this time he's doing it 'properly'. Yet, several weeks or months later you think, "Is he, or isn't he drinking?"

Throw a gun in the mix, and it has a hair-raising potential.

There was always a gun. He kept a loaded pistol in his pocket. I repeatedly made it clear how much I loathed weapons, especially in my home, and demanded he keep it away from me. I couldn't forget the time when we lived in Ruse and I had considered shooting him.

"Hello my darling" I hugged him with a hug, hug, kiss, kiss, as I surreptitiously ran my hands across his growing girth. Sure enough, I found significant weight in his leather jacket pocket.

"Frisking, Helene?" he joked and added, "It's there okay."

I lamely replied, "Don't be silly, I'm giving you a happy-to-see-you hug."

I never knew when a gun incident could happen with Serge, even a dinner at the heavily guarded Great Synagogue, had potential. We had just walked in, and were about to walk through the security frame; "I'll be back" my not-so hero whispered and quickly walked out again.

Now what? I thought, but the mystery was quickly solved when he returned, leaned into my ear, "I put my gun in the car. I didn't want to embarrass you if the alarm sounded off."

"That's so considerate of you," sarcasm covered my imagination of security guards frisking him, and a startled congregation wondering if he was Jewish.

Serge always carried his gun, except one time when he inadvertently left it at my house inside his music satchel. One of my gay friends tried to get the bullets out. It was like a soap opera; Richard pointed the damned thing towards the garden, while I yelled instructions, "Careful!

Don't shoot yourself! Don't turn around you might kill me. Do you want me to have a go at it?"

I didn't want to have a go at it, what I wanted; was to have a go at Serge, angry that his gun had been tampered with, "Who was the idiot that released the safety catch? Did you?"

"No, a concerned friend did."

"How dare you let them do that, you could have killed yourselves," he yelled.

I screamed back, "How dare you leave a loaded gun in my house?"

One day he announced, "I'm not carrying my gun all the time anymore."

"Good, you are finally working through your anger about your father issues, and now, you don't have to feel the need to shoot him anymore."

"You're right. It's taken me this long to realise how much that gun is connected to that anger."

Was it my influence that brought him to this remarkable breakthrough? Therapy, AA, the capacity to analyse his feelings, or a changed mindset, maybe he had finally resolved his anger and addictions. A sliver of hope shaped my fantasy, we would finally walk together into the bright sunset he had promised me.

Complacency is a dangerous place. It's full of fairy dust and it welcomes denial.

I didn't bother with the demeaning task of frisking anymore, yet, when I went to hang up his jacket, I felt the weight of his gun in the pocket. He hadn't relinquished his security blanket or anything else after all.

♪♪

"I'm having my birthday dinner at a local Asian place, out your way. I'm going to order a banquet for a few special friends, I'd love you to come." Serge invited me.

Aware his old nemesis, booze, was most likely back in his life, I kept a reasonable distance from him.

The moment Serge stood on my doorstep I knew he wasn't okay, even though he seemed coherent. He was standing straight, and I couldn't smell any booze on his breath. I ignored my apprehension and allowed him to drive us to the tiny Chinese takeaway place where a handful of his guests were already seated at the only table.

Wearing a cheery grin on his face and a questionable wobble in his step, Serge's alcoholic bass-player friend Jimmy arrived.

I sensed a storm brewing.

The birthday bash was pregnant with gloom and became even more uncomfortable when Serge suddenly announced he had an urgent meeting to attend with an important music producer, "I'll be back real soon. C'mon Jimmy, we have to go see the man," and they left.

Imagine, a disparate group of Serge's people collection, sitting together, like fish on dry land, floundering in an ocean of uncertainty.

Half an hour later, the 'boys' came back. Serge couldn't stand up straight and slurred his words. We stared at him, which provoked his anger: "What are you fuckers looking at?"

Drunks don't need a reason to mood shift. The alcohol does it for them. "Hey guys don't go away. I forgot something at the meeting. I have to go back, but I'll get the manager here to bring out the food, I'll be back very soon. Enjoy the banquet." He called out to the kitchen for someone to bring out the dishes.

The lightly built Asian boss came out. "Okay, I do right away mister Serge, you good customer." He returned a few moments later, loaded with steaming dishes of Chinese food.

Daylight had almost disappeared. The traffic streamed along the busy road outside, while I felt trapped inside the tiny eating place.

Still wobbling, Serge struggled with something in the back pocket of his baggy pants, and with one final yank, awkwardly pulled out his gun, waved it about and pointed it at our food-laden host, "make sure you keep the dishes coming or else – *Kapish*?"

Faced with two drunks, one wobbling and slurring, the other smiling stupidly, it all seemed surreal.

In that terrifying moment I froze, hard breaths came out of my open mouth, and my stomach lurched into frantic cartwheels.

The small white-handled weapon was just an object. The man with his finger on the trigger was terrifying. This hand, capable of creating marvellous music, now carried the potential of destruction.

In that unbearable moment, my insides lurched into a silent drum pounding solo.

Oblivious to the chaos he had created, Serge went off to his fantasy producer while dishes loaded with

Chinese food kept coming and becoming cold, ended up surrounded by empty chairs.

Days later, he bombarded me with his endless phone calls, "Sorry, sorry, I messed up" accompanied by a string of "You know I love you, and I don't do this to hurt you."

I could only answer him with, "I can't keep doing this; either you go away, leave me alone and drink yourself to death or, if you want to be with me, clean up your act."

Wangaratta is a large Victorian town where the annual jazz festival draws musicians from across the globe, including some of the best from Australia.

The entire town is involved; shop windows are decked out with banners and posters. Streets take on a festive energy and more than twenty-five thousand visitors arrive annually.

As one of Australia's foremost improvisation musicians, Serge had been part of the festival at various times. But, because of his infamous antics, it had been a number of years since he was invited to be on the program.

There were colourful versions about a meltdown at one of his Wangaratta concerts. Drunk, he had wobbled on stage and in front of several hundred people, grabbed the microphone, "My band got paid four hundred dollars, and James Morrison got four thousand dollars for his band. Fucking, motherfucker cunts." Making sure he included everyone in his vitriolic tirade, he added, "You're all a pack of arsehole motherfucker parasites. All you jazz clubs managers, fucking don't pay musicians decent money, and …" This may not have been the exact dialogue, but it was similar to what I was told by the musicians who had been present.

Serge's version, "You see, Helene, I had to tell it like it is. The guys applauded me for it and said I was telling the honest truth, but they wouldn't say it. Bunch of spineless pussies."

Several years later, he convinced Adrian Jackson, the artistic director of the Wangaratta Jazz Festival, that the drunken stage behaviour would never happen again, and he was now putting together a new band, reminiscent of the early days of Australian jazz. A long-time admirer, Adrian acquiesced and booked Serge and his band for the upcoming festival. Adrian recently won the 2019 Australia Jazz Bell Award.

Although seasoned musicians, the band consisted of an alcoholic jazz pianist, a semi-retired gent from the jungle, an ex-gaolbird drummer, and a saintly saxophone player.

As an act of good faith, Adrian gave Serge an added two gigs with Odeon Pope, American bandleader/saxophone player. This not only gave Serge another chance for redemption, but the honour of performing with one of the headliners.

"Come with us, Boodgie. We're all staying at a motel in Wangaratta, knowing you are with me will be a great support, and I promise I am not drinking and won't be. This is my last chance to even up with Adrian."

What could I say? I really did want to hear all that great music. Jazz during the Australian summer is enticing. Can you believe it? I still hadn't graduated from the school of life lessons learnt and decided to go. Again, Serge at the wheel, Lenny and his drum kit stuffed on the back seat of the car for the long journey south.

Ever done one of those join-the-dots pictures? You start at number one and continue the line until the last number shows the complete picture. I think maybe our life events are full of dots revealed only when we take our last breath at the moment of the 'big reveal'.

The packed audience in the main auditorium was silent, until the invisible notes enveloped us. At a certain part of the music, Serge played a mesmerising flow of intricate sounds and brought the audience to an uproarious crescendo of applause. He had delivered the most inspiring solo I ever heard him play. During those minutes, he redeemed himself. The success of that first night gave him the deserved high, particularly when his colleagues and fans came over to rave about his unforgettable solo.

Odeon Pope was not a man to be outshone by his band members, and after that performance, he directed Serge to just play what was written in the charts, nothing else. That's all it took to deflate Serge's fragile ego and send him plummeting. He became belligerent and angry, heading towards a downward plunge. With two more performances ahead of him, the timing couldn't be worst.

I kept myself occupied attending several concerts, talking with people, and exploring the goodies on the stalls. I should have known there are no unicorns, fairies, or goblins, but some very wicked gremlins delighting in bringing people undone.

Video camera in hand, I waited for Serge to join his band on stage. After an interminable time, he walked out, sat down at the piano, and addressed the audience. The mobile in his pocket rang; he ignored the audience, answered the phone and went into a lengthy dialogue with a mate in Sydney about meeting him for yum cha.

Into his lacklustre first set, he went on a rave, effusively praising his musicians to a restless audience. "My mate on drums, exceptional. Man-of-God and fucking great sax player, my man on bass has a truly talented artist wife, blah blah blah … Ah, here's Helene my lady with the video camera glued to her eye, we have a … a … turbulent relationship."

That's it… Turbulent? Why get so upset about this comment? In retrospect, I think it was about being diminished in front of an auditorium full of people. To the person who professed to love me more than anyone in the world, all he could come up with was the word TURBULENCE! The word slithered painfully through my heart.

This was the very last time Serge performed at the Wangaratta Jazz Festival. His solo with Odeon Pope became legend, and his behaviour continued to fuel his "enfant terrible" reputation.

I leaned out the car window when we reached Sydney again, "I won't see you anymore unless you clean up and go to AA, for at least six months."

I picked up the dog from his little holiday. His wet snout on my neck, nuzzled away some of my stress.

My mother's comforting bosom soaked up my tears into her button-up apron, and her silent arms wrapped themselves around my emotional wounds.

Leaving the Wangaratta turbulence behind me, I returned to my laughter work, and installed a jolly Buddha fountain in my garden.

Sometimes it's not what you do that's important, it's what you learn. I guess by now, you realise I'm a slow learner.

Often regretting my lack of university degrees, I ultimately appreciated that my knowledge came from the experiences and people I met. And with Serge, I certainly met a collection of interesting individuals.

My father had promised me music, but hadn't envisaged it coming to me through the relationship I found. Maybe I had misinterpreted his intention and choose to travel this strange road to find my real direction, hijacked by my own naivety and the need for a hero to take me through the land of rhythm and song.

CHAPTER 32

Drying Out

"I leave the bar feeling confident and excited by the prospect of checking into rehab. Back in my apartment, I strip off my clothes, change into my sweats, crack open an ale and drink it quickly. I play early 'Blondie' on the stereo. The more I think about it, the more I like the idea of this rehab thing."

– Augusten Burroughs – Dry

The long breaks between us were the winters of our relationship. They lay dormant under a cloak of distance.

In his 'good space', thin, fair hair closely cropped, face hair neatly trimmed close to his skin, Serge made me laugh, made me think, we talked about everything. He knew a lot about cosmology and alternative medicine with an extensive knowledge of vitamins although he swallowed massive doses of them and ate badly.

The 'bad man' was a red-nosed, dishevelled alcoholic man with volcanic eruptions, and this nose, as my mother said in Yiddish, "is where the dog is buried", Ah Yiddish, a language that offers common sense, but often defies translation, I could only imagine a Chihuahua buried up Serge's bulbous nose.

Ultimately, heavy boozing made Serge's normally small nose into an oily beacon surrounded by flaking dead skin, on what became a puffy face. I don't need to tell you the tragedy of this lost soul with his incredible creativity, locked inside this unrecognisable being, suffering from the hellish demons of guilt and self-loathing.

He bullshitted me it was only handfuls of Valium and Normison pills he swallowed by the handful that were the culprits of his erratic behaviour, and I accepted this as a lesser evil than the copious amounts of alcohol he actually drank.

Self-development seminars had taught me some strategies to cope with the embroiled quagmire of our relationship. Reluctant to lose me, Serge accepted some of my attempts to "fix" him.

I sent him to a "fix it" expert, an American anger management psychologist. Serge came back angrier than ever. "What a moron, he made me punch and scream into a towel, and said this would take away the anger of being beaten by my father." The men's anger management group didn't do anything much for him either, although he did well in groups, where he found an audience, and enjoyed his entertainer status, sharing anecdotes with his fellow angry-persons. He told me about the sessions at his AA meetings, and afterwards, going with the 'boys' to talk and drink cups of tea.

I knew that Serge tried to be a better man, desperately wanting to throw off the prison of his alcoholism, but the vicious mistress of the bottle always reeled him back in.

The showman in him enjoyed the bad boy image talking about his booze times, how he ripped someone off, and why so many musicians didn't want to work with him anymore. He loved holding court about his misdemeanours as if they were badges of honour. Sober, he was entertaining.

♪♪

Travelling a great deal with my work, I didn't want another dog after Tooska died, but Serge had a different agenda and bought me a puppy for my birthday. We named the tiny Silky Schnauzer, Rambo and when I told people his name is "Rambo" they laughed and I responded, "Well, he's tough." This was my new love child.

Serge arrived at my place loaded with flowers, a barbecue chicken, and bread rolls.

As if he wasn't burdened enough by his own history, he carried on the back of his jeans, a large bunch of keys attached to a big copper cross with *'Paladin'* engraved on one side, and *knight errant* on the other. Added to this already heavy load, a ferocious looking Marshal Arts butterfly knife.

During a picnic at Stanwell Tops one Sunday, sitting at our favourite secluded spot watching Rambo sniff at the grasses around the edges of the ocean, I asked him, "What makes you pick up that first drink?"

"It's like a voice in my head says 'Go ahead, you can handle just one drink, nobody will know.' It's not actually the alcohol I enjoy, because I don't, it's the buzz it gives me, and getting out of it that I crave. People misunderstand that, they think I love alcohol, in fact I don't."

"I suppose you wouldn't take much notice of a good Merlot then?"

"No, it's lolly-water to me. There wouldn't be enough buzz and a bottle of it wouldn't even touch the edges."

I wonder if inside the brain of an alcoholic lives a little demon stabbing its pitchfork at the craving, making it dance a macabre ballet that pulls the victim further and further into their doom.

Serge's constant battle with booze was his personal nightmare, he knew what it was doing to him, and he hated it. He had solitary drying out periods when his survival mechanism called him to sobriety. That's when he disappeared for weeks, locked himself up in his cave out in Parramatta, and went through gruelling days of detoxing.

Here is an extract recounting the process of his own rehab, to fellow pianist Dave Halls who had attempted to write Serge's biography; *"The bed covers were wet with perspiration and I couldn't move. It was now three weeks and time to come down. But there was a voice—where was it coming from? The wall! It was Mingus and Miles who were talking to me. 'Hey Mister Fingers, play that introduction again.' They spoke out to me while I sat behind a grand piano in a room where walls spun around. I could just see my fingers on the keys but they wouldn't play. 'Come on man, play something.' I tried to cover my eyes but there were no hands. The sweat was pouring all over my bed sheets again as I felt a slight pang of hunger. Time to start eating again. Four days should do it, I heard somewhere from the back of my mind, four days to come down. Lie down and let it swim all over you. I shivered under the hot blankets. I wonder if anyone knows I am like this. I wonder if anyone cares. They'll be sad when I'm gone, won't they? If I were to go, how would they react?*

Can someone listen to me?

I started to laugh but was interrupted by a spider the size of a football running across the ceiling, another eight-legged creature chased it, slightly bigger. As it reached one side, the first spider turned and ran through the bigger spider and to the other side. I blinked, and when I opened my eyes there were four football-sized spiders running across. I was shaking now, not out of fear but because I had no control. I closed my eyes and heard a Thelonious Monk tune played backwards. I couldn't escape for even half an hour. I moved my body over so I could somehow stare at the floor. But all I could see when I looked were ants, millions of them, running around the floor. Crazy baby.

'Focus' I told myself, 'focus on them to see if they're real.' I stared hard but couldn't even make one out clearly, probably because there were so many of them. But that wasn't what worried me. My Telstra bill was $300 and I'd just spent my last $5 ten days ago! Oh no! – Better ring Telstra. But I can't, it means moving over to the phone, which Telstra has probably cut off now that it's three months overdue.

For the next four days I battled the urge to pay my phone bill and just lay there. Other bills came to mind and started adding up in my head – hundreds and thousands of dollars to fix up something small. I tried to sleep but couldn't. I tried to relax but couldn't move. I cringed as the nights turned to day and light rays cut through the drawn curtains. I didn't like it but couldn't be bothered closing the curtains further.

I tried to get up. But I had no legs because they would not come with me. Instead they remained behind as I hit the floor hard. I stayed there for half a night before gaining some sort of consciousness; I was back in my bed. Why do I do put myself through this?

It was living hell, but I knew I could get through it as I had many times before. I was used to the shakes, the sweat, the dry retching. On the third day after deciding to come down I tried eating some stale bread from three weeks ago. As I brought the bread to my mouth I started to throw up, but there was nothing to throw up.

Tears came to my eyes and I cried out, "Why?"

The next dry retch came with the second attempt to eat bread, and this time I brought up blood, blood from broken vessels deep within my poisoned body which was being overtaken by my single-minded mission to get rid of the non-existent food from my stomach as if it was something poisonous. Obviously the only thing that could come up was broken blood vessels. But it still felt good and cleansing, for a moment.

Coming down, this was the third day without alcohol. I'd done this many times before and knew what to expect. I knew that in another day I would be right. Reality was on its return with a throbbing headache and I was just beginning to remember snippets of phone calls I'd made while I was "gone".

I could walk on the fourth day. The world was a lot better. It was time to venture outside of my bachelor pad, surrounded by black and white photos of jazz artists.

It was time for me to do a big shopping trip at Westfield in Parramatta. So big in fact, that it took me two hours to bring the trolley back to the flat and up the lift to my floor. I was almost through with this binge – vowing never to do it again – and ready to start some cooking. But I decided to phone a mate first.

While talking on the phone something happened. My heart began to palpitate. Somewhere inside my chest there were a hundred karate fists belting to get outside. I could actually feel my heart beat speed up, slow down and then just go blank for a few seconds. In a panic, I called Doctor Quan, "Something's going real bad doctor, I'm just coming out of a binge and my heart's beating slow and fast and not at all. I don't know what's going on, I think I'm going to die!!!

"Listen Serge, I don't have the medical equipment to deal with it. Lie down; if it doesn't go away in the next few minutes ring 000 and get yourself an ambulance to hospital."

I lay down praying to God that if he was going to take me, do it now, but please just give me one more chance. My heart missed a few more beats and paced up and down. I couldn't handle this; I had to get to hospital. Not by ambulance, but by car.

On autopilot, I went to my car in the basement, got in and headed straight to the hospital. I was no longer living drunkenly behind the beat, but very much awake and ahead of the beat. This was it. This might be the end – but I didn't want to give up. Not yet. Not until my symphonies are out.

At the hospital I grabbed a guard and told him to get me a nurse urgently. I'm sure it's not protocol that they do these things, but this guy must have seen my face and didn't want to argue. When the nurse came over I grabbed her hand and put it on my wrist.

"Listen to my heart beat — is that normal?" Five seconds of listening to my heartbeat, I was rushed behind a door and looked at by an Irish intern.

Is this what has become of my life, the life of Serge Ermoll, Tronk, Son of Gargoyle? I'm a pianist and composer; I've played the world with great musicians such as Dizzy Gillespie, Branford Marsalis and Odeon Pope. I made twenty-seven albums and apart from my music, I am a karate instructor with three black belts that I earned in Sydney, London and Tokyo.

Still lying there being examined and sure I was about to die, I ran through the list of my credits in my head, and suddenly remembered, oh yes, I was a private eye for twenty years, a long time ago.

Mixed with my prayers, I asked 'Him 'how someone could get so far, yet crumble to an existence like this. I promised Heavenly Father that if I got through this, I would go to AA and win Helene back."

♪♪

I can't remember how many times I sent him home because he was so drunk. Sometimes he sat half conscious in his car in my driveway, or I tried to stop him from driving off drunk, "You can't drive like that, you'll have an accident."

I thought, one day I won't care anymore.

You can't care about someone and then, because they keep behaving badly, you stop. It doesn't work like that, at least not for me. I care about people who have long gone from my life, both dead and alive ones.

I care about the horrors of humanity stretched across the planet. Not because I want to show that, gee whizz, I'm such a goodie-two-shoes, no! It's because that's the way it is, that's the way the ingredients in the cooking pot of my feelings have created the recipe of who I am, and probably why I am so brilliant at bashing the shit out of myself.

CHAPTER 33

Keeping Abreast

"I come to weep. There is no escape from grief. Outwardly, I am silent. Inwardly, you know I am screaming." –
The Talking

– Rumi

I didn't know how long Serge lost himself in his latest self-indulgent alcoholic daze, or how many bottles of pills he had swallowed, or how many spiders had found their way up his walls, or how much money he'd borrowed from buddies to keep up his exorbitant booze habit.

Death was playing hide-and-seek with his body. I was not available to him, friends and colleagues had retreated, all of it culminated in his decision to go to AA meetings and return to the twelve-steps. Step one; admit one is powerlessness over alcohol, and life has become unmanageable. Step two; believe in a higher power to restore sanity.

Although Russian Orthodox, Serge was making peace with all and any connections to God, the Russian one, the Jewish one, The Buddha and the overall Christian God. He stuck a Star of David onto a large cross, adding it to his already heavy bunch of keys hanging off the back of his jeans.

As long as you draw breath and think there is no more, remember tomorrow is more. And when you think you know it all, you are confronted by events confirming you don't. Would there ever be an end to the renovations of this relationship?

In his first email after a long time, he wrote: "*My dearest Helenatchka, I'm completely vulnerable right now and fucked up. I am not a bad man and I do love you with all my heart, but now I'm screwed up in my heart and soul. I'll always love you. Your always Serge.*" An image with a heart on wings and a key through it was at the bottom of the email. Then came another email in a similar vein, "*I'm not in a good space now, please try to understand. I'll always love you, Your Always Serge.*"

After that, silence, no phone calls or emails.

Six months disappeared before my phone brought me his voice again, "I'm doing AA Helene, I'm clean, my mate Tony Barry is helping me and I would love to see you."

Believing this newfound dedication to the twelve-step program had worked, I allowed Serge to creep back in my life, cautiously keeping him at arm's length. Don't be silly; do you believe this shit? I know I did, but you are allowed all the scepticism you wish, and rightly so. You, dear reader, have the luxury of not being involved.

Although his mercurial and inconsistent behaviours still jumped at me like Martian invasions, he was a kind, generous man, coming instantly to the rescue at any sign of trouble or illness in anyone.

"You know, boodgie, if anyone ever hurt you, I would kill them." I knew instinctively he would.

Whenever I was sick, he was there with help and cups of tea. I procrastinate about seeing doctors, so, whatever physical problem I'd complain about, he'd check his Mims, (A large medical manual) trawl the Internet to find a diagnosis, and reassure me it was nothing serious. "You see, because you have gallstones, sometimes the bile doesn't go through enough, and that's why you're feeling crook. It'll settle down if you don't eat fat for a while. Go have the thing out, I love you, you'll be okay." He hugged me and I felt better instantly.

Being diagnosed with breast cancer made it incredibly difficult for me to feel anything but panic and fear. "You have only a few tiny cancer cells in your right breast, and we are going to remove them," the not-too-warm surgeon informed me.

"I'll be there for you, Helene." Serge held me tight, and for that moment I felt he could keep my demons away.

Serge sat in the hospital waiting room, patiently fiddling on his mobile. I was in a kind of mindless mental cocoon going through the preparation process, being wheeled around from one measuring machine to another. X-rays were taken, nurses and doctors filled in charts. You'd never think a pinhead of cells would demand so much attention.

After we left the hospital, we went home to pick up the dog for a walk. I was relieved this day was over. The sunset had spread a soft lavender haze over the horizon; people ambled along the promenade, oblivious of the two new tattooed blue dots on either side of my right boob.

By the time we picked up Rambo and reached Coogee beach, Serge was behaving very strangely with loud, irrational complaints about where Rambo had done his shit. Serge's shit was harder to cope with after the day I had just gone through. I snapped, yelled into that otherwise peaceful evening, creating a very public farewell scene.

♪♪

Chasing all the spiritual help I could get became a daily task of prayers, meditations, and affirmations. I summoned every dead relative I had to watch over me. It may seem as if I had gone totally bonkers, but take my word for it, it all helped, mostly because it diverted my neurotic thinking.

The daily trips to the hospital became routine. I decided to bring my laughter work into my treatment. After all, this was a good time to practice what I taught. I asked the radiotherapy staff to play my ethereal music tapes while my arm was up and my boob was getting blasts of radiation.

I took in one of my laughter toys: a flashing lights ball spinning at the end of a long rubbery string. This was my daily makeshift laughter workshop moment I shared with other patients waiting their turn on the radiation machine. For a few moments, we connected, laughed together and were distracted. I coped better during the treatment than I had anticipated.

Serge rang a couple of times, garbling drunken nonsense. All it achieved was to unsettle me and mess with my tenuous equilibrium. My hand shook so much I could hardly hang up.

I recovered and was left with a pretty scar and lopsided boobs. I wonder if Dizzy Gillespie would still be stumped about whether he'd prefer my left tit or my right one.

CHAPTER 34
Bob Dylan Concert

"How many roads must a man walk down, before you call him a man? How many seas must a white dove sail before she sleeps in the sand. How many times must the cannon balls fly before they're forever banned? The answer my friend is blowin' in the wind, the answer is blowin' in the wind."

– Bob Dylan.

We recover from serious life-threatening illnesses, get over them, and yet, are sometimes brought down by lesser stuff. I was in bed with the flu, unable to sleep all night. My head felt like a cotton wool factory had found its way in there.

The worst came from too much thinking and stirred up crappy memories. A Bob Dylan concert flew in my fuzzy brain with '*Blowin' in the Wind*'. My breath was already short-circuited with gut-wrenching coughs, and I didn't need any more blowin' of anything. Yet, I remembered another of Serge's catastrophic birthdays, the 16th August 2007 when Bob Dylan was scheduled to perform at the Entertainment Centre in Sydney as part of his 'Never Ending' tour. Good title for my never-ending dramas with Serge.

"I'm getting tickets for us to see Bob Dylan, it's my birthday treat." Serge said.

"I didn't know you liked him. I like his song. 'Blowin' in the Wind'."

"You'll have to come. It'll be my treat for both of us, your birthday is only five days away from mine anyway."

Birthday! Surely, no more surprises.

"Okay, I'll go, but I'm driving us there."

A compromise was a good start. "Okay, I'll let you."

In keeping with his need for an entourage, Serge bought two extra tickets and invited his long-lost high-ranking Karate sensei, Gary, another one of his worrisome mates.

I wasn't overly thrilled to learn Serge had previously given Gary my landline phone number. "Who is that?" I asked the unfamiliar voice who answered, "The fucking devil."

Expecting to speak with Serge, Gary seemed pleased that my ear was available instead. Oh boy! I was held hostage on the phone listening to long barrages of philosophical gobbledy-gook Gary had formulated from a mixture of zen, new age, and whatever else. Some of it was interesting enough to engage me in conversation, until I realised that my input was totally unnecessary. Any kind of rational thought was superfluous and best to let the dialogue run its course until I could extricate myself. "Gotta go, someone's at the door."

"How come you always have visitors when I call."

"Popular, I guess."

Gary and his Asian wife lived a quiet life down the South Coast where he painted massive canvases of surprisingly good art.

The evening of the concert, Serge stood on my doorstep to pick me up. It is said that if you keep doing the same thing over and over again and expect different results, you must be balmy or something – Here he was, on my doorstep, and in a state that made me wonder. But still, this Dodo bird drove them in her car to go hear Bob Dylan.

Live lobsters crawled languidly in claustrophobic-sized tanks surrounded by walls covered in Chinese art and calligraphy. Waiters moved around slowly, carrying platters of food. I heard a hubbub of Chinese voices at the Emperor's Garden restaurant near the Entertainment Centre.

We were having pre-show dinner with Gary and his wife, already sitting at the table when we arrived and introductions made.

So this was Serge's esteemed karate sensei. A short, dark haired man, quite ordinary looking, I thought and somewhere during his first sentences to me, Gary announced, "I was in gaol for nearly ten years, you know."

What do you do when you hear something like this? Smile nicely and be polite? Maybe forget Chinese dinner and a concert and make a quick exit?

Not sure how to react, I asked, "No, I didn't know, what were you in gaol for?"

"I killed a man, stabbed him forty times, but it was circumstantial."

"Stabbing a person forty times can hardly be considered circumstantial."

"I was drugged out and didn't really know what I was doing."

What can you say without some kind of concern for the continuation of your own life? "Oh, I see!" and almost added, 'Are you better now?' but somehow it didn't fit.

We continued the conversation, including what his years in prison were like. "I read a lot of books. Mostly about religion and spiritual stuff." This explained his phone conversation themes.

My expectation of this tough, black belt, high-ranking Shotokan Karate champion, murderer and gaol bird, did not measure up to this diminutive, lean, unremarkable man who talked a lot, and a wife who said nothing, except to order Chinese food.

At the Entertainment Centre, the audience had gathered inside the auditorium. We struggled up endless stairs past rows of racked seats until we reached ours; far, far away towards the back, making the stage below look like a shadow box filled with miniature instruments and sound gear.

The support band should have kept practicing their unbearable racket in some backyard garage. I ripped up a Kleenex tissue and stuffed it in my ears while Serge kept going up and down the steps, claiming he was having problems with his water works and needed to get to the loo. I felt certain it wasn't the lower end of his body that connected with liquid.

My recollection of crappy memories includes Bob Dylan's lacklustre performance, a murderer sitting two seats from me, and Serge's trips up and down the stairs.

Another birthday mess-up – This time I discovered Serge's hip flask peeping out of his inner pocket. "Busted" I announced as I pulled it into the air and without another word, I rushed down the endless stairs, out of the building, and into the night's bustle of Chinatown, found my car and drove home.

According to the papers, it had been a mediocre concert.

Times were a-changing, and Like a Rolling Stone, I moved on.

Visceral feelings still held me in this crazy relationship. I had blindly allowed myself another dramatic ending with a gizzard-gripping workout. So what had I learnt this far? My lake of tears was drying up, yet greater wisdom still eluded me.

CHAPTER 35

Oye, Oye, Oye

"Nowadays most people die of a sort of creeping common sense, and discover when it is too late that the only things one never regrets are one's mistakes"

– Oscar Wilde – *The Picture of Dorian Gray*

"Curiouser and curiouser!" said Alice in a moment of confusion when nothing seemed as it was. The white rabbit of possibility goes rushing past us seducing and distracting us with his pretty watch, and we loose the thread of our resolve. Then again, this could simply be the moment when awareness kicks in, we begin to see other possibilities, and go chasing down the rabbit hole to find –another place where nothing is what it seems.

If I were to live in Alice's Wonderland who would I be? Alice, the rabbit, the mad hatter or heaven forbid, the crazy queen? I don't know. I think at times I'm any one of them, even the disappearing Cheshire cat.

Once upon a time, I was like the caterpillar quietly sucking on a hookah with my mates, contemplating philosophical questions with cock-eyed wisdom.

I was crazy enough to allow Serge back into my life, but wise enough not to get embroiled in his next activity.

"No, I am not getting involved in your stuff anymore, Serge."

"You could make some decent bread out of this."

"I don't care. I am not promoting another one of your projects. I told you already."

"You wouldn't have to do a lot."

"No." I was determined not to be pulled in, but couldn't help asking, "What is it anyway?" If you don't ask, the conversation stops there.

"A long lost friend has asked me to write arrangements and produce an album he wants to record."

"Mmm … is he a good singer?"

"I don't know, we haven't rehearsed yet, I've only just started writing the charts."

"I see, well, good luck. Who is this guy?"

"Someone I knew a long time ago. He's a successful businessman and wants to make the album as a Christmas gift for his clients."

"Oh." I didn't voice my scepticism. As musical director and arranger, Serge was getting a great deal of money for this job, and the guy was going to get fabulous music backing.

Unlike previously, writing charts on the dining room table, Serge was now settled in his flat with a proper keyboard.

After the first rehearsal, he walked into my house, clapped his hand to his forehead and muttered, "Oye, Oye, Oye," over and over.

"Hello darling, what's with the Oye, Oye, Oye? Are you converting to Judaism?"

"I don't think I'm going to be able to take it."

"Why?" I was used to Serge's moods, behaviours and interactions with people.

"We had our first rehearsal today, and Tony's singing is unbelievable."

"That good hey?"

"That disastrous."

"Can't he sing?"

"Intermittently."

"That doesn't make sense, either he can sing or he can't."

"Listen for yourself! Where's your cassette player?" We set it up, and he inserted the tape. "Before I push the button, I want to know what you really think of this, Helene."

I became curious; why was he so interested in my opinion?

Maybe he thought I would get drawn in to be part of the promotion. Nothing on this planet was ever going to induce me into another misadventure with Serge.

The voice floating out of my cassette player began with so much promise, rich, deep and in full tone, I settled in for a treat, "Grenada, I'm falling under your spell…" My mother would have loved it. "…And if you could speak…" a few more sweet sentences and … suddenly there it was, Serge's Oye, Oye, Oye lament, justified. The voice wobbled, hit some strange off-key notes and continued, "of an age…" and again lovely notes followed by more strangled ones that hit the air.

This was more "*Oi Vey!*" than anything else.

"Are you kidding? Was he mucking around?"

"No, Helene, this guy actually thinks he's great, I can't stand this, we did hours of it. It's agony."

"Are you joking, is he paying you money to record this?"

"Yes, and it gets worse. Listen, here's another track, *"If you go down to the woods today, you better go in disguise, for every bear that ever there was will gather there... because today's the day the teddy bears have their picnic."* At first, I was lulled by a lovely baritone voice, until somewhere inside that first verse of the Teddy Bear's picnic, the vocal wobbles happened again. It was hilarious; not only that, as the songs continued to fracture my ears, and the airways, the dog started howling, which gave me the idea to suggest, "Maybe Rambo could do the backing vocals, it couldn't get worse."

As the album progressed – Another mangled song, "Sixteen Tons" had a few pounds of lacerated notes, making us feel we couldn't get another day older without laughing. Goes to show, if someone is willing to pay a stack of money, discordant notes are irrelevant.

Bum notes and epic egos between Serge and Tony, made the recording of this album a convulsive endeavour.

"Oye, Oye, Oye thinks this is going to be a historical album."

"Sound more like hysterical." I added, "How did you go today?"

"Same shit, more bum notes and what an ego. Fuck man, he thinks he's better than Caruso and that everyone else is an idiot." Thrown into this mad mix, was an escalating amount of drinking, ongoing payouts for musicians, studios, rehearsal rooms and any other expense that Serge could think of so that over twenty thousand dollars were poured into this ego-driven project.

The astounding irony was that after the CD was sent around to all the radio stations, the ABC guys loved it, and played it on air quite a lot, proving my point that mediocrity too often prevails.

Normally, being involved with such a talentless singer would have sent Serge out the door, but sadly to the detriment of his own reputation, as if it wasn't tarnished already, and the desperate need to pay bills, he stayed on the project and created some wonderful arrangements.

They had discussed a second album, but the musical romance between the two men had gone sour, also fuelled by their ongoing love affairs with booze. One track, "Some Enchanted Evening," was anything but enchanted, adding to their dissonant relationship, which by now, had descended into soap opera proportions.

Months later, Tony rang me to complain Serge had ripped him off, and that the arrangements were shit. I was compelled to defend my hero, he might be an alcoholic, difficult, and impossible, but lay off his arrangements and talent, you cretin! I restrained myself from telling Tony what a crap singer he was, and how fortunate he was to have the best orchestration behind his wobbly voice.

Needing someone to blame for the rift, Serge decided I must have said something on the phone to set Tony off; it had to be my fault. Much later, when he got over that piece of tantrum, his new mantra became; "Tony is an arsehole."

In the end, I saw it all as, "An Impossible Dream" and was pleased with myself for having kept out of it.

CHAPTER 36

Heroes and Villains

"History is moving pretty quickly these days, and the heroes and villains keep changing parts."

– Ian Fleming, creator of James Bond

Though he died when I was ten years old, my father remained my hero all my life. My memory of him kept alive by my mother who often talked about him, his activities, his passion for what he believed in, helping family, and his escape from the Russian army that took him on a solitary trek across Europe. When he finally settled in France, he became a political activist, helping many refugees relocate to other countries after the war in Europe.

I've been filled with regret my father did not live long enough to love me, guide me through life's whims, and those I mindlessly jumped into. I longed for his lost promise to send me to music training. He died much too soon. I wonder, had he been alive, would he have approved of the way music played out in my life. Would he have been disappointed I didn't study composition and gone on to perform. Would my one hit-wonder 'Barefoot Boy' have made him proud? I feel certain it would have. I also wonder, how dad would have responded to my choice of relationship with my genius musician who was the source of so much of my misery. I don't think daddy would have been happy for his 'Ketzele' (kitten.)

Sometimes the music, and his kindness, elevated Serge onto my hero's pedestal and collapsed when his demons pulled the construct down again.

Serge often talked about his great hero, friend, mentor, and jazz promoter, Horst Leopold.

Horst produced many albums, concerts, and other career opportunities. He held Serge in check from the 'enfant terrible' reputation he had created for himself in the jazz scene.

"Okay baby, ve vill be schwingin' und groovin'." Serge loved to mimic Horst's heavy German accent and famous comments, sending everyone in stitches of laughter, "Hey guys, remember when Horst tried to explain something to us and he couldn't find the words? He stumbled looking for a way to say what he had to, and finally came out with, 'I tell you, I know, I know. I know … fuck all.'"

The big daddy of the early days of jazz, Horst can easily be called a legend. In the seventies he initiated the Melbourne Jazz Centre 44 and the record label 44 on which he produced many jazz albums. He also booked bands at the Basement, ran the fledgling Manly Jazz Festival, and created his own series of "Music is an Open Sky".

More than an entrepreneur and mentor, Horst filled a great need in Serge as a father figure. "You know, Helene, in those days I haunted Horst, making myself useful and to reciprocate, he got me into concerts, produced my Free Kata albums and put me in the loop." I heard the love in Serge's voice when he talked about his hero.

Horst and his artist wife Clarita moved to the United States, where jazz was more dynamic and accessible than its limited population in Australia. Making New York their new home base, he carved out a prominent career and together with some business partners, went on to open two jazz clubs, Sweet Basil and Lush Life. He continued to nurture musicians.

Legend people can do your head in. We create fantasies with larger than life stories we hear about them and then expect a kind of god-like creature. Maybe it's their persona or bad breath or shit dress sense, that when you meet the imaginary hero in real life, the magic bubble bursts, and you are left with an ordinary human. Horst was anything but ordinary.

After many years in the States, Horst was scheduled to come to Australia for a short visit and many of Sydney's jazz musos eagerly anticipated his arrival. As for Serge, beyond his usual excitable nature, he was filled with expectation and talked of little else.

The timing was great. Serge was doing a regular gig at Round Midnight in Roslyn Street, Kings Cross. This was a smart, elegant, comfortable jazz club with a great stage area for bands and singers, and busy most nights.

The difference on this smoky, packed, hubbub-filled night – Horst was here – He sat at one of the tables listening to Serge play. I waited, not wanting to intrude on the magic moment when these two lions of music arrived at the moment they connected again for the first time in decades. I saw the tears form on Serge's face as he and Horst were locked in an emotional clinch.

Finally, I was introduced to Horst. Light coloured hair, rotund face and body, eyes that seemed to take in everything around him, I found it easy to like this larger than life individual who lived up to all the stories about him: Charming, intelligent with a delightful sense of humour. "Ah, zo you are the great love of Serge's life. He tells me he loves you ferry much and that you look after him und help him, is ferry good, Helene. It's a pleasure to meet you." How could I not be instantly captivated with an opening like this? Accompanied with a warm, encompassing hug, he made me feel like we were old friends.

Squeezed in between all the jazz musos who'd heard he was in town, we enjoyed some great meals and conversations together. Horst returned too soon to New York, his music epicentre.

Years disappeared before I spoke to Horst again. By about 2017 there were too many deaths in between. At first, we had an occasional phone call to say hello and talk about what was happening in the world. For a start, the forthcoming USA elections that voted in Donald Trump as President. Our phone conversations moved on to reminisce about Serge's talents and misdemeanours. Horst and his wife, Clarita were now busy artists preparing for exhibitions.

When I asked for input for this book, Horst was generous with his memories, words rushing out of him like a runaway train, "I booked all the great guys for my club and made many recordings. Miles Davis lived around the corner and came to the club to speak to Stan Gets. The place was always packed. I booked Chet Baker. I had no problems with him. The other clubs asked if he turned up, considering he was such a heroin addict. No problems with me, always happy days."

During one of our phone conversations about the jazz scene in New York, he told me, "The money is so much better in the United States. McCoy Tyner got a thousand bucks a week. Art Blakey on tour got $10,000 a night. Keith Jarrett made $20,000 a night per concert. Gil Evens used to play in my club Monday nights. He got $15,000 per record. Money over dere is the big, big difference."

I pulled him back to ask about his views and memories of Serge, "Was he difficult to handle?" And got an unexpected response, "Serge was a very good player. He had imagination, but he had a problem with his language, completely over the top. People don't walk around swearing like that over dere; he wouldn't have lasted five minutes. Apart from that, there was really nothing to handle, I don't put any restrictions on people."

I was concerned to learn, "I had a stroke last year and had to have open heart surgery. I was in the best hospital in New York. Most doctors were Jewish, the best, they all love me, because I didn't demand anything, they were just great."

Later that year, he rang me again once or twice, and we chatted about his life, retirement and how much he enjoyed immersing himself in painting colourful abstracts.

He was also very proud of his wife's art, "She is a ferry good artist."

Way before my time, Serge had dedicated an album to him. And on the Jungle Juice album I produced, he wrote the composition, "Blues for Horst".

During late 2018, I received a couple of emails from Clarita that Horst was in hospital with kidney problems. She wrote he was looking forward to reading this book. Sadly, he won't be doing that; Horst died in January 2019, leaving many people who respected and loved him, in deep grief.

♪♪

Back in the sixties, Horst helped set up a jazz club in Jason's restaurant, owned by Bert Mendelsohn, Graham Marks and Eddie Santos. Originally a French restaurant, Jason's at 269 Crown Street, off William Street, became a vital jazz venue for the cream of Australian musicians: Allan Turnbull, George Golla, Julian Lee, John Pochee, Kerrie Biddell, Johnny Nichol, Marie Montgomery. Evie Pickler and her brother Arthur who played double bass, were regular performers. Eddie had his regular trio there, playing drums and doing vocals. David Levy was on piano until Serge got the gig.

Jason's also boasted occasional visits from famous Hollywood movie stars. A date had once taken me there for dinner – Not yet time for us to meet, it was possible Serge was there and we were oblivious of each other. The pond was full of other fish for each one of us.

Loveable, down to earth Eddie was one of the most stable friendships in Serge's life. Eddie didn't buy into bullshit or pretence I often saw in others. He laughed with the rest of us when Serge mimicked him, wrinkling his face, pushing invisible glasses up his nose with one hand and with the other, pulled forward equally invisible balls in his crutch. "This is Eddie adjusting himself. Man."

Eddie Santos was another sad loss when he died of lung cancer.

♪♪

A match made for the twilight zone: the friendship Serge had with Ben Tranter, a fellow musician, often descended into the quagmire of couple's dysfunction. The relationship vacillated between love, hate and drama. And boy, did I hear all of it!

A car accident badly damaged his legs and his ability to play music. Disillusioned and angry, Ben ended up in a wheelchair.

Two angry musicians found their commonalities, fuelling each other with their frustrations.

Trying to make sense out of the weird friendship, I questioned Serge, "I don't care what you say Serge, no matter what a great musician he once was and who he played with, he keeps bringing you down, and I can only imagine how he makes a living."

"Better you don't know, he's got to survive, and there's not much he can do. He can't walk, right hand is almost unusable, he has no other skills than to play the cello, anyway, he's my buddy, actually no, he's my brother."

"Pity you didn't have a real brother with a better influence on you, one that could show you the positives of life, not Ben's constant misery, and hatred of the world."

"You're just jealous of our friendship. He's a very smart guy."

"I know that. He can be charming, until you listen to all his bitterness about people, not to mention his boring as hell self-centred ego."

Sometimes, their friendship reminded me of little girls skipping hand in hand, happily babbling away with each other, or screaming and crying over a broken dolly.

"He's a cunt." I heard on the vinegar days. Other days Serge claimed, "He's my best buddy, he bails me out when I have serious financial problems. That's a real mate."

"That's a real schmuck. How much money have you manipulated out of him?"

He told me proudly, "Thousands. Well he's got it and I'll pay him back when I can, and I would do the same for him if I had it. Besides he's investing a lot of money into that legal wrangle I'm having."

Please don't ask about that, it's a long, complicated saga I was never too clear about, all I can tell you is: there was talk about gazillions involving dodgy people, and a character called Leo Ronin, you know, the one who ripped off all the media for the Paddington Jazz Festival. Ben's financial input into that piece of nonsense was the fuel for one of the bromance major bust-ups, when the friendship was 'off', finished, kaput; for months.

"Helene, I just got a call from Ben."

"Whacky doo, what does he want?"

"Don't be mean. He rang to tell me how much he misses me and that I am his best friend, and that he's sorry."

"So?"

"I'm going to pick him up for lunch tomorrow. We are brothers at heart."

"When did that relationship evolve? Did your mother know about it?" Sometimes I had genius moments of sarcasm.

The relationship resumed into what could have been an award-winning sitcom, with one final episode putting the finishing touches to it.

Ben bought himself a superb whizz-bang electronic wheelchair allowing him freedom of movement, and as an act of dedicated friendship, he spent several thousand dollars more to buy one for Serge. By this time, Serge was in a lot of pain with arthritis, hip problems and gout. Ben's idea was for the both of them to wheel down the streets together on their mechanical chairs.

The response to this act of brotherly love was epic, and I heard all about it from the comfort of my lounge room. Cushioned in my soft pale blue leather lounge, little Rambo the dog glued to his side, Serge was on his mobile, screaming.

"You fucking arsehole Ben. How dare you? I came home to my apartment and there it was, the fucking wheelchair. What are you trying to do, you fuck, make me a cripple like you?"

During this mobile warfare, I went to the kitchen to prepare lunch, "I'm getting a courier to take the bloody thing back to your place, and you can shove it up your arse," Serge's voice bounced around my walls.

He returned the offending chair. Ben got a refund, and put all the money into Serge's bank account, amicably settling the birthday present.

It was sad to see two intelligent, talented men so broken they were unable to face the failures of their own making. Yet, they found validation in each other, mirror images of their jagged broken pieces, painfully fitting together.

Like everything else about Serge and me, my friendships were very different. To start with, my mother was also my friend. We went on many companionable journeys together. She sat next to me in the car and chatted about her life or family history. Her deteriorating health forced different trips on us; to doctors and waiting rooms. "Oye vei, I not like this vaiting und vaiting." Even in ill health, my mother was feisty.

Squeezed in between the 'good parts' of life, we get the tough ones, invading us like carrion birds ready to peck away at the flesh of our happy existence. They challenge us to learn how we can overcome them, and hopefully grow to become better human beings. I had plenty of those, they bloody well hurt like hell, tore my emotions to shreds and showed me how much resilience I still had in me. The deterioration of my mother's health and mental capabilities did that to me, she was going through the early stages of dementia and some frightening aspects to her diabetes. I had to make excruciating decisions about placing her in a nursing home.

CHAPTER 37

Liquorice Allsorts

If you accept reality for what it is, you can either change it or adapt to it. But you cannot do either if you are not aware that it exists

– Abraham J. Twerski, M.D. – *When do the Good Things Start?*

Ever eaten little square layers of black liquorice allsorts with the soft, sweet coloured candy in between? The candy parts easily dissipate in your mouth, but the liquorice is thick, bitter, hard to chew, and leaves a black residue between your teeth.

I think life is often like that, the sweet times disappear too quickly and the black, unpleasant hard times linger inside you with their dark memories.

My last times with Serge were ambivalent, filled with the layers of sweet and hard. Despite our dramatic finales, there were still doors left ajar.

Behind my door, I lived with sometimes the music, sometimes the laughter, and sometimes the silence.

Inside the layers of his life, Serge had just about run out of people and places to play his music. He justified it by saying it was someone else who was responsible. His attitude reminded me of the fable '*The Fox and the Grapes,*' about a fox trying to quench its thirst by reaching for grapes hanging over a wall, and when he failed to get any, walked away telling himself they were too sour, and he didn't want them anyway.

Alternatively, Serge lamented, "I'm too unpredictable, that's why no one wants to book me."

"That's true, but you know they appreciate your talent." My words were aimed to make him feel better, "I know you've left yourself limited choices, but there could be other ways."

A creative mind finds ways, and he did. "I'm going to create a new project. I'll show them."

He needed an audience; a platform where he could lose himself, direct his fingers over the black and white keys to wrench the music from the guts of the piano.

Not quite done yet, he still had a flickering flame of defiance in him, which he directed toward a new target. The NSW government funded Sydney Improvised Music Association (S.I.M.A.), was set up to create concert opportunities for Australian jazz musicians. Once upon a time, Serge had been on the committee as a revered improviser of his Free Kata music, until the association ostracised him.

An ongoing vendetta with the president of S.I.M.A. brought out mostly ugly, unpleasant tirades on the phone. I overheard him when the call was at my place or when he later moaned to me about it. A 'nice' call sounded like this: "When are you going to give me a gig, man? You always put together great programs", but the angry, frustrated

Serge hurled his colourful language down his mobile, "You fucking piece of shit! You use government funding for your golden-haired guys, but I'm not politically correct enough for you." Those rising verbal abusive improvisations made me wonder at which riff did Mister President hang up. All I could do was cringe.

All that vitriol created more damage, excluding Serge from any S.I.M.A. programs at their regular venue, The Seymour Centre located near a large department store and a park with communal swimming pool, and beyond, the grounds of The University of Sydney. This venue included several theatre and performance spaces and a small, intimate area for live music.

The frustration of no gigs from S.I.M.A. gave Serge the impetus to find another way to generate an audience, I must admit, I admired his determination to stick it up them by hiring the same venue for one night only, organising his 'Love Jazz Concert' for the 5th December 2007. He also booked a fine line up of musicians and guest vocalists. As usual, he ignored costing details.

"I'm doing all the organising Helene, but could you please just do the door, that will be such a great help."

"I dunno." And that was enough to bring me to do the door. In showbiz, doors are to let the punters in and unless there is a designated box office, a person has to sit there, collect tickets, and sometimes the entry fee. Normally, it would be easy enough – be charming, efficient, smiling. Serge had promised too many people free entry and some got quite nasty when I insisted they pay. Amazing, what people will or will not pay for.

During the early days of my laughter workshops, when I had no one to help me, my multi-tasking included door duties.

The snake charmer sits crossed legged in front of his basket and makes music to summon the cobra from its dark bedroom, and for as long as the music lasts, the cobra remains undulating in the light. I now think I was like a mesmerised snake weaving around Serge's life, drawn by the notes flowing from his fingers.

Black trousers and shirt, closed cropped greying hair on his head and face, Serge sat masterfully at his piano once again, dominating his space for the last time. A small audience was seated in this dusky jazz environment, drawn to the creativity flowing from his playing. I believe creativity is the essence of life, and can't imagine living in a world without it. I knew that hearing Serge play was a great part of my attraction to this tortured genius. Sometimes, I heard beyond the notes playing out the melodies of his life, and it was almost impossible to imagine this same human could hurtle jagged discordant tones from his mouth, or crawl up drunkenly from the floor.

Our after gig post mortem was unusually positive; together with the miracle that we had collected enough money to cover costs, probably because I had been such a relentless doorkeeper. We were also excited about Tony Barry's fabulous rendition of "Seattle."

All good – Afterwards, I returned to my laughter work, and Serge to writing his symphonies.

♪♪

Laughter took me to many diverse platforms: I was constantly changing, adding, researching and playing with new ideas I felt would be beneficial to others, and in some way, gains for me as well.

I came home for a while, until the next out of town booking. I boarded the dog, got on a plane and flew off into another unknown or else I drove down the coast, up the coast, or westward for conferences, development days, short presentations, and day workshops. My brief was always to: lighten people up, bring humour into the workplace, and generate creativity for staff to be more productive.

Sometimes I stayed a night or two in plush hotels, resorts or dumpy motels, people's homes, a tent in Dubbo zoo where lions roared all night. In Port Macquarie, I stayed in a woman's house where her living room had a strange waterfall filled with garden gnomes, plastic flowers, and bits of cacti.

Often, my hosts extended themselves; like the couple from Cooma who owned the local accountancy firm and a large sheep property. They invited me to stay with them while I conducted several workshops, including one in their home for local drought-stricken farmers. During my stay on their property, I went out early one frosty morning to hug a tree, and saw many large kangaroos hopping across the landscape.

The Snowy Mountains enchanted me so much, I almost bought a quaint little house in Cooma, until I realised that freezing snow winters were not my cup of hot wine.

I made many transient friendships when I stayed with people in different parts of Australia and South East Asia, but although we agreed not to loose touch, we did.

One of the saddest aspects of life, for one reason or another, are the gone-friends. They take with them the vulnerable parts of yourself you have shared, and the knowledge you have of each other's joys, regrets and dreams. It's as if the glue that held the friendship together has hardened, crumbled, and become yesterday's shadows.

Despite briefings and discussions beforehand, I frequently faced a different situation. For instance, I might have been told the people with disabilities would be attentive and able to engage in the activities. Turned out, they were either in wheel chairs or had speech difficulties, making it totally inappropriate to ask them to speak in gibberish. This challenged my ability to be of value to people, so I had to draw on the other parts of my background to summon activities that would be fun. I included improvisation exercises by asking my 'different' participants to be trees or birds flying through the trees. It generated a lot of mayhem and laughter.

Corporate settings presented other challenges, mostly about people not loosing face when confronted with some of my outlandish requests.

A mental health organisation booked me for a couple of sessions at Nambucca Heads for a large group of people with Down syndrome. Afterwards, I stayed in the area for two more days, and not knowing anything about the surroundings of the motel I had booked, I was disappointed to find it was out of reach of transport or car hire facility, too far to walk anywhere and too cold to hang out by the pool. All I was left with was to sit outside my room, enjoy the scenery, and write:

Nambucca Heads – Motel... Friday 17th October 2008

Awareness awakes in me a rustle of palm leaves playing through the breeze. I hear trucks rumble along on the Pacific Highway, a burst of cicadas fills the spaces between the roar of traffic, distant birds, and a dog barking.

Sunshine dominates the clear blue sky and settles on lilac coloured lilies.

After wandering around the gardens and writing on the porch of my motel all day, I am now inside the darker confines of my room, where not even a slice of sun to throw a light pattern on the pale blue walls, or the stained carpet.

The solitude drapes itself around me, my memories invade my thoughts with longing for 'what might have been'.

Tears start and just as quickly dissipate, and like undisciplined butterflies, memory floods me as spontaneously as breathing. My yesterdays invade me and I trawl them in as if I were a fisherman with a net full of squirming fish – And retrace my relationship with Serge: the first time I found his alcohol bottles in the pocket of his jacket hanging in the wardrobe, he was in bed with the 'flu', mumbling, getting louder, aiming vicious dialogue at me. I didn't know then how to handle him and was led into a verbal battle that reached the edges of violence.

Pain happens in the heart, memory sends its fingers creeping around the pulsing organ, and there is no barrier strong enough to stop the tears.

Shadows of the late day opens other vistas, and I look for good times, at first refusing to come, instead, I find the memory of a birthday when Serge arrived at my place, drunk. I remember the disgust I felt when I saw the exposed crack of his bottom above his baggy pants when he clung to a chair, pulling himself up to stop his fall. Patches of long hair dangled from his balding head and clung to his thick neck like underfed orphans.

No! I force myself to remember better times: a family day at my half-brother's place, the raw metal of a screen door slams into my foot making it bleed profusely, blood drips onto the floor. Serge instantly throws me over his shoulder and rushes me to the local hospital, past all the people in the waiting room, finds a doctor and demands immediate attention. Needles go into the wound; the excruciating pain is diminished with Serge holding me so tight, he absorbs some of the agony of the stiches piercing my foot.

The sun moves around the sky. The shadow of my hand plays across the paper. This interminable day slowly disappears leaving a patch of the sun's heat on my arm.

Nobody, anywhere; all I hear is the flow of traffic and the birds.

The next day I flew home.

CHAPTER 38

End Play

If my slight muse do please these curious days, the pain be mine, but thine shall be the praise

– Poems of William Shakespeare.

Many of my years with Serge were filled with the battering rams of his words accompanied by endless tears. Although I survived the emotional wounds I don't think anyone could withstand that kind of turmoil and remain untouched. Still, I had arrived at an understanding where I could choose to be martyr, victim or victorious warrior. I couldn't tell you of any particular way I arrived at this insight, but I think it was a culmination of all the yoyo years of dealing with Serge's temperament, the dives into my inner oceans and having to swim like crazy to find my sanity and balance.

The distance I created between us helped me recharge my batteries and rejuvenate my sense of sanity.

It seemed like forever since we had seen each other. After another one of those dramatic ends of the relationship and months of separation, here he was, standing on my doorstep, again. I noticed his pale blue eyes were clear.

His beard, although quite grey, was neatly cut close to his rounder face made him look like a chipmunk. I used to call him that when he put on weight.

Like a Phoenix reconstructed from burnt-out ashes, Serge always returned to me with his life, music and the force of his personality. Yet, each year his plumage lost more of its lustre and the movement of his flight, restricted.

"Hello, Helene."

I didn't know what to say, let alone what to do. Words can be impossible.

"Aren't you going to ask me in?" He moved one foot onto the lowest of the four steps to my front door.

"Not for long; I have an appointment," I lied, and being a crap liar, it must have shown.

"I just want to talk to you and tell you something very important." Ah well, talk! You can't blink away a chunk of a lifetime.

I watched him walk down my long hallway; Rambo was annoyingly welcoming, waggling his tail and running around Serge's legs, woofing loudly, and leaping up in excitement.

"Hello my boy, did you miss your dad?"

This was not going well, I thought. Rambo is a little shit and a traitor. Serge picked him up for a close facial-hair mingle, and long-lost love affair.

"Would you like a cup of tea?"

"Yes, that's what I came to tell you, I haven't had a drink for months and I'm going to AA now."

"I hate to burst your bubble but what else is new?"

"I'm seriously doing AA and my twelve steps."

"Are you here to make amends?" I couldn't help the sarcasm.

"That and to tell you how much I miss you and little Rambo. You are my family you know." It was obvious Serge was trying to pry his way back into the fortress of my emotions.

A mental flash of the last drunken drama dug into me like a sharp fingernail. But he charmed me with the tenacity and consistency of his feelings for me. There is an old Jewish saying from my mother's bottomless supply of wisdom, "You throw him out the door, and he comes back through the window." He had cleverly climbed back in through the window of my life.

Our cups of tea were getting cold, and before I could reach for another sip, his hand dwarfed mine, "Helenatchka, I do love you, you know, forever, no matter what I do or where I am."

"So why do you put me through that crap?"

"You know I don't set out to hurt you. I do this to myself, it's self-sabotage."

We talked. My pretend appointment was forgotten and a temporary amnesia set in on my decision to keep him out of my life.

I finished my tea and before daylight changed into evening, we had rekindled love and made new plans.

For a while, all was well. He went to AA, and I went to Al-Anon.

I developed my work to include attitude, gratitude, so I decided to produce a CD, 'Lighten Up'. My book Laugh Aerobics that Harper Collins had published years earlier was sold out, and I have no idea if the two thousand copies translated to Japanese found ha-ha's in Japan.

Spending intermittent weeks recording my CD in Mal Green's studio in Castlecrag's lush bushland was fun and productive. As a musician, artist, and drummer with some top Aussie bands, as well as being a recording engineer, Mal's creative input was invaluable.

I sold enough discs to maybe recover costs, but sitting in cardboard boxes in my clutter room is probably the cockroach's favourite meeting place.

♪♪

By now, I had overcome many challenges of venues, people, external noises, broken-down air conditioners in forty-degree heat, an in once case, I was informed the training room was next to a crocodile infested river. Outside the window in another place, Kookaburras competed loudly with my laughter training. Another time, a woman-interpreter translated my words into Arabic, however, the lunch provided was delicious and we all laughed at jokes we shared. My one, about a suitcase made from circumcised pieces of skin brought uproarious laughter. The ladies insisted I come back another time to share lunch and more humour.

I enjoyed the vagaries of being a travelling laughter lady.

On the 18th June 2009, a recruitment company invited me to conduct a laughter seminar in Adelaide for delegates from around Australia. Later that year, in November 2009, Serge was engaged for a concert arranged by John Howell, his promoter friend from Kuranda, who had moved back to Adelaide.

I ultimately saw the live session of that Adelaide gig on YouTube. I was deeply saddened by it. It was obvious Serge was battling with a great deal of pain. His fingers, once in charge of his instrument, the power and energy of his music, now moved tentatively across the keyboard. The ghost of his former self played a shadowy version of his beloved jazz, hesitant notes drifted out onto a forlorn platform. He did his best, but lacked the fire and passion of former times.

I hurt for the lost forever music.

Serge and I had travelled such a long, formidable road together, but by now, had stepped into different directions.

CHAPTER 39

The Last Lily

"Love is the flower of life, and blossoms unexpectedly and without law, and must be plucked where it is found, and enjoyed for the brief hour of its duration."

– D. H. Lawrence.

How are we ever to know when we do something for the last time that it will never happen again?

This was his last birthday email to me.

Saturday 21st August, 2010 – 4.25am –
To: Helene Grover
Cc: jazzsergery
Subject: Happy Birthday my Helene

"To my Dearest and most special Helenatchka,
Happy Birthday my most dearest and sweetest
Eternally I'll always love you
With loving heart I'll always hold you
My whole being always by your side
For our God given most holy ride
I love you so much my whole essence gives to you
And wishes to forever hear you and be with you

I pray every day to my Father in heaven
For us to grow together and learn with love's heaven
Always I'll repeat that we go into God's sunset together
Eternally with God blessing us, and loving each other forever

Your always and eternally

Serge xxx

He wrote far better music than his heartfelt birthday messages.

By this stage, three fingers of his right hand were so arthritic he could barely move them. I cried seeing them, and knew he would never be able to play piano again. He walked painfully, dragging his left leg, shorter than the right one from an accident when he was very young. No matter what, I still felt sad to see this once larger than life man diminished, and his body bloated from years of pills, alcohol, and greasy foods.

The fire in him had become barely a spark. He began to talk about his mortality. "You know, Helene, I have been thinking about what is this life all about, I don't think I'll last much longer, I am in so much pain and can't play anymore. People don't give a shit."

Serge was retreating into an inner world of pain and loss; a fragile man wearing a worn out mantle of resilience.

After all I had been through, I still had emotional spaces for him I can't explain.

My feelings for my mother were less ambivalent. I hung on to the last pieces of her life, unable to say goodbye to this little person who had shaped so much of my existence. This human being had given me love, anger, frustration. I felt I had to protect her, no matter what.

Unbearably frail, she didn't recognise me anymore. Serge drove me every day to see her, and helped me grope with the inevitable. Nursing staff at the hospital told me my mother was reaching the end.

"You have to let your mother go," one nurse told me.

"Let go of your mother, Helene," Serge echoed.

"What the bloody hell do you all think I am? God? It's not up to me when she goes." I sat next to her bed in silence and watched her breathe, her tiny face shrunk, the round rosy cheeks had disappeared, she was no longer the feisty little mother who had given me the loving forty five of the ninety three years of her life. She was somewhere in a between place.

I was alone, present and witness to the juggling of life and death.

Light was almost gone and the outside shadows slithered through the window. Twilight dropped into the room prompting memories of my long lost family: my father, aunts, and grandmother. I had an uncanny sense of them being here, waiting. I closed my eyes, and imagined holding my mother in my arms: "God, here is Mum, I give her to you, she's a good person, please look after her."

That evening I received the phone call to let me know my mother had died.

A week later, I emerged from sitting *Shiva*, the Jewish custom for the dead. I was a long way from relinquishing my grief and tears as I walked along the boardwalk of Coogee Beach, oblivious of passers by, I looked past the sandstone wall, across the sand and upwards to an intermittent blue sky. I imagined my mother peering over a big cloud, chastising me as she used to do, "Listen *boobale*, stop mit der eye pishing, I am so busy making cheesecake for everyone. The whole family is here."

The idea made me smile. Nowadays, when a friend loses a loved one, I tell them I will ask Mum to make them her welcome cheesecake. They were the best on the planet.

After my mother died, and with no other relative in Australia, I clung to Serge, hanging on to his familiarity, and the certainty he understood me better than anyone else.

♪♪

By this stage, chunks of my world had disintegrated together with some of my friends, leaving a trail of memories.

As for Serge, there was little left in him or for him. His fingers couldn't hold the music anymore. The people he had invested in with degrees of emotion also evaporated. Some remained on the periphery, the subjects of his ongoing pain. Years of self-abuse, addictions, and disillusions were tearing him down.

I was grateful for his support, and in return, I wanted to make him happy, so did what I could to give him little joys: my chicken soup, baked lamb shanks, chicken ragout, and my special risotto.

"I'm taking you to one of my new café discoveries in Randwick, they make the best prawn linguine. You'll love it."

"You know I don't like cafes, Helene. Let's just go to the noodle joint in Randwick for lunch."

"Come on, as an improviser you have to look for innovation. My shout."

"I really don't feel like it."

"Do I have to pull your gun out of your pocket and aim it at you just to go and have a meal with prawns I know you love."

"You're still on about my gun." Oops! Dangerous territory. I quickly changed the subject. "It's a lovely day we can sit outside and take Rambo." That was a good strategy, the dog, the prawns, and my persistence. He enjoyed the meal on the café's footpath. Rambo enjoyed the passing paws.

Reading the Sunday paper while eating one of Serge's perfectly cooked breakfasts, I spotted an interesting ad, "There's going to be a one-night show at the El Rocco about the life and music of Chet Baker, played by an award-winning actor, Tim Draxl."

"Chet Baker, you're kidding, my favourite trumpet player. When? We have to get tickets straight away." He stood up out of his chair, ready to go.

"Hold it, first, I'll phone and see if we can get tickets today." I just had to do it. I actually love Chet Baker who died much too young from his heroin addiction.

I wonder how often serendipity delivers coincidences. This time, it brought us back to the El Rocco, the minuscule underground venue where it all began so many years ago.

The heavens draped sheets of water over the buildings of Sydney's underbelly, and rain gushed into gutters and drains, the night of October 2010, when Serge and I went to the El Rocco for the first time, after all our years together.

Fluctuating from always being broke or flush with impulsive acts of unrequited generosity, Serge bought extra tickets for a couple of friends to join us, Peter and Linda Stein. Peter another soul mate musician friend of Serge, died in 2019.

We gathered on the footpath outside the El Rocco and just as we were about to go down the steps to the jazz cave, Serge went off to buy packets of Smarties. Don't ask, I could only guess.

I munched on the little chocolate pellets, my mouth full with sweet and my ears filled with Chet Baker's music: 'My Funny Valentine', 'Lets Get Lost' 'Look for the Silver Lining' and 'There will never be Another You.' The lyrics echoed so many parallels of my life with Serge. This was the last best evening we had together.

A profound sadness was to come.

♪♪

Imagine, two strange looking critters sitting on either of Serge's shoulders, the red demon of drink on the left, and the white angel of redemption on his right, battling each other for his soul.

The alcohol monster had imprisoned him for too long and he was never again able to explore the intricacies of his music.

It's not all good, it's not all bad; it just is.

I never set out to have the hardships I experienced. No one ever does. My youthful objective was: To pursue a life of creativity and freedom, hit the road of music, escape the demands of my mother, and find out who the bloody hell I really am.

Still unknown, was whether I was wishy-washy weak with flashes of strength and rebellion, or unable to move entirely away from my relationship with Serge. If only I could have had a huge rubber to erase what didn't work.

By now, our relationship had shifted to something quite different from twenty-six years ago when it was alive with the joy of meeting and the promise of exciting things to come. The initial flow between us had stagnated into complacent inertia, and as he sat in the vase of my life, my feelings for him had begun to wilt.

Serge gave me one more bunch of flowers to show he loved me, always. Made up of roses, tulips and filler-foliage, it included one white lily with its tight bud offspring clinging to the stem of its parent.

I took special care of this fragile lily that lasted longer than the others until its petals curled with a pre-death translucence. As for the unopened bud, it hung on to its tenacious life as if it knew the struggle was futile. I wasn't ready to give up yet and nurtured this fragile flower that gave me its beauty for a few more days until it became a brown, gelatinous glob. I buried it together with the debris of my daily meal.

This 'Last Lily' reminded me of what I shared with Serge —A spectrum of wanton destruction or nurturing kindnesses within the layers of our relationship.

CHAPTER 40

To Hell and Back

'If you can laugh at your problems, you'll never run out of something to laugh about'

– Helene Grover

"Okay everyone, turn to the person next to you and make your thumbs face each other for a friendly wrestle. Now, press them together, kissy, kissy, kissy, pull them back, now attack! The first thumb that holds the other one down, wins." My instructions engaged everyone in the room to laugh and have fun. I was happy to be responsible for this childlike behaviour of nurses and other health professionals at the Canterbury Hospital, and explained the reason for doing this. "As silly as this seems, doing something fun and unexpected provides a few moments of respite from stress. It's not rocket science but, the objective is to confuse the brain from overthink and give you a mini mental holiday from tension."

Several suburbs further to the west, Serge was engaged in a more serious activity – Writing his music. That's what I believed.

After I completed my laughter workshop at the Canterbury hospital, I felt pleased with myself. I packed up my bag of funny stuff, got in my car and headed home along the busy Parramatta Road – The lights turned red at the same time as my mobile rang, and holding the wheel of the car with one hand I answered my call. In October 2010, there was no Bluetooth yet. Serge was on the line. Although pleased to hear from him, I was frustrated I wouldn't be able to speak with him for long, "How did you go, Helene? How was your workshop?"

"Really great, thanks darling. I can't talk long, I'm in traffic."

He seemed reluctant to finish the call, "I had dinner with Ben last night and he gave me back those pills I got on prescription for him, he said they were too strong and spun him out."

"What pills?"

"Oxycontin, they really help when I'm in bad pain."

"Serge, they are morphine based, please don't take them, I know how you throw handfuls of pills down your throat, just don't, its very dangerous. Please promise me you won't take any. Shit, the light just went green and I'm in very heavy traffic, I'll phone you back when I get home please, please, don't take those pills. I'll be home soon, so wait for my call, okay?"

"Yes, sure baby." I heard a chuckle trailing the end of his call.

Later, there was message from him on my mobile asking if I had arrived home yet, and after that, nothing.

Two weeks before, he came all the way from his studio in Parramatta to Coogee to take me to my doctor and sit with me for the result of my mammogram. The cancer was gone, but the fear returns every year. Fear diminished me into a childlike state.

"You'll be fine, Boodgie girl, I know for sure you'll to be okay."

"How can you know for sure?"

"You know that I know when I tell you I know." He squeezed my hand. "I'm never wrong." He was right.

This was the last time I saw him.

♪♪

The inner sanctum of his ninth floor studio had a crowded tiny kitchen and bathroom with pieces of ad-hoc furniture filling most of the constrained space. A sleeping nook separated by a screen hiding a huge television set, surrounded the mass of clutter where he ate, drank, cooked elaborate Chinese meals, and composed his symphony on a run-down second-hand electric keyboard pushed tightly against the wall.

Daylight struggled to get past the never-washed windows, closed blinds and disintegrated original curtains hung there since he had first bought the place many years ago. The interior darkness made it necessary for him to have a lamp switched on.

Even the bathroom was overrun with partially empty shampoo bottles, half used soaps, and sink spaces so full, a fly would have had problems to find a landing.

I once offered to decorate the studio, "First, we'll get rid of all the extraneous junk, crappy furniture and all the window shit. Get the sliding glass doors washed. You might even be able to sit out on your little balcony and see the flow of traffic below on the Great Western Highway. We'll get someone to paint the place, buy some stuff at Ikea, the place will feel bigger, brighter and better for you to create your music in comfort."

At first he loved the idea, but quickly relinquished it.

The studio reminded me of his father's music room in Punchbowl, where every inch of wall had been plastered with posters from his career; album covers, photos, and newspaper clippings.

Without daylight, fresh air and the lack of space to move, Serge's studio felt claustrophobic, it also had an overwhelming ghastly odour, one of the reasons I rarely went there.

This was the place where Serge spent days and nights of alcoholic binges stumbling around, being sick on the ever-increasing sticky carpet he covered up with a multitude of cheap colourful rugs.

When his intermittent sobriety came back, he made attempts at cleaning up, but was never able to fully get rid of the molecules of old age, sweat, stale vomit and greasy cooking. No matter what it looked, smelled or felt like, it was his comfort zone of escape from his world of endless struggles.

"I know I caused you a lot of pain in all our years together, my Helenatchka, and you are still here, so I am dedicating my first symphony to you. I've called it "To

Hell and Back". He told me his symphony was about his journey into madness brought on by drugs and alcohol, and his return to sanity.

The main theme of "To Hell and Back," was a track from the Jungle Juice album, recorded all those years ago in Kuranda.

The original sheet music for the symphony sits in the dark spaces of my wardrobe, never played or heard. Attached to it, is the signed dedication to me. This is one of my most treasured possessions, stored next to the many pieces of my own scribbled writings, humbled by his massive talent.

When I think of the great composers and their lives, I make concessions for Serge and feel his pain when all his attempts to bring his symphony to fruition, failed. He contacted people he believed could help, and although they loved the score, they told him it would be too costly to do anything with it, particularly at the Opera House where it really belonged.

One woman, an expert in transposing music arrangements, billed him for several thousand dollars and the only remuneration he could offer her was his run-down keyboard that she accepted. Personally, I think it was heartless of her to take away a musician's only instrument.

Serge was very proud of this work. This composition was a kind of rebirth for him, but for me, it signified my journeys to hell and back; the madness, the anger, the hope and the despair I experienced with him.

Maybe one day, when someone clears out my cupboard, the symphony will become the great discovery of the music world. You never know.

CHAPTER 41

The Music Stopped – Monday 11th October 2010

I would say that jazz is my own language

– Amy Winehouse

A week later, I faced a different kind of fear not being able to reach him on the phone, no matter how many desperate calls and messages I left on his landline and mobile. Nothing! Another day of silence and my concern skyrocketed. Panic spread in me like a sinister presence, overwhelming me with the feeling something was wrong.

Much as I loved travelling to my workshops, this time I wished I had not committed to fly to Canberra for a one day training session. How could I make other people laugh, when it was the last thing I felt like doing? My frantic phone calls, interrupted by the short flight, continued as soon as I landed, and kept making all the way to the conference room. I rang anyone who could find out for me, what was happening with Serge.

My mind spinning with dread, I put my forebodings on hold to face a corporate setting and deliver training on how to reduce stress in the workplace. Ironic, considering my stress levels could have scraped paint off a ceiling!

The bright sliver of humour I had generated during the session dissipated as soon as I was outside again, and stood under a storm-filled sky waiting for a taxi to take me to the airport. I would have liked to share my apprehension with my taxi driver, they often are quite chatty, but he was playing loud, Arabic music. My nose was attacked by wafts of B.O. and I wondered if he would have been able to understand my tear-muffled waffling.

Laughter and optimism are incompatible with anxiety spinning out of control. After all, I didn't have any concrete reason for my anxiety, and had no way of knowing if Serge was in any kind of predicament. He had pulled himself back from hell so many times before.

The airport in Sydney was busy and noisy. Announcements blared loudly, people were coming and going dragging luggage, and trolleys filled with suitcases were moving past me, arrivals and departures signs flashed. Peripheral goings on couldn't diminish my feelings of helplessness.

After collecting my suitcase, I turned on my mobile, and phoned my loyal friend, Jeanie.

"I'll pick you up from home and drive us out to Serge's flat. Just relax. You could be worrying for nothing."

Who was she kidding? Me! I'm a post-graduate from the University of Worry.

"I don't have his key anymore. I suppose his friend who lives in the building will let us in."

The traffic along Parramatta Road moved at a snail pace, and made me want to pull my buttocks forward to make the car go faster.

My fingers twisted the fronds of my scarf, my breath intermittently stalled in my chest.

Nobody had a key for Serge's apartment, not even Dimitri, his friend who lived in the building. He too was concerned, and after he let us in, he went up to knock on Serge's door. No response.

No one seemed to know what to do next. I kept repeating, "He's dead, I know he's dead, I bet it was those pills he told me about a few days ago." The "few days ago" had been almost a week.

The foyer of the building provided no answer, and the only thing the caretaker could do, was to call the police who calmly did what had to be done. After all, they had no emotional investment. First, they established that Serge's car was in its allocated space, then went to the ninth floor and broke down the door.

The days, hours, minutes and seconds that brought me to this moment, all fell into the abyss of dread – a place of lost hope. I had to confront the reality of death – the final instant where denial became impotent and disbelief threw a grey cloak over me.

I felt all of it, the moment I was allowed into the room.

The double bed mattress on the floor held Serge close to the edge, his colourless face turned sideways on the pillow. Curled into an S-shape, he had returned to a foetal position without a breath moving through his body. His life was gone.

A palpable stillness manifested itself and for an instant, the room disappeared leaving only me and this lifeless man, and everything of my life with Serge, dissolved into nothing.

I noticed the bed sheets he lay on were the ones I had bought for him his last birthday. No top sheet covered him.

Silent hands pulled me out of that room.

My brain momentarily lost its capacity to think until I remembered a distant echo of my words to him, "If you don't stop abusing yourself, I'm going to find you dead one day."

The coroner, who carried out the autopsy, sent me details of the cocktail of pills in Serge's stomach: Oxycontin, Valium, and Normison. While these drugs did not exactly cause his death, they precipitated it. Officially he died of a heart attack.

Research has shown the chemicals of tears vary according to our emotions; laughter, grief and onions. My tears tasted of grief.

For all the times I had said goodbye forever to him "I never want to see you again," "I'm done." None of them had carried this finality, making me powerless to retract my words. No more could his letters, cards, emails or phone calls have the potential to pull me back into the 'him and me' life. I grappled with the reality of 'this is forever.'

Death, as many of us have experienced, often brings to the forefront the trail of aftermath; loving relationships or nursed grievances, all buried with the one we have lost. The chaos, discord and jealousies of Serge's life, inevitably reflected this.

I was left to wonder what would have happened if Jeanie and I hadn't driven out to find him. How long would he have lain there? The last note played.

CHAPTER 42

Funeral

"Don't cry because it's over, Smile because it happened"
– Dr Seuss

More than forty years earlier, my mother and I had been in Australia for barely one year when my father died, and not knowing many people, it was difficult for us to organise ten men to be present for the traditional Jewish funeral. And to think I had problems sorting out the last ritual for one man.

Serge loathed mournful dirges of Gregorian music, and would have cringed if he were alive to hear them pouring down from the gallery of the Russian Orthodox Cathedral in Strathfield, I'm sure he would have preferred his own *"Sergery"* composition to accompany his last exit.

I can't remember what I wore that day, except I didn't turn up naked.

Feeling strange in the cathedral with its sparse seating around the walls, mostly for the elderly, I sat there flanked by my long time Russian friend George, born in Shanghai, same place and year as Serge. The familiarity of George's shaved head with its wispy grey ponytail was strangely consoling, and so was his blonde lanky Estonian wife, Reet, sitting on the other side next to me holding one of my hands while she wiped my tears with a rough paper serviette. Sitting inside our silence I felt the comfort they brought me.

My buddy, comedian George Smilovici who often made me laugh, took time out from his busy schedule to come to the funeral because at some stage I had introduced him to Serge and they had planned to write music together, but it never came to fruition; a combination of lack of time and a clash of personalities. There was no music or jokes on the day of the funeral, instead, George was serious and warmly gave me support. A tiny smile played in my head remembering one of his comebacks to a heckler, "Why don't you wear a headband to hide the circumcision scars."

During the lengthy, unfamiliar service, I fluctuated between grief and observation of my surroundings. Nothing felt real: the rosewood coffin appeared too small to contain the once larger than life Serge, and the delicate pink roses covering the lid seemed incongruous.

In spite of my grief, I was painfully aware of my unaccustomed surroundings. The cloying citrus aroma of incense evaporating into crevices. Cluttered around the walls, hung gold-leafed icon paintings. My eyes landed on the shadow play of palm tree fronds on the opaque window, while strange conversations were going on in my head: "Hey, my Sergie, how you like dem roses?"

"Nope. You know I like carnations and wild things." I was clutching at some kind of mental respite from the finality of death, knowing this was the last place and time I would have any connection to him.

Present to pay their last respects, the assortment of mourners were sparser than I had imaged: Family members, musicians, friends, his, mine, the reformed murderer, the shot policeman, the drummer dressed all in black, a bandana around his head. For some inexplicable reason, they all reminded me of seagulls facing the ocean.

My friends Phillip and Jessica were flustered when they arrived late at the graveside. They had inadvertently gone to the wrong funeral.

"How could you follow the wrong hearse?" I later questioned them.

"We didn't know the way but saw a priest go to his car and figured the logical thing to do, was to follow him along Parramatta Road behind a hearse heading in the same direction, and that's where it got out of hand. The priest drove down a side street and we decided to follow the hearse instead."

I got impatient, "So?"

"So, little sis, this hearse didn't seem to know where they were going and wove around all over the cemetery. Finally, we followed them to a mausoleum where a bunch of people had gathered. Somehow it didn't feel right till we found out we were at a Lebanese funeral. We had followed the wrong hearse. Luckily there was a gravedigger nearby, and he showed us the way to the Russian sector. And that's why we were late."

Funerals have stories, not just about the departed, but also the pieces of events that weave around cemeteries:

My mother told me about my grandmother's funeral, how my brother had cracked up laughing when he saw all the ladies dressed in long black garb.

As sad as loosing loved ones is, there are anecdotes of humour generated from the odd behaviours of people during their time of grief. My mother and I reminisced about a friend who had thrown herself down and pounded the ground of the freshly earth covered grave of her husband.

I don't know why, and it must be a kind of Freudian slip, I sometimes mix funerals and weddings up. Not meaning to be disrespectful, I unconsciously asked a friend, "What time is the wedding? Oops, sorry, I mean funeral." It wouldn't be so bad if I asked someone getting married, "So, what time is the funeral?" especially, if it ends in divorce.

My grief was sharpest when my godson Allan, held onto my arm when my mother was lowered into the ground, and we clutched each other with our shared sorrow.

For several reasons, Serge's death rituals were not followed by the musicians' final jam session – Usually, a gathering of drinking, playing and anecdotal memories. Serge had taken me to a couple of them where I heard some of the best jazz played, music for the angels.

"I bet nobody will come to play at my funeral," Serge had insisted a long time ago.

"Don't be silly, you're such an integral part of the jazz scene, and you know what they're like. Any excuse for a piss up and a jam."

"That's true, but I'm so out from it all."

"Well, you have been a very naughty boy, but there will be music and speeches about what an interesting mother-fucker you were."

"Ah well, at least I'll be up there with Miles, Keith, 'Trane and the others checking it out from our cloud."

"Why are we getting so morbid? Eat your chicken soup before it gets cold."

There is an invisible container holding the ingredients and spices of my life and who I am. It helps me dispel the gremlins of bad times, and lean on the memories I cherish.

♪♪

A large blackbird perched on the fence outside my office window. I absentmindedly thought, "It's almost time for Serge's AA meeting to be finished, and he'll be here soon." For the briefest moment I forgot and grappled with the permanence of death.

When I go through my cupboards, I find mementoes of him. CDs, rehearsal tapes, photos of gigs and events, videos I took of him playing, piles of love letters held together with rubber bands, cards and emails filled with effusive declarations of never ending love and riding into the sunset together. In my jewellery box are all the dainty pieces he bought me for birthdays, Christmas, Chanukah or because he thought I would like it. There were odd things too, a large purple sand egg timer, a soft toy German Shepherd dog to remind me of Tooska.

Even though the battery is dead and impossible to replace, I still hang on to a laughing bag his father bought me for my workshops. There are no more ha-ha's left in it.

No matter how many breakups, how many months of distancing myself from Serge, I always had a sense of return, of one day, when he'll get over this rubbish of alcoholism and get clean, we will get married, like he wanted to so many times, and I kept saying, "When you will be sober for two years, I will marry you."

I wonder if a hand of fate, or a mischievous being somewhere in the ethers, chooses to make fun of us puny mortal, perhaps lead us to lessons we need to learn, or awareness epiphanies jolted by situations we are dropped into. Two weeks after Serge died, the next laughter workshop I had previously been booked to conduct, was for a social welfare organization located in Parramatta, Serge's last dwelling place.

Crazy! Getting lost driving to a suburb I had been to many times before. My GPS was giving me a hard time sending me around in circles and dead ends. A voice with an unidentifiable accent, gave me incomprehensible messages like, 'take the third exit to the right'. What was this imbecilic electronic device telling me? What the hell was the third exit? I was running late and screamed at the little screen stuck to my windscreen, "You're a shit! What are you doing?"

The electronic shit responded: "You have reached your destination."

Bag of tricks over my shoulder, I raced into the conference room, grabbed the mike, "Hello ha-ha, sorry I'm late. I'm reminded of the woman who sailed on the Titanic; just as the ship went down, she grabbed a waiter by the coat tail, and said, 'I know I asked for ice cubes, but this is ridiculous' and If we don't find fun and humour in our life, we will sink like the Titanic."

As a trainer of I-know-it-all, I asked participants how they overcame bouts of seriousness, acknowledged that everyone has problems, and talked about how to deal with it. Bloody hypocrite! Here I was in desperate need of taking my own advice, and dishing it out like I had all the answers.

Still petulant, my GPS had the temerity to send me home through a lengthy tour of suburbs I didn't know existed. My colourful language had no effect on it until I reached my destination, an empty house and a welcoming dog.

♪♪

When the individual pieces of yesterday's jigsaw surfaced, I remembered that during my twenty-six on and off years with Serge, we always gave unwavering support to each other and rushed to the phone to share pet peeves and joyful successes.

"Hi Serge, I just got a call from a promotion company called Mango, they want me to do a massive gig for Sanitarium Food products." And his excited response, "Good on you, my darling. I know you'll do a great job, you have such wonderful stage charisma, I watched you on the Today Show, and I'm so proud of you."

On the other side of the spectrum, he would phone me full of plans: "I just signed up with a new music promotion company called Blue Pie. The boss, Damien Riley loves my music and he's planning a whole new career for me."

"That's fantastic, can you trust him?" The music industry was full of entrepreneurs out for a quick buck, and skyscrapers full of promises.

"I hope so. He's a really nice guy, has a large office with a lot of staff, it looks Kosher."

"Then I'm excited."

As memories and past conversations with Serge emerged, I realised I had gained some emotional backbone making me who I had become. Tougher, more sceptical, not as prone to chasing frivolous butterflies or dancing to the tune of someone else's song.

Once the curtain of life had tightly closed between us, I was able to mourn for the quarter of a century of a life shared.

"Hello mum, could you please bake another cheesecake, Serge is coming."

"Oi Vei."

CHAPTER 43

Sea Change

"It struck me then how much the past – not just the past but history and family – was like the ocean tide. It was always the same ocean, but the waves made it fresh and new each time"

– Aimee Friedman, Sea Change.

The ship's movement was barely perceptible as it sliced through the Pacific Ocean on its way to paradise.

I stood on an upper level of the ocean liner looking at an elderly white-haired couple gracefully waltzing across the marble dance floor. Every now and then, they disappeared under a giant glass sculpture hanging from the ceiling, and reappeared again, moving slowly to the music of the live band. Watching them, I remembered Serge telling me many times that we would sail into the sunset together, and this couple looked as if they were heading into the sun's horizon.

There were a number of aged life travellers seemingly at ease with each other as they walked hand in hand on the deck, shared their meals with us, laughed, talked, and restored my hope in humanity. Some people do live happily ever after.

Cruises are easy, you get your luggage on board, someone takes it to your cabin, you unpack, and then, that's it. I am a chronic over-packer. Even for one night away I pack enough just-in-case stuff to see me through to the next decade.

Away from home, away from the last twenty-six years, the cruise cleansed me. I ate, slept, swam, talked with strangers, read a book and laughed with my friend Jane. An unknown person made my bed everyday and left pristine white towels moulded into little animals propped up on my pillows.

Every day I watched the expanse of ocean surrounding us like yards of glittering fabric, studded with precious droplets of water catching the Pacific sun. The tranquillity of the sea and gentle chugging of the ship's engine had a transforming effect on my years of turbulence, and left me with an inner peace where the landscape of my emotions changed.

Over two thousand people on a liner, and I found one person who partly reflected my own experience.

She looked like a life-size kewpie doll dressed in black lace; Cyclamen lipstick clung to her bow-shaped lips, blonde hair held tightly to her head in ancient waves. She had a lost, forlorn look on her face, as she sat quietly sipping her cocktail. Next to her was an empty seat.

"Excuse me," I asked smiling, "is it okay for me to sit here, or are you waiting for someone?"

"Yes you can sit here, the guy I'm with is around somewhere, at some bar on the ship."

I began a conversation with the woman in black.

She looked so sad underneath that mass of her old fashioned hairstyle.

"My beautiful daughter died suddenly from a blood clot, and I can't get over that." She informed me after our initial cursory conversation.

"When did it happen, if I may ask?" It was difficult to know whether I, a stranger, had the right to dig a hole in her pain or show compassion by listening.

"Eighteen years ago. She was twenty one years old, it should have been me." What words can you possibly say, what sign can you make to show that you care about a stranger? I put a hand on her arm, looked in her face, and within the unspoken spaces, we understood.

"You told me your partner is on the cruise with you."

"Yes, he's an alcoholic, he's gone off for another round of drinks." Words poured out of her, "We've been together for two years, he wants to move in with me, but I'm not going to let him because he's been drinking more and more, and he started being verbally abusive to me in our cabin, and I am so embarrassed. People in the cabin next to ours can probably hear him."

I began to tell her about my recent loss, but I saw she was a long way from wanting to hear me, so I let it slide.

We became silent. The band started to play *"Fly me to the Moon"*. We sipped our colourful cocktails, and listened to the music. Beyond the windows, the indigo ocean cut away from us.

In this moment, I felt a sense of peace: released from my angst and anxieties, conscious of that long ago self, one that had been filled by the years of hard times with a man that had brought me pain, laughter, and the demons of alcohol addiction.

♪♪

Months later in Centennial Park, I watched Rambo fossicking under the trees. "I miss you, Serge," I cried into the air. As if on cue, a myna bird flew down and perched on the old wooden bench, looked at me from the yellow pouch of its eye, twisted its grey-feathered head, screeched, and flew onto the tabletop.

Maybe it was a messenger from Serge to remind me of when we had spent many hours in Centennial Park, talking about our parents and wondering if the dog had done his poo yet, followed by "What are we having for dinner?"

I sat there, alone and forlorn. Like the layers of bark on the surrounding eucalyptus trees, I peeled back the layers of my existence and remembered all the boys and young men of my life, brief romances, and career paths fluctuating from one choice to another.

The self-development gurus will tell you, "You can't change the past, but you can change how you feel about it."

I finally transcended the memories of my relationship with Serge. All of it was one large experience with one person. There can be no hate, no regret, only the memories of a deep connection.

♪♪

I am conscious of him late at night when the invading television noises fill the stillness. I wonder if he's in that other place finally playing with all the greats he always said he would. Are they discussing the music, raised ninths, chords, who was the greatest, and who plays like shit? Is he telling his heroes they are real motherfucker players, and how much he loves them, man?

There can't be a hell because he lived it during his lifetime.

I once had an unwritten kind of bucket list – it went something like this: I want to go to Disneyland, see the Grand Canyon, visit The Taj Mahal and the pink city of Jaipur, go to New York, be a singer, have a number one hit song, write a book, fall madly in love, get married, go to Russia and find my father's birthplace.

I didn't see The Taj Mahal or the pink city of Jaipur, and never got to Russia or New York.

Funnily enough, I am satisfied that in spite of being waylaid in transit. I did many of the items on my list.

I would have loved to see many more places in the world, yet, when I trawl my memory, a standout is the visit to Euro Disney, the year it opened in Paris. I refused all my cousins offers to take me, opting for an uninterrupted day to do what I had longed for many years. The gates opened, I paid for my day's ticket to see EVERYTHING – and did. That day is firmly entrenched in my happiest memories. I was a child again, lost in the wonders of this magical kingdom. I rode on a pirate ship, spun in a teacup, barged around three times in a Small World, lunched at Cinderella's eatery, grabbed at three dimensional images of Michael Jackson, and ran away in fear from the haunted house.

Together with the other stragglers, I was the last to leave before the gates were shut.

My childlike wonder was ignited and still lives in me.

What matters, is that I replaced a blank canvas with the vast tableau of the life I created, and filled my palette with the many colours of experience.

I have yet to learn where the music of my life will lead me.

The End

The Warrior

I left the safety of a homespun cocoon to cross a jagged terrain

Danced to the music of experience

And succumbed to the call of love

I am the warrior returned from dangers and battles won

And at the edge of the battlefields –

Discovered the secrets of acceptance – hg

ACKNOWLEDGEMENTS

Cynthia Sachs – Author "Kismet"
Darren Saul – Photographer
Evan Shapiro – Cilento Publishing
Susan Child – Author "Smash"
Randwick Writers Group – Dina Davis, Author 'Capriccio'
– Geraldine Star, Susan Beinhart
Jane Chaynor – Catherine Varga –
Maree Montgomery
Mosey Aaron

And my many caring friends who never gave up that one day the book will be published.
Eli, Hazel, Rose-Marie, Sheila, Jeanie, Tania, Hilary, Philip, Monique, Robert in the USA.

My lovely Randwick Library writing students and staff.

My dearly departed Rambo, who provided me with furry hugs and unconditional love.

And … If I have left anyone out, it's not because you don't matter, it's a matter of brain malfunction.

www.ingramcontent.com/pod-product-compliance
Lightning Source LLC
Chambersburg PA
CBHW071232290426
44108CB00013B/1390